doubleday

NEW YORK   LONDON   TORONTO   SYDNEY   AUCKLAND

mad house

GROWING UP IN THE SHADOW OF
MENTALLY ILL SIBLINGS

clea simon

PUBLISHED BY DOUBLEDAY
a division of Bantam Doubleday Dell Publishing Group, Inc.
1540 Broadway, New York, New York 10036

DOUBLEDAY and the portrayal of an anchor with a dolphin
are trademarks of Doubleday, a division of Bantam
Doubleday Dell Publishing Group, Inc.

Portions of this work have appeared in an altered form in the
Boston Globe and *Detroit Free Press* Sunday magazines.

To protect the privacy of various individuals, I have
changed some identifying details and the names of some
people in this book. —C.S.

The quoted lines appearing on page 1 are taken from "A
Shower in June," by William Corbett, *New & Selected Poems*,
Zoland Books, Cambridge, Massachusetts.

Book design by Gretchen Achilles

Library of Congress Cataloging-in-Publication Data

Simon, Clea.
Mad house : growing up in the shadow of mentally ill siblings /
Clea Simon. — 1st ed.
p.   cm.
Includes bibliographical references.
1. Schizophrenics—Family relationships   2. Brothers and sisters.
I. Title.
RC514.S5445   1997
362.2'6—dc20   96-26893
CIP

ISBN 0-385-47852-6

1   3   5   7   9   10   8   6   4   2

FIRST EDITION

FOR JON

contents

preface

Katherine was screaming again. Her high, frantic wails had alerted the house almost thirty minutes before, and they continued in a constant barrage, each cut off only when she sobbed in breath. The bathroom walls seemed to tremble from the force of her voice as my father labored to remove the hinges of the door, and my mother, standing behind him, tried to pass some reassurance through the barrier, through the din. Katherine, my sixteen-year-old sister, had gone into the bathroom sometime in the past hour and had turned the simple lock for privacy. But then she had panicked, had somehow forgotten how to release the catch, and now she believed she was trapped. "It's OK, we're here. It's OK, we're here," my mother said, repeating the phrase like a mantra, trying to calm Katherine down. My father gave up on the hinges and began unscrewing the door-knob, taking it and the lock off to free my sister.

Although this scene is burnt into my memory, I have no clear recollection of where I was as Katherine's wails made that wood door vibrate. I must have been in the house to witness this. I was probably right across the hall, in my own bedroom, undoubtedly curled up with my nose in a book while the drama played out, in an attempt to avoid the pandemonium. Scenes like this had grown increasingly common as Katherine descended into schizophrenia. I was eight years old.

This was neither Katherine's last crisis, nor my family's only bout with mental illness. Not long after this scene, my brother, Daniel, then eighteen years old, would break down during his freshman year at Harvard and would be hospitalized, the first of many times. My beloved, normally outgoing brother had progressed from locking himself in his room for hours, with his music and his pot, to hearing voices. My brilliant brother could no longer differentiate between his mind's creations and reality.

By the time I was ten and moving from the *Black Stallion* books to *The Diary of Anne Frank,* both my siblings had been diagnosed with schizophrenia, with its delusions of persecution and bodiless voices telling of terrible things. By the time I was twelve and graduating to boy-girl parties, my brother and sister had been in and out of various institutions, hospitals, and halfway houses. Over the next few years, my siblings seemed so out of control, so potentially dangerous, that both were forbidden to return on any permanent basis to our family house in suburban Long Island. By the time I was fourteen, I lived as if I were an only child, growing up in a moderately affluent seventies suburb, and I let myself enjoy my solitary standing. Daniel and Katherine were out of the house, and I believed the problems that had come from living with them belonged to the past. I could not have been more wrong.

As one does with an embarrassing memory, I avoided thought of my brother and sister and believed that since they had no role in my current life, they had no effect on my behavior. It would be another ten years before I realized that, far from having escaped my family's problems, I was buried in them. The illness that had taken control of my siblings' lives had made an indelible mark on my own, and denying the impact of their illness simply kept me from seeing, and countering, its effects. I wanted a life without mental illness, without the pain and confusion that my brother and sister unwittingly brought to me, and so I sought to leave them behind. But all my efforts at creating a new life scenario without my brother and sister, without their illness, sank me deeper into denial and despair.

In many ways, my family situation was not unique. Most of us grow up with some kind of dysfunction, as it is now known. Most of us carry it with us. We can do only what we know, and that for many of us means repeating the behaviors learned in our family, or reacting against them. I tried to break that pattern. For years after I left Long Island and my family home, I tried to pick up life as an adult by mimicking those around me, those who had what I saw as healthier families. It didn't work. I had poor luck with jobs and romances, but I couldn't see why. After all, I had functioned, and done very well, without much support during my early years. A smart, compliant, and outwardly cheerful child, I had chugged along through elementary school, junior high, high school, and into Harvard (like my brother) on my own little high-functioning track, avoiding the craziness around me. But in so doing and without any conscious realization of the consequences, I had shut off my ability to interact with the outside world and cauterized many of my reactions to life, simply to keep going. More than a decade after that terrifying afternoon when I held my tongue as Katherine screamed, I found that I couldn't open up to the present—not if I still kept other parts of myself closed down. If I wanted to go forward, I had to go back.

Thus my journey of self-discovery began with a retreat into my childhood and my family's sad and frightening past. To reclaim my own life, I had to reexamine the traumatic effects of watching my only brother and sister "lose" their familiar personalities as they "lost" their minds. I had to let myself feel the fear of living with two mentally ill people and also the fear that I, too, would develop the disease that had destroyed our family's peace. I had to confront the distorted family dynamics that their illness created, dynamics that, in many ways, worsened a bad situation and in which, in some ways, I participated.

What I was discovering was how the illness that controlled my brother and sister also defined my life, although in subtler and less devastating ways. Their illness had been present in my life for years before those first breakdowns, and it would be present for years to come, as I lived out the patterns set in those times of noise and fear.

The work continues. Even today I occasionally find myself reacting as I would have as a child in that house, with panicked anger, with unexpected courage, or with terror. I don't always know they are coming, these leftover emotions. During my best times, I see them as shadows—a quick flash of panic, a wave of sadness that follows hard after a more expected response—images from another time that dog my present life. Still, sometimes, I act as I would have then and realize only afterward that I hid from a co-worker as I would have from my sister, or saw the ghost of my brother's face on my lover's. Although I have not lived with my brother or sister for twenty years now, their illness has been woven into my life in ways that I am still picking apart.

Not much is known about severe mental illness, partly because these diseases are so hard to pin down. Not that they are uncommon: About 1 percent of the population—that means more than 2.5 million people in the United States alone—has been diagnosed with schizophrenia. This disease, arguably the most disabling and most difficult to treat of all mental illnesses, is a thought disorder, which the experts classify as psychosis, the category of mental illness in which the patient loses the ability to distinguish reality. But this is a rough definition, and many serious mental illnesses cannot be so easily classified. For example, bipolar (or manic-depressive) disorder, which afflicts somewhat less than 1 percent of the population, is usually characterized as a mood (or affective) disorder, but it may produce episodes of psychosis as well, as may various other disorders that defy classifications.

These illnesses are better defined by symptoms. Both schizophrenics and bipolars, for instance, may have visual and auditory hallucinations, seeing or hearing things that are not there and sometimes responding to the commands of illusory voices. For many people with bipolar disorder, such psychotic episodes often occur after days or weeks in a manic episode. Beyond that, bipolar disorder is primarily defined by its recurrent cycles between manic, mixed, and depressive modes, cycles that usually slacken with age. Schizophrenia, however, is further characterized by delusions, in which the person with the illness believes in untrue ideas, such as the suspicions of paranoia or grandiose fantasies. Many people with schizophrenia will also exhibit disorganized behavior and speech and can seem to babble incoherently or lapse into catatonic stillness. These are considered positive symptoms—active traits that define the disease. Negative symptoms include a lessening of revealed emotion, called flattening of affect, in which the ill person appears not to react to the outside world or responds to normal situations in grossly inappropriate ways. The psychiatric world's codification bible, *Diagnostic and Statistical Manual of Mental Disorders,* also lists a deterioration of functioning skills and further refines the definitions of other symptoms. Otherwise, it classifies schizophrenia as psychosis that is *not* bipolar *or* suggestive of an organic cause (such as drugs or head injury) or mental retardation. Neither is it the split personality popularized by books such as *Sybil* or movies like *The Three Faces of Eve*; multiple-personality disorder, an extremely rare condition, is what is known as a dissociative disorder.

Prognosis and treatment for serious mental illnesses have achieved only a moderate success. As many as 90 percent of people who experience a single manic episode, experts say, will go on to have future episodes, although the majority will have periods of stability in between the extremes. And while the use of lithium has been considered a magic bullet for bipolar disorder, some experts suspect that as many as 50 percent do not respond to it. The prognosis for those with schizophrenia also varies widely, and has greatly improved in recent years with such new (or newly approved) drugs as clozapine and risperidone, which seem to reach some—but still not a majority—of the most severely ill. With schizophrenia, a basic rule of thumb still seems to hold true: The patients who have the most sudden and acute "breaks," whose lives seem to crack open and drop them into madness, have a better chance of recovering than those, like my brother and sister, whose lives crumble slowly, eroding into unreality. Following the same basic rule, those who are the quickest-diagnosed, the most promptly treated and hospitalized, are also often the ones who can best recover, getting their feet under them and continuing with life after a single hospitalization.

The new drugs have prompted some wonder stories: people who reawaken to "their old selves" after decades of repeated hospitalizations, of years lost in delusional states or rambling hazes. Perhaps these drugs will eventually change schizophrenia's disheartening prognosis—currently, only about 20 percent recover fully enough to return to work or school. But neither these miracle drugs nor the research that created them has been able to answer the basic questions, such as what causes these types of diseases and what influences their progress and severity. Genetics seems to play a role, but none of these diseases appears in the predictable patterns of a strictly inherited trait. The latest research from major universities and the National Institute of Mental Health suggests that an interaction between genetics and environment—possibly a virus, or repeated attacks of a virus in utero or immediately after birth—is responsible for both schizophrenia and bipolar disorder, and perhaps accounts for the widely differing severity of the illnesses.

At least one long-lingering theory, which places mental illness's roots in the emotional environment of the home, has been put to rest. After decades of locating the cause of mental illness in the mother's "schizophrenogenic," or crazy-making behavior, major researchers no longer believe that mothers in particular or family dynamics in general cause schizophrenia or manic depression. The image of the disease has shifted as a result, and a huge advocacy movement, spearheaded by the National Alliance for the Mentally Ill, has been created in which family members as well as those affected by such diseases can lend their weight to push for education and research, in the hope of finding a biological cause and, eventually, a cure.

After decades of blame, it is no wonder that many families and advocates seek a physical cause for mental illness—a chemical imbalance, specific DNA site, or some interaction with a contagion that can be held responsible. Such a medical model would preclude blame and minimize the guilt that has kept families from getting support. Fortunately, in the past ten to fifteen years, thousands of people have spoken openly about their suffering. Destigmatizing the mentally ill and their families has been instrumental in encouraging sufferers to seek treatment and counseling.

As siblings of the mentally ill, we have watched our parents work through their guilt, face down blame, and finally, tentatively, come to terms with their children's illness. We have heard our parents proclaim, "It's a disease, it's not our fault." But more often than not, we have been left out of the dialogue. Rarely is the impact of the illness on the "healthy" children of the family talked about when a disease like schizophrenia or bipolar disorder surfaces in families. As siblings who have watched our brothers or sisters "go mad," who lost our peers to psychosis, we share a unique experience: Our brothers and sisters are the ones we were supposed to have played with, learned to get along with, emulated if they were older or taken care of if they were younger, the people with whom we should have navigated the shoals of growing up. But instead they broke down.

This is a hard topic to tackle; there is a great variety of sibling experience within families, even healthy families. Whether the ill sibling is older or younger, the same or the opposite gender, and at what point in the healthy child's development the ill sibling's disease appears—all these factors influence the functional sibling, as do the number of children in the family and the number of children who are ill. The severity of the sibling's illness also plays a role in the effect on his or her brothers or sisters, along with the success of treatment and the ability of the ill sibling, when under treatment, to function, to finally in some manner grow up.

We share many of our issues with the siblings of the chronically ill. We, too, have had to adjust childhood behavior to accommodate illness: We have had to hush when someone was sleeping, not have friends over for visits during "bad times," and, with quiet resignation and understanding, accept less of our parents' energy and attention. We, too, worry about the implications of our siblings' illness on our own genes and fear for our children or future children. Like the brothers and sisters of children with leukemia or polio, we often carry hidden burdens of resentment, which may mutate into guilt. We also share certain weaknesses, such as our difficulty in detaching from our parents and proceeding into a developmental phase our siblings never would, never could navigate.

But the nature of mental illness adds another dimension in disorientation. Even with the efforts toward destigmatization, mental illness remains hard to understand—harder, often, than a strictly physical condition. Instead of visible symptoms or a physical decline, we often must face down wild mood shifts or bursts of anger in a seemingly "whole" person; when we might expect in our siblings a longing to rejoin our childhood games, we come up against the closed doors of isolation, of depression and delusion. We live on a daily basis with personality changes that cannot be predicted or completely explained. And even when these alterations are not dangerous, they can still be confusing and terrifying.

Sometimes we fear with reason. Some of us were abused: It is estimated that 10.6 percent of schizophrenics act out violent aggressions toward family members and that 12.2 percent directly threaten to hurt a family member. These actions may be understandable—lost in a psychosis, a family member may be reacting to commands we cannot hear or acting in self-defense against a danger we do not see. And, of course, these numbers can be refuted on various grounds. Some experts consider them a high estimate, since they come from a self-reported survey of NAMI families, and these families may represent only the most flagrantly ill. (NAMI may not include, that is, the families of those who can function with their illness and do not desire a support and advocacy group.) Other experts regard the numbers as low, because these figures take only direct violence and intent to assault into account, and not the menace and insinuations—the attacks on property, childhood toys, or pets—that may accompany the illness.

At the other end of the spectrum, some of us saw our siblings abused, abandoned by our parents, or lost in a health care system that is not attuned to the care of the chronically ill, especially those who often cannot speak for themselves. Sometimes we have served as their advocates; other times we have stood by and watched as our brothers and sisters sank, which brought burdens of its own.

Obviously, all families are different. But in the course of researching this book, I found that certain patterns surfaced in the lives of those who grew up with mentally ill siblings. We can all name landmarks in our particular hells, no matter what the family size and structure. We share certain behaviors. Some of us have become involved in the care of our siblings; many have extended this umbrella of care and gone into helping or health professions. Others have fled, afraid of the violence and confusion of our family members' illness or chased by the tremendous guilt and rage that almost always accompany such disease. Some of us have cut ourselves off entirely. Many of us have vacillated between these extremes.

All of us have at some point felt fear, and some of us can admit to our anger at having our home life disturbed by a sibling's problems. Many of us have shared the frantic desire to overcompensate, to somehow make up to our parents for the ill child's failings. Other of our responses are insidious—the dread, particularly for younger siblings, of being overtaken by mental illness as we approached the age of the ill sibling's initial breakdown. Or we might have experienced the fear that we were already ill, had already made some psychotic break but were already so out of it, so lacking in self-awareness, as to be unaware of the shift in reality. Perhaps most disturbing is how, for those of us who did not have any other frame of reference, our situation seemed to grow normal, no matter how terrible or terrifying it might have been. What happens when violence, illogic, denial, and terror become part of the daily discourse? Do we replicate these scenarios in the larger world and in our future relationships?

In examining my own life and talking to others who grew up with mentally ill siblings, I have heard in many different stories similar responses repeated like fugal themes, including that of perceived complete isolation—of feeling utterly and totally cut off from our friends, neighbors, the rest of humanity. But our experiences are not isolated.

This book recounts my own stumbling journey growing up in the shadow of my siblings' mental illness, along with excerpts from the tales of adults who grew up in similar circumstances. Research and clinical observations of experts who have studied mental illness and family development in all its forms explain some of our reactions, as well as the many manifestations of the illness we witnessed; this science also give us the vocabulary to discuss the landscape and to see where our experience resembles that of others. Many of us have found ourselves doubly wounded: first by our family experiences and then by a lack of comprehension—in ourselves as well as others—as to why we are needy, hurt, angry, and disconnected. As "healthy" siblings we have wondered if our experience even counts; after all, we are not suffering the tragic and inexplicable illnesses of our brothers and sisters. But we, too, have come through tragedies, no matter if the degree and details differ, and we have all been changed by them.

Using my story and drawing on others, I hope to illuminate the issues that haunted our childhoods and in some cases threatened our ongoing development. Though we feel alone, we are not alone, and for this reason a road map, no matter how sketchy and incomplete, can offer at least the possibility of safe passage.

chapter one

After an earthquake, geologists and structural engineers are quick to point out why what happened was inevitable. Similarly, those of us with mental illness in our family can't help examining our lineage for evidence of fault lines. Since severe mental illnesses are often as devastating and impossible to predict as any natural disaster, this retroactive search rarely isolates definite causes. Still, when we look back, we can't resist that search for clues.

I was born lucky. As the youngest of three in East Meadow, an upper-middle-class suburb at the tail end of the baby boom, I had all a child could want. Our family had a nice house, we all had our own room, and there was a full acre of woods behind us. We had money for sleep-away camp and a boat. I had many pets, toys, and records—even my own portable hi-fi.

Things came easily to me: I can remember sitting on my father's lap with a book opened flat before me as he read aloud. And I recall laboring to make sense of the words, watching those printed symbols fill out with sound and meaning, seeing them transform into something beyond their composite alphabet and turn into stories. Early on, life seemed like those stories, brimming full with more to come. Application and a little patience, I learned quickly, would open many doors.

My early years seemed filled with great tenderness, populated by people and things I held dear. I loved my parents and named my big, plush frog toy Daddy Frog. When Daddy Frog grew nearly bald, I got Gaty, a green speckled alligator with a red flannel mouth and plush tail that I held on to during my first school years. Happy regularity ruled my life: I had cereal for breakfast, bologna on white bread for lunch, and when my father came home at six, dinner. We all sat down at the table together: my parents at either end, my sister and I at one side, and my brother across from us. I never questioned any of this; my brother and my sister, along with Gaty and "The Flintstones" on TV after dinner, made up my safe world.

My first pets were turtles: green disks about the size of my fist, but with clumsy paddling feet that propelled them slowly around their plastic dish, or up on the dish's island with its propped-up palm. I knew Yertle the Turtle from my Dr. Seuss book and named one—or perhaps a succession—of small, cherished pets after the heroic character. I remember paddling after my brother, still small and awkward myself, and having him scoop me up in his arms. He treated me like a pet, I've been told, but I don't remember much about him from those early years. I think of Daniel—ten years older than I—as big and strong and good. When I try to conjure him, what comes is his voice. If I try, when I close my eyes I can still hear him talking.

Whenever I think of my sister, I think of the great pop music of that era. Eight years older, she gave me my entree into rock and roll. I recall lying on the floor of Katherine's room, entranced, as she played the Beatles' "A Hard Day's Night." That record came out in this country in 1964, becoming a huge hit during her eleventh summer, when I turned three. Earlier that year the hit had been "I Want to Hold Your Hand," and a neighbor boy, just a bit older, had sung the chorus and then tried to kiss me. I ran back into the house crying, or so I am told. I can recall hearing the song, but nothing else.

Partly, probably, because of my pets, I loved the band that called itself the Turtles and listened whenever they came on the radio as well. My sister and I both had transistor radios, presents from our father, brightly colored balls with the tuning and volume dials set in silver. I always wanted to listen to music with Katherine. We went through all the bouncy pop of the midsixties together: the Lovin' Spoonful; Peter, Paul and Mary; "Incense and Peppermints"; and "C'mon Marianne." From Katherine and her friends I learned the jerk, the swim, the monkey, and, by 1966, a real twist, where you followed the movement in your hips.

The next summer, when I was to turn six years old, I saw an ad on TV for a festival in Montreal. Expo '67 had rides and games and exhibitions from around the world. I insisted, my parents told me years later, that we had to go. And we did, driving up to Canada in the family Buick. That was the summer the Turtles made it big on the radio, and as we drove we heard, over and over, "Imagine me and you/And you and me. . . . /So happy together!"

These are the images I had of my childhood until I was in my midtwenties. While they are true, there is also a selection process in my mind that casts these memories in an unnaturally golden light. That selection is evident to me now by the great lapses I still cannot explain. In actuality, I have very few memories from those first few years when the five of us lived together as a family, and many of those recollections have been pieced together out of family lore.

Most of them take place outdoors. I remember games. I can see myself playing in the small yard behind my father's office. I remember what must have been my brother's bar mitzvah, standing for what felt like hours at the end of a concrete walk outside the Jewish center when I had been told not to move; probably some caretaker had momentarily left me to run back for some forgotten parcel. My feet felt big and leaden; the pebbly path seemed very long and the center's door far away.

I remember Katherine playing in the yard of our big house, the one we moved to when I was just one. She had a tetherball game, a big padded ball that swung from a cord attached to the top of a pole. The image freezes my sister in midgame: Katherine batting the ball, while her friend waits to slap the ball back. I can see her then, and she's young, maybe eleven or twelve. Unlike me, a portly toddler, she is slim, with delicate features and straight dark blond hair I would envy a few years later. That hair, pushed back in a hairband, swings in one piece behind her as she jumps. I can imagine a soundtrack: the slap of the ball and the yells of excited girls, the hum of late-summer crickets in the shaggy grass, sprinklers and lawn mowers. But none of those sounds seems to belong to the picture, not as I remember it.

I have one memory that combines sound and movement: Katherine and her friends again, probably a year or two later and this time playing red light, green light on that same infrequently mowed back lawn. This time Katherine is it. Her face is turned toward the door at the back of the garage, her hands cupping her eyes. She yells out, "Red light, green light, one-two-three," and then turns around and opens her eyes. The point of the game is for the one who is it to spot anyone moving, to catch the others as they close in on the one counting. And so Katherine sets off to fool her friends, saying the words slowly at first and then speeding up to finish all in one breath before whirling around to see who remains in motion. At four or five, I'm too young to be included in my sister's preteen crowd, but it seems a game worth study. I watch how her girlfriends try to anticipate her call, how they sometimes playfully choose absurd stances—statue poses—to freeze in. I concentrate on every detail, studying Katherine with an intensity I can still recall. Perhaps I thought it a terrible thing to be caught by her, to have her spin around and see you.

As my older brother's pet, I was often in his company. Because of Daniel's willingness to play with his much younger sister, he frequently looked after me when my parents were busy. There's a photo I've found of us in our respective roles. I am a little roly-poly thing, about three years old and sitting on a sofa next to Daniel, then thirteen. He is reading to me, leaning toward me in the act of showing me a picture or a word, focusing all his attention on me and seemingly oblivious to the camera. I am sitting straight up, staring directly into the lens, smiling, my chubby legs and feet aimed directly ahead. We make a cute pair, I know. Though the photo betrays nothing but a loving brother and sister, I look at those two on the sofa and I get a strong feeling that the bright-eyed child was not happy. Thirty years later, I'm not sure how I know this. But at times, even before I was six years old, I knew I had reason to fear.

I remember Daniel, big and strong, giving me piggyback rides or hoisting me onto his shoulders and carrying me, laughing and yelling, as he trotted through the house in the evening, while my mother prepared dinner and we all waited for my doctor father to come home from his office. Usually those times were lively and fun, with other people bustling around. But there was one weekend afternoon, the kitchen still cold and lit only by the late-winter sun, when

Daniel carried me in and simply left me on top of the family refrigerator, on that white and shiny monolith, my legs hanging over the edge as if it were a cliff. I screamed and screamed. This memory stays with me, I'm sure, because it was a first betrayal. My trusted big brother had left me, abandoned me during what had been a game. He made frightening what had always been fun, riding high on his six-foot frame.

In retrospect, I've wondered if his leaving me up there was more than the obnoxious stunt of a big brother. Daniel had always doted on me, but by his middle teens he was already falling prey to certain symptoms associated with the mental illness that would eventually take his life. Could it be that he turned away, distracted by voices or in response to a command that I couldn't hear? Did I scream for fear of being left up there, at play ending, or because I saw my brother's focus turn inward in some strange way? As often as I've imagined that terrible moment, I can picture only his back, receding through a doorway, not his face.

The emotions connected to this time have come to me as nightmares, both as a child and in subsequent years. In all of these I see something of enormous proportions, a decidedly nonhuman character threatening me—something like a giant wave, a monster whale outside a ship's porthole, or a towering building that leans over me ready to fall. Always the shape is so preposterously huge that I cannot make out its edges, which is terrifying to me. Always it has a mindless quality, as if it is a force of nature rather than a malevolent but directed spirit. But always it is menacing, and always it is unavoidable. Even when I've been awake this dream image has caused me to shudder: when swimming over large dark patches of sand or vegetation in otherwise clear water, when passing through the shadow of certain buildings or overhanging piers. I think now that this dream dates back to the time Daniel stranded me, or even earlier. I wonder if my brother, while holding me at other times, sometimes seemed to vacate the daylight world. This shadow scared me then and continues to intrigue me now. I have trouble regarding it as a metaphor. I keep looking to see if I can remember something more. But perhaps the shadow was simply that: trouble looming.

My last memory of my family as happy was that trip to Expo '67. There we all strapped ourselves onto giant benches that dropped into the smoke of a man-made volcano and took us all the way to the earth's core. We ate crepes in the old French part of the city, where the bubblelike cobblestones made the streets seem like another Expo creation. It was only after our return that my parents seemed to begin to worry about Daniel. With no classes to attend, no other summer activities, Daniel, then sixteen, had withdrawn into himself and begun spending days alone with his records. With all his years in medicine, my father must have recognized that Daniel's behavior was not healthy, and soon after our grand weekend in Canada, he took Daniel on a long sailing trip. Alone with his son for several days, my father hoped to draw him out, to hear his troubles and bring him back home happier. Perhaps he already suspected that his outreach would not be enough. A photo from this trip says it all. My father, hunched over the tiller, looks grim and preoccupied, older than his years. My brother, staring straight at the camera, is smiling broadly, but blankly. His features are handsome, but his smile looks as vacant as an infant's.

During their absence, I think, is when I began to invent dreams, such as the one I'd tell my mother when I came down for breakfast. She'd been in a garden, a bright and beautiful place, I'd tell her as she fixed my cereal and juice. She'd been standing there beaming, I'd say, and all around her had been turtles, up on their hind legs, clasping their front paws together to make a ring around her, to dance and sing for her. Although I told her of this dream repeatedly, I never had it. I made it up to give my mother the cheeriest scene I could imagine. I needed her to be happy and was young enough to associate happiness with an abundance of turtles.

Something in our family had changed, but I was too young to comprehend exactly what. Now I can see that both Daniel and Katherine were going slowly mad, with the form of schizophrenia described as insidious because it creeps in on the patient over a period of years. The hardest to treat, the hardest even to recognize in its early stages, this type of schizophrenia can begin to show up even in very young children. By adolescence, when a great majority of mental illnesses first become apparent, the symptoms are chronic and may be accepted as normal behavior. With hindsight, my mother tells me, she knew her first two offspring were not healthy, saw a strangeness in their behavior early on that I never displayed. Daniel would forbid other children to touch anything he claimed as his, becoming violently possessive as early as kindergarten. Katherine, even in grade school, would regularly erase small errors in her homework until she wore holes in the paper, insisting on its being "perfect." And Daniel regularly came home from elementary school with tales of being beaten by other children, stories that, when my mother called his teachers in a rage, could not be confirmed.

Were we already observing symptoms? After the fact, after a breakdown and hospitalization, it's easy to pick out these early signs of illness, but if full psychosis had not developed later, would these quirks be viewed as anything other than the personality changes of a growing child or of adolescence? Would they be recalled at all? The nature of serious mental illness lends itself to second-guessing. I've done this; I think most family members of the mentally ill do. Because we feel helpless to cure, we look to see if there was, instead, some triggering event we should have taken seriously. And we nearly always find something that we feel ought to have clued us in.

Almost every family member recalls just such a moment.

"She was a nervous child," recalls Sal, whose youngest sister was finally hospitalized with schizophrenia when she was twenty-two. "Even in elementary school, she was afraid of her teachers and didn't want to go to school, but there wasn't a particular reason. Later, she became paranoid at work. She would come home saying that the people at work were talking about her. But we were kind of in the dark as to what we were dealing with."

"I remember," says Samuel, whose older brother Stu had schizophrenia, "having a meal at our aunt and uncle's over Christmas holidays." This was at least a year before Stu clearly became ill and dropped out of college. "When the cake was served, we all started digging into it. And I remember one of our first cousins said, 'Stu, are you gonna eat your cake or look at it?' Evidently, he had started to eat his cake and had suddenly frozen in place, his fork an inch above the cake. Fifteen years later I look back and that was probably the first symptomology he had." Samuel would later learn, from his brother's medical records, that Stu was plagued by voices, aural hallucinations that distracted him from whatever matter was at hand. "That day, with the cake, he was frozen, listening to the voices."

Samuel's story sounds painfully familiar. Such clues sound like small things to outsiders, but we siblings, we who have lived with what comes after, know what they portend. This clarity in hindsight isn't purely subjective. According to Dr. David Shore, chief of the Schizophrenia Research Branch of the National Institute of Mental Health, some experts have suggested that relatives may often be the first to spot the signs of deterioration, in part because the first symptoms of these diseases vary and can be extremely subtle. Even if we limit our consideration of mental illness to the most serious, to psychosis, with its wild ideas and alternative realities, its unseen voices issuing rigid commands, we often cannot pinpoint the start of a breakdown. Such serious mental illness may begin with an almost imperceptible withdrawal from regular activities. One person may start sleeping later than had been his or her custom. Another may get fired from a job or may simply drop out of an old circle of friends. A person beginning to fall ill may seem agitated, may become hostile and angry, or get tearful, or show no feeling at all. Often there is nothing you can really put a finger on.

"It's hard to know what's going on," says Dr. John Strauss, professor of psychiatry at Yale University, "because people do these sorts of things all the time without necessarily being mentally ill. Often, it's a gradual thing, and the more florid symptoms don't come out till later."

What, after all, is a breakdown? Statistically, we can sometimes pinpoint *when* one is likely to happen and what the prognosis will be, but not much more. And even these numbers are vague. Bipolar disorder may appear at any stage of life, although the twenties and thirties are considered the most dangerous period, according to Dolores Malaspina, assistant professor of clinical psychiatry at Columbia University, and in their authoritative *Manic-Depressive Illness,* Frederick K. Goodwin and Kay Redfield Jamison note that some studies show a smaller surge of onset around the age of forty-five. Most schizophrenics, however, will have what is commonly considered a breakdown—that is, a flagrantly psychotic episode with such symptoms as hallucinations or delusions—somewhat earlier, usually between the ages of sixteen and twenty-five. The numbers (as compiled in Dr. E. Fuller Torrey's *Surviving Schizophrenia* and Richard S. E. Keefe and Philip D. Harvey's *Understanding Schizophrenia*) also show that women diagnosed with schizophrenia commonly break down somewhat later than men, and that although it is rare to develop schizophrenia after age thirty-five, some have gotten it after age fifty.

We also know that some go quickly into psychosis and others slowly develop some form of the disease. The figures on recovery vary and tend to be more optimistic for bipolar disorder than for schizophrenia, but we know that roughly 30 to 45 percent will recover from an initial psychotic episode to the point of being able to function in society, to hold a job and live independently. Perhaps as many as 30 percent currently will not, while the remainder will rely on the latest advances in drug treatment and supportive environments. And while theories abound as to why many of the new drugs work, and what social and living situations make the transition back to full life possible, we do not know why people develop such severe diseases. We do not know why these various diseases progress differently in different people. There are numbers, but all they provide are odds. We do not, in fact, know much about serious mental illness, about psychosis, at all.

Despite the best efforts of diagnosticians, psychosis is less a disease than a state, a catchall name for the broad category of mental illnesses distinguished by a lost or defective contact with reality. Because of this loss of contact, the illnesses classified as psychoses are considered thought disorders, as opposed to mood (or affective) disorders, which largely work on the emotions, such as bipolar (manic-depressive) illness or depression. However, the distinctions do not remain clear, and definitions and diagnoses change. Currently mental health professionals define schizophrenia (and the disorders that seem to share at least one of its symptoms, such as schizophreniform, delusional, and schizotypal personality disorders) as psychosis, but the same psychotic traits sometimes show up in bipolar and autistic disorders as well.

Because these illnesses are largely defined by symptoms, they may be misdiagnosed as one another, and different doctors may also arrive at different diagnoses for valid reasons. Although my father was a physician and undoubtedly suspected the onset of a mental illness when he saw his son withdraw, he could not be sure of what was happening. Schizophrenia, for example, is characterized by the "positive" symptoms of psychosis and by the "negative" ones, in which some healthy trait is missing. The latter include flat affect (the lack of emotional responses), alogia (the lack of either speech or content in speech), and anhedonia (the inability to experience pleasure). But social withdrawal—which may be one manifestation of anhedonia—is common in depression as well as in schizophrenia and the schizoaffective and schizotypal disorders. And delusions, which often afflict schizophrenics, may show up as well in bipolars during episodes of mania.

Many of these illnesses overlap: Schizoaffective disorder, for instance, seems to combine the mood swings of bipolar illness with the hallucinations and delusions of schizophrenia, and has been classified as its own illness. Delusional disorder is characterized by one overriding "wrong idea," such as the belief that enemy planes are buzzing the house. But since other aspects of a delusional patient's life seem to be unaffected by mental illness (patients, say, may not exhibit the flat affect of many schizophrenics), this disorder has been broken off diagnostically from schizophrenia. Schizophreniform disorder looks like schizophrenia but lasts less than six months, which is how it has earned its own classification. Sometimes one illness may lead into another. A patient with schizoaffective disorder may be reclassified as laboring under schizophrenia, and there is often debate as to whether the patient's illness changed or the original clinician missed something.

Some researchers speculate that their work will further divide what are now considered single diseases, such as schizophrenia, into many smaller categories, and that only then will treatment grow more uniform and prognosis more accurate. Maybe, at that time, research will also be able to pinpoint when the disease starts.

"He stopped hanging out with our friends."
"She stopped eating."
"He wouldn't get out of bed."
We hear these complaints so often about all adolescents that we have trouble noting when they signify the onset of a disease. What, after all, is normal teenage activity? Separation from the family and from the outmoded habits of childhood is healthy at this stage. At what point does it constitute withdrawal?

Neither of Bob's parents thought anything was amiss when their youngest son, Steven, stopped hanging out with his older brother. After all, Bob and his crowd were close to two years older, a big gap in high school socializing. But Steven was a surfer, just like Bob and his cronies, and when Steven dropped out of their circle, taking up with one quiet friend instead, he also started to surf by himself or with his new buddy in a much less desirable area of shoreline. Maybe he was just striking out for himself, a high school sophomore trying to distinguish himself from his brother the senior. Within three years, however, his parents would call for emergency help: Their youngest son had become catatonic and stood still in the family yard for hours as if he were one of the trees. Originally diagnosed with schizophrenia, Steven has since been rediagnosed as schizoaffective. He has now been in and out of hospitals and group homes for close to twenty years.

Bob wonders if that initial distancing should have served as a warning. But among close siblings such differentiation may be normal, may even be encouraged, and Bob's family didn't recognize the first signs of mental illness. This is often the case, as seemingly small abnormalities slowly stretch the envelope of what the family considers "normal" behavior. Parents in particular, trained as most are to watch for trouble yet at the same time aware that they may overreact, will talk themselves down from the idea that their child may be mentally ill—that conclusion is too frightening, too permanent-sounding. Instead, they give themselves excuses. This seeming strangeness is due to the emotional upheavals of adolescence. That crazy act may be due to drugs, and we can get him or her off of those. With the kind of subtle breakdowns that are typical of insidious, early-onset schizophrenia, the rationalization develops as slowly (and as steadily) as the disease, particularly among the adults in the family, the ones who can reason.

Neurologists have a name for this familial reaction, based on the way mechanical joints, in certain situations, will not move at all and then suddenly give way. The "clasp-knife reaction" is characterized by a slow buildup of rationalization that—when it starts to go—completely collapses. "We go from thinking, 'This is a person, this is my brother. He's just being a little strange,' " Yale's Strauss explains. "Then all of a sudden, 'He's a schizophrenic.' You've lost the person/brother part."

We have no vocabulary for talking about that middle ground, and we fear to give words to our worst suspicions. To avoid having to do so, we deny seeing anything wrong until the problems are too obvious to ignore.

Granted, many people develop serious mental illnesses quite suddenly and with symptoms that cannot be overlooked. In some ways, however, such an illness—even if it is significantly incapacitating—is easier to deal with if only because the behavior is indisputable. And, for reasons that do not seem to be related, those who suffer such swift breaks also seem to recover more often, faster, and more completely. One of Samuel's other brothers makes a perfect illustration. After finishing college and a year of graduate school, this brother was living and working successfully in Los Angeles. Then, in the course of a few days, he slipped into a manic stage so severe he became psychotic. That brother, now diagnosed with bipolar disorder, became convinced one Friday in 1972 that he no longer needed to sleep, and pushed himself through the weekend. That Sunday, he had an accident while driving. The police found him incoherent at the scene and had him taken to an emergency room. He was hospitalized and largely incoherent for close to three months before his doctors tried lithium, to which he responded.

Even in such cases, with the illness obvious, acceptance of a diagnosis can be long in coming. E. Fuller Torrey saw his younger sister break down within a few weeks, during the summer between her high school graduation and freshman year at college. Returning from a trip to Europe, she became delusional and began to hallucinate. Torrey, who was then in college, recalls, "She would lie down on the front lawn and talk about the British coming to attack." Diagnosed with schizophrenia, she was hospitalized for the first of many times. (Although such a rapid decompensation, as a breakdown is called, usually augurs better for recovery, there are no guarantees.)

A florid psychotic break, as this type of quick and complete breakdown is described, affects the family differently from an insidious-onset case. Both, certainly, are horrible, and both leave the family stunned with grief, but the slowly developing illness is harder to grasp as an invader, a *"thing* that one can combat," as psychologists Stephen Bank and Michael Kahn write in *The Sibling Bond.* A quickly developing disease has borders that define some issues better. When Torrey talks about his sister, he can at least say with certainty: Here is when she was well, and this is when she got sick.

In these cases, while the severity of the symptoms precludes the clasp-knife response, most of the same pressures for rationalization are present. Consider Torrey's family, who were confused at first and had no experience of mental illness. They tended to downplay the situation. Torrey was not yet a doctor, and much of the family's information came from a friend of his mother's, a psychiatrist, on an informal basis. "There was no sense up front that something was gravely wrong," Torrey says. "There was a certain denial of the seriousness of it." The family recognized unhealthy behavior but did not understand the severity of the illness. Torrey recalls that his mother even minimized his sister's psychosis as a "passing phase."

As the ill person becomes only slowly, incrementally different, no single act seems drastic enough to justify what must be one of our parents' worst fears. No matter how horrible the behavior, if it is gradual, it can be explained, at least until the point when the illusion snaps—when the clasp-knife joint gives way. Our reactions are not unlike the story told about frogs: Drop them in hot water and they will do their damnedest to jump out. Put them in water and heat it slowly, and they will sit in the water until they boil to death.

Herpetologists give frogs more credit than that, but the analogy holds as our reactions tend toward the extreme when faced with the tragedy of a loved one falling apart. For humans, of course, stigma and blame add their own heat. Although these theories have now been discredited, up through the 1960s and into the 1970s, when I was growing up, mental illness was believed to be caused by unhealthy family dynamics. In the case of schizophrenia, the blame was usually laid on a schizophrenogenic mother, one who places her children in a double bind, a situation in which the children feel pressured to act in two contrary ways, both of which will be punished as the "wrong" choice. The child's illness thus becomes completely the fault of the mother's bad parenting. The late psychologist-poet R. D. Laing put a more romantic twist on the illness and spread the guilt more widely. He blamed society, claiming schizophrenia was a healthy reaction to an unhealthy world. Either way, the family could be held responsible. And for many of us, when we and our siblings were growing up, that upped the pressure to not recognize mental illness.

These days, research, particularly studies on identical twins, sees these illnesses as primarily organic, usually with a strong genetic component or tendency. Researchers, using techniques such as magnetic resonance imaging, can actually spot the exact physical changes in brain structure and chemistry early on when these illnesses are present, but long before the psychosis develops. Why the illness occurs at all is uncertain. We know, as stated earlier, that schizophrenia occurs in about 1 percent of the population at large and bipolar disorder occurs in about 0.7 percent of the population, but also that the rate within families can be much, much higher. Therefore, it may be that the genes that control normal brain development are defective or that obstetrical complications may activate the genes that cause these illnesses. Other possible triggers, such as early oxygen deprivation, are being studied, as is the flu. "Influenza may play a role, probably in combination with genetic factors," the NIMH's Shore says. "The parent may carry certain vulnerability genes, and exposure to flu during pregnancy, when studied in very large samples, has been associated with an increased rate of schizophrenia twenty to thirty years later in the children."

The combination theory would also explain a statistical glitch that researchers have been aware of for many years: An abnormally high number—about 10 percent more than in the general population—of schizophrenics are born in late winter and early spring, which would place their gestation in the fall and winter flu season. In Australia, a few studies point out, the incidence is reversed. Less research has been done in the Southern Hemisphere, but the results point in the same direction, that severe mental illness seems to tie in with babies carried during that hemisphere's June-through-September winter. Both Daniel and Katherine were May babies; I was born in July.

Some such interaction may explain why the disease does not follow classic inheritance lines. Unlike eye color or other inherited traits, severe mental illness does not occur with predictable frequency in certain families and cannot be linked to a specific gene site.

Dr. Stephen Faraone, associate professor of psychiatry at Harvard Medical School, who conducts research on the genetics of mental illness, describes this interaction in terms of poker. "Some people can just get dealt a bad hand," he says. "They get schizophrenia, get bipolar, regardless of the environment. Then there are other people who are likely to need some environmental trigger. And there are other people who are probably invulnerable, who will survive anything."

Still, we try to trace lines of descent, to explain or to excuse what we fear is our own culpability. Years after her sister developed a borderline-personality disorder, Debbie remembered hearing about her great-aunt who had some form of mental illness. "She was always hoarding things in her house, and she used to send us gifts that were really bizarre. One year for my birthday she sent me a giant pair of underwear. I think, in retrospect, they must have been hers." At the time, Debbie recalls, her parents described her behavior as merely "eccentric."

Years after Bob's brother became ill, he says, his father explained that his own mother, Bob's grandmother, had been schizophrenic. "I thought it was bullshit at first," Bob says. He remembered his paternal grandmother's shyness and an almost childlike insecurity. She seemed quiet and nervous to him, but not irrational. However, his father told him that this same woman moved her family from apartment to apartment almost every year when he was growing up. She feared persecution from some outside enemy and fled from home to home to escape.

Samuel remembers his mother's bouts of severe depression, characterized by crying spells and "a little bit of paranoia." She was diagnosed with a delusional disorder late in life. One of Samuel's cousins, on his mother's side, also seemed to have some emotional or mental problems. Although Samuel doesn't know much of his cousin's history, he knows that this cousin dropped out of college and, although he received some form of medication, never really reentered adult life. "He hung around the home area, and did this and that for about five years," Samuel remembers. The cousin later committed suicide, prompting Samuel to guess that he had had a schizophrenia-type illness all along.

Posthumous diagnoses tend to be that highly speculative, but they do add circumstantial weight to theories of genetic linkage. My grandmother Anna, for example, supposedly suffered from paranoid delusions throughout much of her life. Although never diagnosed as having any mental illness, she believed at various times that poison was being gassed through certain radiators and that enemy planes were looking to bomb us. While these delusions were not so severe as to interfere with her functioning throughout life, they may have indicated a family tendency toward psychosis.

For many families, however, there is no genetic trail. Sometimes nobody in the family that anyone can recall has ever had a psychotic episode, or even a severe depression. Then, suddenly, someone breaks down. Somebody begins hallucinating and is hospitalized. And then the disease takes on an aspect of particular horror: a personal and specific curse visited on one individual and that person's immediate family. Those of us who can locate earlier cases at least share some consolation that this disease may be genetic, may not be particular to or—as our worst fears suggest—caused by our immediate family or our own actions.

But even retroactive family diagnoses (my family's speculation about my grandmother, Bob's father's thoughts about his mother) cannot quite be trusted. We wonder if we are overinterpreting. Are we fabricating evidence to free us from the fear that we caused the illness, or to make the present less terrifying? The research of psychiatrists such as Lenore Terr and Judith Lewis Herman shows that "magical" thinking—the belief that we should have seen warnings and thus been able to avoid the horrible situation—is common among survivors of trauma, especially children. Such thinking gives us the illusion of control, even if retroactively. At any rate, when we are seeking hard facts after an event like a breakdown, the relatively young science of psychiatry is little help. So many illnesses have been covered up over time, so many ill people have been sequestered within their families, and so many psychiatric breakthroughs have come about only so recently that delineating family histories of mental illness is hard, if not impossible.

With all these factors, particularly with gradual-onset cases, it is easy to understand why the adults in such families often do not see the obvious. But for the other children in the family, the siblings, the experience is different. Perhaps because we feel more free from responsibility than our parents do or because we judge our own behavior by our siblings', we may be more aware, sooner, of their early symptoms. However, our awareness of what these new and confusing behaviors mean varies with where we are in our lives when these changes begin. If we are older, we may be less often in the company of our brother or sister and more independent of our family, more able to look to our peers for the norms of healthy behavior. Therefore, we may recognize our brothers' and sisters' behavior as increasingly abnormal. Or we may respond more like our parents, bending our definition of normal to include our increasingly ill siblings for the same reasons of denial and fear. For younger siblings, however, those options don't exist. We don't yet have an adult's repertoire of possible explanations. And because we do not yet have a large scale of reference, we may also be less aware of how abnormal our siblings' behavior has become and more prone to blame ourselves for not keeping up with their changes.

"He was my big brother and I just thought that he was very critical," recalls Lincoln, who was not even six years old when his older brother first became psychotic. "He was very critical about my taste in music and literature, and I just tried to please him, to change my taste to the things that he wouldn't get crazy about. And those changed from day to day. I didn't have a clue that he was ill. I thought I had the problem. I thought I was just an inadequate person and had to try harder."

Many of the cues we look for to determine what is healthy and what is not come from how our parents react, or fail to react. A good six or seven years before her older brother would be diagnosed, or, in her family's terminology, "become ill," Zoe can recall him killing a frog. "He was torturing it in front of me. Mashing it with a shoe," she remembers. Her parents dismissed that act as the thoughtless but normal violence of a young boy, much as they dismissed her later complaints about his aggressive behavior as simple sibling rivalry. Zoe still remembers the scene with horror. However, she was young and, because her parents did not seem alarmed, she adapted. "It was weird, but it was something I got used to," she says, and her definition of acceptable behavior changed.

Talking to other siblings now, adults who grew up watching their brothers and sisters fall ill, I was struck by how vulnerable children are at all ages. A woman whose brother became ill when she was a preteen will discuss how she never resolved issues of intimacy. Another, whose sister broke down when they were both in high school, feels she never had her chance to separate from her family in a healthy adolescent fashion. Author and University of Pittsburgh professor of psychology Diane Marsh notes how the age at the time of a sibling's breakdown can determine how much one is damaged, as if we are trapped at that point in our own developmental amber. If we experience a psychotic family member as an infant, we may not totally complete that stage's task and may end up having problems with trust. If it occurs in our early childhood, we may have difficulty with learning and with friendships; if in adolescence, we may struggle with our sexual roles. Even when we cannot link exact times or stages with the crises in our lives, this much is obvious: The younger we were when illness came into our home, the more profound the effect our sibling's breakdown had on our image of ourselves. The younger we were, the less normal life we had as a basis of comparison. As Herman's studies (recorded in her book *Trauma and Recovery*) conclude, an inverse relationship exists between the amount of psychopathology (that is, damage) we suffer and the age we were when our lives went bad. Common sense confirms this. When we are small, we have fewer defenses, fewer tools to protect our feelings and our view of the world. If someone close to us does something scary or hurts us in some way, we have no way of understanding it or explaining why it has happened. And we are left with a profound confusion about the world and about ourselves.

That, certainly, is how I experienced my brother's distancing, his and my sister's increasingly bizarre and frightening behavior. Something had changed, and I knew it. But I didn't know what. And that core confusion surfaces again and again in the stories of the siblings I've interviewed. We repeat what we've heard: "My parents thought he smoked too much pot"; "My mother thought it was a phase." Without a clear understanding of what was happening to our siblings, many of us internalized their problems and our own family's denial. Unless and until the adults in our lives explained to us what was happening in terms we could follow, we often didn't understand that our siblings were ill, that the problem was outside ourselves. And as a result we began to doubt ourselves and our perceptions. For me, those doubts would multiply as I grew older and my siblings' illness progressed.

chapter two

EVERYTHING FALLS APART

The boat trip with our father didn't help my brother. That fall, Daniel returned to high school, to advanced-placement physics, European history, and Latin. He did not return to me, however. More and more of his time was spent in his bedroom, the music of Bob Dylan and the Rolling Stones coming through the shut door, along with the heavy smell of marijuana. The little time I did spend in his room seemed different than it had, our once-warm playfulness somehow cooled. Not knowing what had changed and wanting to find out, I sneaked into his room one day to spy when he was not home. I remember looking through his opened bureau, finding paper clips and small change pooled in a shallow drawer divider, and socks below that. I was looking for secrets, but no clues to my brother were to be found.

At school, Daniel continued to ace his courses and won early acceptance to Harvard, to the class of 1972. He was brilliant and had planned, while still in high school, to follow our father into medicine. Sometimes, also, during these two years, as he turned seventeen and prepared to graduate, he would lose his sense of appropriate behavior. I remember hearing my mother yelling at Daniel one night shortly after I had been taken to bed. She sounded uncharacteristically upset, nearly hysterical as she screamed at him to go to his room. Her voice had woken me, and what I saw when I stepped out of my bedroom seemed impossible. There was my mother, red-faced and yelling, and my brother, calm, still, and totally nude. He faced my mother with a beatific smile on his face as he proudly displayed his erection to her, to my sister, and now to me. His body looked bizarre to me, but it was my mother's loss of control that frightened me the most. Although my father soon emerged to throw a robe over

Daniel, and my mother quickly hustled me off, again, to bed, I thought about that strange scene for a long time. I did not know what to think, but I knew that something very bad had happened.

As my brother drifted away from me, Katherine, in her own way, began to focus on me. She had always seemed jealous of the attention my brother had lavished on me in the past, and now that he had withdrawn she began to tease me with a vengeance. "Clee-ah-pee-ah-belly-pee-vis" she'd call me, a nonsense name that made her laugh with its suggestions of bathroom humor. I hated when she did this and learned quickly to turn away as she called out in a taunting singsong, "Cleapeabelly!" She wasn't easily discouraged. I remember her starting in on me as we finished dinner at a local restaurant. Her rhyming began as we were getting up from the table, and she continued hounding me as we got our coats and walked out. I was the baby, and she seemed to be determined to make fun of my chubbiness and my days of wetting my pants. "Cleapeabelly. Cleapeabelly Peavis!" Against strict orders—I was only about seven—I pushed ahead of the family into the parking lot. But my plan to get away was aborted as my father ran after me and scooped me up. By the time the rest of the family caught up to us, Katherine had locked herself into a rhythm. Even after my mother, exasperated, ordered her to stop, Katherine kept laughing and reciting her mocking singsong, softly, audible only to me in the backseat that we shared as my father drove us home.

Things were definitely getting weird, and I began to retreat. I made caves for myself all over the house: in the studio where my mother painted and engraved her etchings, in the back of my closet, and in the alcove tucked into the base of our stairwell. In one such niche, between my father's recliner and the extended frame of our fireplace mantel, I envisioned a complex world for my smallest play pets: round-bodied plastic mice I had nabbed from one of Katherine's board games, called (appropriately) Mousetrap. In this hideout, which was only a few inches deep, I figured out how my little mice would arrange their home, where they would sleep and eat, how they would run from one place to another in times of danger.

The challenge was always to make do under difficult circumstances. I was practicing protective magic, preparing for a crisis. How would my mice order their lives, where would they sleep, how—given certain unchangeable conditions—would they survive? I planned carefully enough so that they would fare very well. And myself? I played another game with my own living space. The high ceilings of our old home had been altered through remodeling, leaving interesting cutouts and dips: an arching entrance where a foyer had been built onto a front stoop, or a lowered ceiling where a room had been extended. All these uneven ceilings and doorways intrigued me, as did the long stairwell that cascaded down to our front hallway. What if the house were turned upside down? I didn't envision destruction or smashed glassware, just a neat inversion. How would I order my furniture, where would I store my toys: in the built-in bookcases that would still retain their basic shape? In the fireplace that, upended, would resemble a cupboard? How would I make my home comfortable if it were all, somehow, flipped? This didn't seem a serious concern, although I kept at this game for years and still sometimes find my eyes straying upward toward the molding of new places. But I was getting as ready as I could.

I still have a story I wrote during one of those early years, printed in block letters set down on widely spaced lines. We'd been asked in school to write a story to go with a colorful drawing of a green frog sitting on a lily pad. On the frog's wide green head was a golden crown, much like Daddy Frog's. I picked up the implied magic of the setting. An evil witch, I explained, had turned a good prince into a frog. Then she had told him he could be a man again if he traveled to the tower at the end of the world. He wanted to do this and tried to go to the end of the world. He tried to run there, but he wasn't a human anymore and he didn't have a man's long legs. He tried to fly, but he wasn't a bird and he didn't have wings. So he hopped and he hopped, but he didn't get very far. He was very sad, I wrote. I saw no way out. So I had the frog prince find a nice girl-frog. On the tall ruled lines I carefully printed out that the prince-frog and his girl-frog fell in love. They got married and lived happily ever after in that pond. I got a "Fair+," with points off for creative spelling, and I was very pleased to bring that home. A careful observer might have noticed how little faith I had in help from outside, how even in my fantasies I made do. But in my world, no matter what happened, everybody was happy.

Although our family fabric was fast unraveling, nobody talked to me about it. My parents were not sure what was happening, I think, and they sought to shelter me from their worst fears, seeing me as innocent of trouble at the age of seven and eight. I had my turtles and my stuffed animals. But I was also beginning to get the nightmares, the ones of total catastrophe, that would stay with me for years. First they came as fever dreams—whenever I was sick, a huge ball of fire would rush in to engulf me as soon as I fell asleep. Then the images began coming to me even on nights when I had no fever. Sometime in those last years, before Daniel left home, the dream became more sophisticated, culling its setting from a school field trip.

Our elementary school went often to the Hayden Planetarium in New York City. I loved the planetarium and the colorful, glowing displays in the darkened rooms surrounding the theater that we would visit before the shows. That's where the dream begins. In it, I would be walking in a similar space, a darkened hall winding through a planetariumlike museum. As in real life, the displays were backlit and glowing, providing the only light in the huge room, and the deep shadow intensified a feeling of great loneliness that grew in me as I passed from exhibit to exhibit, almost as if I were realizing I was lost and alone and wandering farther away from my class. Then I would see that I was following a time line, a history of our solar system. In the dream, I'm captivated and follow the line along until I reach the final display, the last bit of colored light in the black hall. The display, I would then see, commemorated the day a comet, a burning sun, crashed into our world and destroyed it. The placard would be dated "Today." As I read it, I never feared an impending apocalypse so much as I had a growing sense of dread that it had already taken place. And as I stood there, alone in the great hall, separated from my class, it would dawn on me that I was the only one who had realized that the world had ended.

This image only recently stopped haunting my dreams. I have successfully placed it—perhaps not for the first time but with the final recognition that comes with the work of therapy—in Daniel's prebreakdown period. The subconscious, I had always read, loves a pun, and I had been living with one. Before he was hospitalized, before my parents acknowledged his illness, I had recognized the decline of the big brother who served as center of my world. The comet, a burning sun/son in my lexicon, had already crashed.

The actual crash, when it came, was out of my direct sight. Daniel had gone off to Cambridge, Massachusetts, to his freshman year at Harvard, and lasted barely a semester. There his hallucinations and delusions overwhelmed him, and his behavior became so odd that counselors at the university's health services feared he might hurt himself. The university recommended that he sign himself into McLean Hospital, a well-respected private mental hospital in the nearby suburb of Belmont. Everyone hoped his stay would be brief, and he remained enrolled in his class.

Since he was a freshman, his name was included in the annual housing lottery. Harvard students spend their first year in the cocoonlike dorms of Harvard Yard but move out for the remaining three undergraduate years, usually into one of twelve residential colleges called houses. While he was still at McLean, Daniel's number came up lucky and he secured a space in Adams House, the dorm famous for artists and activists where my father had also lived during his upperclass years. That spring was my father's twenty-fifth class reunion, an occasion for the old grads to be feted and enjoy a grand welcome back to Cambridge. What I remember instead were my parents, grim and tired even before they started, leaving early on Saturday mornings for the four-and-a-half-hour drive up to McLean, and the gray, worn looks they had when they returned late on Sundays.

During one of these trips, I learned later, my parents participated in family therapy, with other McLean patients, their parents, and a social worker to facilitate discussion. This was early 1969, when new ideas about mental illness were gaining acceptance, but this social worker chose to focus instead on family interaction. "Why are you putting such high expectations on your son?" she asked my mother, accusing her by implication. "Can't you see what such a high-stress environment has done to him?" Nobody told my mother that her son's deterioration wasn't her fault. And nobody suggested that any other type of family therapy, perhaps one that would include me and help me cope, was possible.

Daniel's wildness wasn't helped much by McLean. Although he had committed himself voluntarily and therefore would have been free to leave, his mind saw imaginary enemies surrounding him. Late one night, he made a rope of bedsheets and climbed out of a second-story window, "escaping" when he could have walked out the front door.

He came home for a while then, to rest up, and tried repeatedly to rejoin his class, but the fiction that he would return to school permanently, to any semblance of normal life, soon grew thin. Each return seemed to end in a rehospitalization; after each release he came home full of optimism and plans to try again. Everybody hoped that each time would be an improvement, but after a few of these back-and-forth trips, even that hope became frail. I remember watching Daniel through a window during one of those leaves between college and hospital. Stripped to the waist, he split logs from a downed tree. The tree had been buzz-sawed apart, the slices of its trunk piled carelessly like huge coins scooped out of a giant pocket. And Daniel, no giant but big and strong, hoisted each of these logs in turn on a stump, and with a metal wedge and a large mallet cracked them into fireplace-size fragments. With one powerful strike, the slab would split open with a loud crack. Daniel would then stoop and gather the pieces, sometimes opting to divide a segment still further, sometimes piling them all in a pyramid and beginning on the next. He looked sweaty and muscular, the picture of health, but I kept my eyes glued on him for protection. Should anything go wrong, should I look away for a moment, I feared, the vibrant young man would splinter, too. And if anything went wrong on my watch, I felt certain that damage would have been my fault, as surely as if I had swung the mallet.

I wasn't cognizant of my sense of responsibility then—it hadn't come clear to me just yet. What I sensed was a great weight on me to get things right, to keep life on track, at any cost. I believed that I needed to control my thoughts as well as my actions and began to concentrate very hard on whatever was immediately in front of me. A good reader from an early age, I immersed myself in books. The weekly stop of our library's bookmobile several blocks up the road and my visits with my mother to the main library provided necessary refuelings, and I soon outdistanced the scholastic book club, which let me order only two thin paperbacks a week. The bookshelves my father fixed onto my wall filled quickly, and the top shelves of my closet gave up their hats and sweaters to hold the overflow. These were the years in which I developed a reverence for bookstores, and I can still picture the musty, two-story Paperback Bookseller where a knowledgeable clerk introduced me to C. S. Lewis and his magical world of Narnia with its talking animals and evil witches.

Lewis, in his best British storytelling manner, sends four children, exiled from London during the Blitz, into this marvelous place via an old cupboard in the country house of a distant relative. How like my own hiding places, that old cupboard, and how sympathetic these children, particularly the youngest girl, who would crawl into a secret and private space. And to find a world there! Their England seemed grand enough: four siblings, all friendly, more or less, to one another. But Narnia itself was ideal, a park without mosquitoes. I loved the talking horses and deer and worshiped the great lion Aslan, who ruled over Narnia with a heavy, although velveted paw, and I ate up the logic of these books. The wardrobe, we learn later, came from the wood of a tree that had sprung from a seed of Narnia. And the old professor, in whose house the children first discover the magical land, had been one of the first humans to visit there during his own childhood. Everything was well ordered in these books; everything made sense.

They provided a world, complete with friends and adventures, true, but also with laws and regulations. Hungry for order, I ate up the ethical code of the rigidly moral Narnia, where even magic had rules and good characters as well as evil had to pay when they transgressed. Narnia's strict code felt reassuring in comparison to my quickly disintegrating family world.

Daniel continued to dissolve, as if the brother I'd known were a torn cloth fraying at the edges; he seemed to shrink and change, become ragged and haphazard. Several times he left us—another attempt to return to school, another hospitalization—and each time he returned diminished from the brother I knew. And increasingly, instead of coming home to recuperate, he began to wander, sometimes heading out for the West Coast. It was then we would get late-night calls from police and from hospitals. My parents would intervene, my father calling on his medical colleagues in a dogged but futile effort to find the right combination of therapy and drugs. And then Daniel would be hospitalized again or enter an outpatient program, be placed under supervision and put on medication. Sometimes he would start a job, but these would usually be low-level and theoretically low-stress positions, and with his quick brain, he quickly found such work tiresome. His boredom would mix with his growing paranoia, fueling his delusion of being a hobbled genius, and he would refuse to take his medications. The pattern became familiar as he would then pick fights with his co-workers, explain in lucid and convincing tones how he was being kept from fulfilling his potential by the brain-numbing drugs forced on him by his doctors and his parents. He would begin by shrugging off my father's advice and then erupt angrily at him, accusing him of joining the rest of the medical establishment in its conspiracy to keep him down. And he would end up hospitalized or on the road, and in a month or two or three, the cycle would begin again. At first, when he was doing well, he could still rally some of his former charm, his jaunty, teasing charisma. This served to render the inevitable declines that much harder to bear.

Decades later, I would hear from one of his high school chums, a man who defended Daniel as a sensitive soul with a highly creative mind who had been tragically misunderstood by all of us. He recalled how even back in high school, Daniel had told him of the persecution he faced from his family. And he'd known the pressure had gotten worse, our family more rejecting, as Daniel had dropped out of college—his father's college, this man pointed out accusingly—to follow his own star. Even I, then an eight-year-old child, had supposedly taken part in the effort to squelch Daniel's original fire. Nothing was ever "wrong" with Daniel, this man asserted. We simply never understood him.

At first I was incensed by his accusations. But knowing my brother at his best, I understood how difficult it was for his friend to believe what he had become. How could he not defend him? Daniel could be so charming, this letter reminded me, bringing back as it did some of the anger, confusion, and despair of that time. I never responded to it and told myself that my brother's friend must not have seen him during those last years at home. Daniel didn't seem to have much use for his old cronies on those occasions when he came back to us. He'd do chores, work out back some, but mostly he spent his time alone in his room. And soon he would be off again, and we wouldn't always know where. At some point he brought back a black-and-white kitten he called James from Nashville, a reference to the singer-songwriter James Taylor. James grew into a rangy, battle-scarred tom, the terror of the neighborhood. He used to bring us his prey, squirrels and voles. The first of many cats we would make a home for, James was supposed to be with us only temporarily, but Daniel never retrieved him. I loved James, wasn't bothered by his scars or his smell, and didn't mind assuming care of him. Perhaps I imagined I was taking care of Daniel. I have been told that there were other visits in which Daniel made himself less welcome. My mother said later that at one point she hid all the knives and other sharp objects in the house, for fear that he would harm himself or one of us under the prompting of his delusions. At some point soon after this, my parents decided he could not live with us anymore.

Once Daniel was out of the house, it was Katherine and I. Her annoying habits were quickly becoming scary. Her moods could change in a moment. When she sensed a reaction from me they would get worse, often starting her on another round of screaming, and I learned to compose my features into a mask of calm. With Daniel no longer joining us at the dinner table, she had moved into his place, directly across from me. In this new arrangement, I learned to eat without making eye contact and studied how to avoid her without seeming to, how to wait until she was looking away before taking a reading of her face. If I was caught in the act, she'd start right in: "Why are you looking at me?" Her accusing tones escalated with each charge. "You're giving me a *dirty look!* Why are you giving me a dirty look?" She was right, in a way; I was not looking at her in a casual manner. She saw in my eyes my wariness as I waited for her rage.

All my caution did not suffice. One Chanukah, our parents treated us to two roly-poly hamsters, one for Katherine and one for me. I had picked a lighter-colored variant on the common brown variety and named him Honeybun. Katherine chose an albino from the pet store's litter, a pure-white animal with red eyes she called Butterball.

Like my turtles, Honeybun was a small but perfect creature in my eyes, active and responsive. I could spend a half hour at a time watching him eat, seeing him tuck seeds into his voluminous cheek pockets. Unlike my turtles, Honeybun was warm-blooded, nearly human in some of his fur-swaddled movements. I reveled in the feeling of his compact and warm body in my hand, the push of his little feet as he waddled up my arm, the softness of his fur. I immersed myself in caring for Honeybun, studying several *Know Your Hamster* booklets from the pet store. Honeybun had chew sticks to work his constantly growing incisors on. He had fresh water in his drip bottle, and cedar shavings in his cage, which I changed once a week. Having spent enough time with my plastic mice and with my Narnia books wanting to be an animal, I became a conscientious caretaker of animals. Honeybun was my family, and I loved the small animal dearly.

While Katherine's pet died after a few months, I believed my care would ensure a long life for Honeybun. Although he was the first of several hamsters, he was the one I adored. Thus I was horrified when Katherine said she wanted to play with my precious pet. She had been teaching me "Chopsticks" and now, she said, she wanted Honeybun to play piano, too. I tried to stop her from placing the little round animal on the keyboard of the upright in our playroom, but she ignored my protests and soon was chuckling, then roaring with laughter as his pink feet depressed the keys, making a disproportionately loud sound for such a small animal. As he ran up the keyboard quickly, arrhythmically, urged along by the piano's great booming, Katherine and I held our hands up along the front edge of the piano. Ostensibly we would keep my pet on track and keep him from falling to the floor, but still I held my breath in nervous anticipation. Powerless in the face of her single-minded zeal, I watched my golden-furred pet, wide-eyed and frantic, run his chromatic scales.

Then, glancing up at her, I saw her manic grin turn vicious. I held my breath, waiting for the explosion, hoping that if I was quiet, maybe she wouldn't lash out. Looking back, I think I knew at that moment that I couldn't protect Honeybun. I sensed that he was a symbol and that my own safety was on the line, although I didn't yet recognize the panic rising in me. Moments before she "accidentally" slammed the keyboard cover down, crushing my pet, I was ordering myself: Don't care. You can't do anything, so don't care. I was already retreating into my own safe inner space.

My mother was called in, and Honeybun's still-breathing body was placed in a shoe box, on a bed of cotton. His sides rose and fell, but not his legs or his alert pink nose. By bedtime, he was still.

After that, I tried to avoid being alone with her. If I heard her coming toward my room, I would duck into my closet hiding place or sink deeper into the beanbag chair partly obscured by the door, in the hope that she would pass without a confrontation. As Katherine neared the end of her high school years, she would ramble on end-lessly in conversation, would walk in on me without notice and begin talking no matter what I was doing. My father installed a small bolt lock on my door, asserting that I deserved my privacy, though I believe he and my mother had to have been concerned about my safety as well. In any case, the lock was a blessing, and I used it whenever Katherine and I were both in the house. I also continued my habit of monitoring Katherine's movements. Terrified of her quicksilver explosions, I became expert at holding perfectly still when she came to my door, unable to relax until she gave up calling to me and walked on.

As her behavior grew more bizarre, my parents took pains to see that we were not left in the house alone together, nor was Katherine ever without supervision. "I'm too old to have a baby-sitter," I re-member complaining to my mother. I was right. Close to my tenth birthday and certainly responsible for my age, I did not need the older woman who came around when my parents went out for an evening at the opera or on those occasional weekends when Daniel would end up in some hospital within driving distance and they would arrange to visit.

"She's coming to keep Katherine company, too," my mother explained to me. She assumed I knew. And I did understand that something was wrong with Katherine, although I didn't know exactly what or even how to broach a subject that, while not taboo, would certainly dampen any conversation. The price of bringing it up was the grief I saw in my mother's face as she responded. At the time, I felt responsible for that sadness and would do anything to keep it at bay. I realize now that she was making impossible, necessary choices, setting up safeguards to protect one of her children from another.

By the time my sister turned eighteen, her mental health had crumbled. Despite weekly visits to a psychiatrist, she could barely hold her thoughts together and nearly flunked out her senior year in high school. Simple concepts threw her off, as when one English teacher told the class they could have their final paper in "anytime before graduation." He meant it as hyperbole, stressing, no doubt, the laid-back attitude of a young teacher in 1971. She took him literally and didn't start preparing her notes until classes had ended. Graduation wasn't until the next week but her grade of incomplete was already filed for the record. Katherine lacked Daniel's amazing intellect, but still my parents were shocked by the letter informing them that their older daughter would not graduate from high school. My mother took on the task of explaining the situation to the principal, of discussing Katherine's illness and her literal interpretation of the teacher's careless words. The principal understood and made provisions for Katherine to graduate as long as she handed the paper in by the end of the month. We learned later that the principal also had a schizophrenic child.

That must have cost my mother dearly, to appeal for clemency for Katherine. They fought nearly constantly in those days. Fights between adolescents and their same-sex parent are expected, even normal, as the teen grows up and away from the parents, but the conflicts between my mother and Katherine were full-fledged battles. Katherine would shout strings of obscenities at my mother as loud as her voice would bear. When her store of dirty words was exhausted, she'd run to her room, slamming any door in between with enough force to make the walls in our old house shake, and then she'd shriek her rage wordlessly. Sometimes I could see those fights coming, my sister set on an idea and my mother just as determined to talk her down. Silently, I would will my mother to ignore Katherine, to simply walk away and not respond to her daughter's growing paranoia, her accusations of dirty looks or of malicious interference with her dates and friendships. I thought, perhaps groundlessly, that if my mother could stay calm, then Katherine might run out of steam. More often, the charges turned into curses as the volume rose, and after the doors had slammed I would find my mother sobbing. Sometimes Katherine would still be screaming in her room hours later.

I think those fights drained my mother of her energy, depressing and exhausting her. It was around this time that my parents tried to explain, and began giving me definitions for Katherine's increasingly erratic behavior. As I turned eleven, I learned that Katherine was "disturbed," that she had a sickness called schizophrenia.

I still didn't understand. The gap between my comprehension of these technical words and the day-to-day reality I experienced rendered these terms practically useless. They were labels, descriptions of a static situation. They could not tell me what these conditions sprang from or where they would lead. I needed more to understand what the disease meant to me, to know how to cope with the loss, the mood swings, and the violence. When I wanted to ask questions, however, I saw in my father's eyes an overwhelming fatigue that silenced me with fear. What I saw in my mother's face, whenever I started to speak on the subject of Katherine's scary "disturbed" episodes or Daniel's absence, was worse: I saw her grief for the child she felt she had already lost and grief for the child she was losing.

With the confusing changes of my early youth still not understood, I had been thrown into deeper crisis. The shock of change, my apparent abandonment by my brother, and my betrayal by my sister happened too fast to be absorbed, and I was thrown into coping with floridly psychotic behavior. My brother was gone. My sister had turned into a monster, capable of violence. I didn't understand what was happening, but I experienced her attacks on my pets as attacks on me—soft, warm things I loved and identified with could be hurt, could be killed by her. Even though I tried to decode her behavior and became exceedingly careful in following her intricate and rapidly changing rules, I also started to withdraw. Behaving properly was not a reliable safeguard. Life and death depended on escaping notice, and I chose to become as invisible as I could.

Even more threatening to my world was the great sorrow I saw in my parents. My mother heard herself being blamed for her children's illness, and my father, even with his years of medical training, found himself unable to cure or even slow the decline of his own son and daughter. The pressures were great, and I feared they too would crumble. Needing them desperately, I tried to save them. Now, more than twenty years later, I see the extent of my decision: As both my brother and sister grew more ill, I, like my mother, began to perform triage on my family. And I extended that harsh selection to my own emotions. As in a wartime hospital, I discarded what I felt I couldn't save and ignored what I thought would take care of itself. My brother and sister were beyond my influence, and I tried to forget them. My own grief and fear could be shelved, in fact were easier put on hold than dealt with. How, after all, could I explain my brother's absence and my sister's attacks? But my parents still seemed to respond to my actions, and with them I could get something done. I sensed that they would do better if they saw me being happy, and so I acted happy.

Once I realized how well my charade was going, I believed I was stuck with it, trapped into being solely responsible for helping my parents function. I assumed a permanent smile, and this allowed me to postpone indefinitely my reckoning with my own emotions. It also, perhaps, kept anyone from reaching out to me, but I never expected that anyway. Even in my fantasies, in my story of the bewitched frog, I could not imagine anyone understanding my problems or helping me. After all, I truly was the happiest, most successful child in my family—that fact fed my fantasy while at the same time distancing me further from the people around me. The brother and sister I knew had disappeared, but I had no cause to complain, I told myself. And by the time I was eleven, I believed this. I no longer could tell what was real in me and what not. My nightmare had come true. I found the world I knew had indeed ended. I was cut off from my family and had done my best to cut myself off from my own emotions. I was entirely alone.

I wish I'd known then that similar situations existed and that other children with mentally ill siblings felt just as isolated. Thrust into adult responsibilities by our siblings' decline and, often, by the confusion and panic of adults around us, we all felt very much alone. We believed we had to take on the care of the world. In many ways we were stranded. Although differences in age and birth order influence our roles in our families, most of us recognized this predicament. At some point, to some degree, as our siblings grew ill, we prematurely ceased to be children. We believed this assumption of responsibility was expected of us. Sometimes, if we were near in age to the sibling who had become ill, we went through the confusion of role reversal and became parent figures to our older siblings.

For Rachel, whose older sister Callie developed schizophrenia as she finished high school, the reversal happened in one day, Senior Day. "It was the day before Christmas," explains Rachel. "Seniors took over the classes; graduates came back. I was a freshman and my eyes were popping out of my head, I was so excited." Callie had always been an ideal big sister, talented and very smart, and Rachel looked forward to her triumph. "Then I saw her walking down the hall toward me and crying," remembers Rachel. "She was saying, 'I don't know what's happening, I don't know what's going on.' " Rachel calmed Callie down and then took her home. On what should have been her big sister's big day, Rachel assumed the role of older sister. "And I felt so awful," she still recalls. "It was Senior Day and she was a senior."

Samuel's brother went from being a role model and surrogate father, what he calls a "classic older brother," to a dependent. When his brother broke down, Samuel, as the next in line since their father had passed away, assumed the care for all of them. "The whole family burden came down on me," he recalls. "It was kind of like the whole family was coming apart. I felt an ominous, oppressive responsibility to help them." In his case, he was old enough to assume many of the practical functions of that role. It became his job to seek out care and treatment options as his brother's schizophrenia grew worse. It became his job to counsel his mother on his brother's condition and to inform the family of its options—"to get these people directed to the right source to get them fixed," as he puts it.

If we are younger, we cannot take on such practical responsibilities. Still, we do what we think we can to shoulder the family's burden. "I was the homecoming queen. I was in majorettes. I was the epitome of the social aspect of my school," says Gretchen. Now in her late twenties, she readily recalls those high school years. Her older brother, then a senior, had his first major breakdown when Gretchen was a freshman. "I did want to do all those things. I did want to be in the band, and I did want to be on the swim team and have a lot of friends and go to parties, but I think I was doing them because I wanted to be seen as so normal. I was almost beyond normal." To everyone in the school who had witnessed her brother being removed from class, she recalls, she was trying to say, "See, our family isn't just my brother. Our family is normal too!"

Lincoln remembers thinking, from the age of five on, that "I had to hold it together or my mother would die." His older brother had become psychotic that year, with what Lincoln now thinks was either schizoaffective or bipolar disorder. "My mother was always yelling because of my brother," he remembers. "And I felt like she just couldn't take any more." Lincoln recalls one incident when he was six years old. His mother dropped him off at the dentist, along with his five-year-old brother and four-year-old sister. "She said to me, 'You'd better be good. And make sure they're all good.' And I did. I felt very responsible. I always felt that I really had to be good or I could kill her."

"I had to be happy. I had to be successful," adds Rachel. "I had to be the good girl, because my parents had enough to worry about." This sentiment is echoed repeatedly by siblings of the mentally ill, like the West Coast woman who recalls, "There is a lot of happiness in me that's inherent, and I think that's what my family clung to."

Our joy, our optimism and faith in life may be real. But once they become our duty, something we owe to our parents, they become strained. In her book *Families and Mental Illness,* Diane Marsh notes a resemblance between families with a mentally ill child and those in which a child has died. In both, she says, the remaining children may develop what grief literature calls replacement child syndrome, in which we try to compensate for all the sadness our sibling has caused and to fulfill all the promise our sibling seems to have lost. In this effort to lessen our parents' grief, we may bury vital and true parts of our own personality.

The pressure grows even greater for those of us who lived with our ill siblings while they were exhibiting psychotic behavior. At the same time that we felt obligated to appear happy, we were often terrified. Sometimes we were afraid of changes that we didn't understand; often we feared our siblings themselves. But we believed we had to keep smiling to keep our parents together and to keep them sane. We lived with dread, with a level of anxiety that our parents did not know how to defuse and that we believed we could not express.

Hillary remembers constant fear and implied threats for much of her early life. Her older brother, who was eventually diagnosed with a mixed-personality disorder, then displayed a number of disturbing behaviors. These included torturing the family pet, a cat, once trapping it in a metal milk box for hours before she found and released it. "I don't know if he would ever have let it out on his own," she recalls. On another occasion when her brother was left alone with a cat, she heard the animal "let out an ungodly yell." Such incidents are not uncommon and carry with them an implied threat of more personal violence. Another young woman recounts in detail how, twenty years earlier, her schizophrenic brother had trapped and drowned bees, all the while making her watch.

"If you are a child and your pets are threatened," explains Julie Tallard Johnson, "it is a threat to you, quite literally." The Minneapolis-based psychotherapist, author of *Hidden Victims, Hidden Healers: An Eight-Stage Healing Process for Families and Friends of the Mentally Ill,* discusses the kind of subtle, chronic abuse that can't be proven physically but may be just as costly to our mental health. In the course of her workshops and support-group training classes, Johnson routinely asks siblings if they as children lived with a threat of or fear of violence. "Almost one hundred percent have said yes," she says.

"You live in threat . . . and you learn how to live and react to that kind of experience."

Often the violence isn't personal, but it can still be very frightening. Alice, recalling her brother's sudden breakdown, explains. "We were sitting at the kitchen table eating lunch and he got up and he started to tease the dog." At the time, she was fourteen and her brother was seventeen. "I asked him to stop teasing the dog and . . . it seemed instantaneous. He ran down the hall and he slammed the door to his room. He locked it, and he started destroying everything he owned. He destroyed all his records and all his belongings."

Sometimes the fear of being personally assaulted is real. Although the threats I lived with, toward my pets and perhaps toward myself as well, are not the norm, neither are they entirely unusual. Advocates for the mentally ill point out, correctly, that people with mental illnesses, made especially vulnerable by their disorientation, are much more often victims than aggressors. Until very recently, efforts at squelching stigma by the National Alliance for the Mentally Ill and the National Stigma Clearinghouse of the Alliance for the Mentally Ill of New York State have asserted that "a mentally ill person is not significantly more likely than anyone else to be violent." However, a 1994 paper by Dr. E. Fuller Torrey, himself a sibling and advocate, has pointed out that when not medicated, the seriously mentally ill are more threatening than the general public. Quoting studies from the National Institute of Mental Health as well as private university, prison, and hospital research, he found that when not medicated, seriously mentally ill people were more likely to exhibit violent behavior than the general population and that mental health professionals are familiar with this behavior. Although the "rampaging maniac" of B-movie fame is rare, he or she will be found more often among the mentally ill than not.

Family members may be at particular risk. A 1990 NAMI survey of 1,401 families found that 10.6 percent of people with a serious mental illness had physically harmed relatives in the year preceding the survey and another 12.2 percent had threatened harm. These numbers sound low to Johnson, who has spoken with more than 1,000 siblings in the course of her work. "To prove violence in this society, there has to be a mark," she points out. Her older brother developed schizophrenia when he was in his late teens and she was twelve years old. "My brother would threaten to kill me," Johnson says, "and I often thought he would."

Many siblings have similar stories. Hillary, now in her late thirties, tells of how her older brother, then ten or eleven, pushed her down a flight of stairs. At the time she was not even seven years old, but she remembers her shock and pain. "It was the first time I'd ever had the wind knocked out of me," she says. "I could not breathe or speak or even cry."

"My brother would taunt me and come after me and try to physically toughen me up," recalls Lincoln. His brother probably has a schizoaffective disorder; he has never been treated and was violent toward Lincoln from an early age. "We often fought physically. He actually stabbed one of my sisters once. I was very, very frightened of him."

Zoe remembers milder but constant physical harassment from her brother, before his schizophrenia was diagnosed. "He was always poking, and there were times when he would hit me," she recalls. Her brother also threatened their mother, "physically pushing her against a wall," Zoe says. "And at that point he was probably six foot two and he was this looming figure."

Dr. Edward Shapiro, medical director of the Austen Riggs Center in Stockbridge, Massachusetts, a not-for-profit psychiatric hospital and continuing treatment center for the mentally ill, explains that such behavior is not unknown. "I've seen a number of siblings of schizophrenics who experience really bizarre assaults on them," says Shapiro, who has worked in adolescent and family therapy for more than twenty years. "Killing the pets, tearing their underwear. And because of the parents' denial they couldn't tell them. So they feel very unprotected."

When inappropriate behavior develops a sexual component, siblings are traumatized in yet another way. As with violence, we younger siblings seem to be more vulnerable. Adolescence is sexually charged and confusing for the most well adjusted of us; under the circumstances, the behavior of our ill siblings is often understandable. A newly psychotic, and thus often unmedicated, family member may easily have an overload of urge and a lack of boundaries. Says Shapiro: "Some schizophrenics don't have the capacity to deal with sexual stimulation, so they play it out in all sorts of ways that terrify normal kids, and the other kids are exposed in ways they can't manage."

Lily, a quiet woman now in her twenties, found herself fondled by her teenage brother during a "touchy-feely" game he suggested a year before he was first hospitalized for schizophrenia. Her brother was seventeen at the time and she was fourteen, too old for such exploratory play, but he groped her breasts and inserted a finger in her vagina before she was able to push him away. Around the same time, he slammed a bathroom door on her hand during a fit of rage and then nearly immediately tried to compensate for the pain he caused by showing her his penis. "He tried to cheer me up," she now recalls, still shaken by the memory. "He said, 'Oh, here's some fruit! A banana and apples!'"

Johnson's brother harassed her as well, usually by verbalizing sexual fantasies, which were naturally disturbing to Johnson, then twelve years old. As is so often the case in the early stages of such an illness, her family let this harassment continue. The message she says she got from her family was "he's mentally ill." Implicit in that message was the understanding that because he didn't know what he was doing, his actions should be overlooked, a practice she says she has found to be "very common in a lot of families.

"What often causes the sibling the most trauma is not the mental illness, it's how the family has responded to the mental illness," says Johnson.

As Hillary remembers, even when her brother tormented the family pets, she was told to ignore his unusual behavior. Although he did things that made her fear for her life, her parents seemed more concerned with avoiding stigma for him. "They would rather think I was a little off and telling lies," she says. "That was better than to think I might be telling the truth." She now believes they saw her brother as the only one in the family who needed support. "We all experience these people as powerful," she now explains. "But the message we were getting was just the opposite."

———

To understand our own trauma, we have to recognize how alone we were, how often our parents fully or partially abdicated responsibility for our well-being. While wanting to protect us, our parents did not want to acknowledge the dangerous capacity of our ill siblings or simply did not know how to cope with their illness. Lily's mother told a school nurse that their oldest son was "under a lot of stress." Within the family, they blamed her brother's pot smoking for his erratic behavior, but he remained the "golden boy." Zoe's parents, like mine, stepped out of the loop while she was fairly young, leaving her to defend herself. "I had a lock on my door because [my brother] had pounded in my door before," she says. "He had broken it down." Rikki's parents took the same step. "They put a deadbolt on my door," she says. "They said, 'We don't feel like you're in danger, but we just want you to have this.'" That kind of parental response—to protect one child by giving her or him a lock—is fairly common, according to Johnson. Unfortunately, it puts the burden of responsibility on the healthy child to ensure his or her own protection once the lock is installed. "The parents don't know what to do. It is not like they have the resources available to them. But, nevertheless, the sibling is traumatized by the parents' response."

In her autobiographical book *The Four of Us,* the playwright Elizabeth Swados talks about how her parents withdrew from her when their son became ill with schizophrenia. She describes a lonely, scary existence. "I was a constant silent witness and I despised the violence in our home, didn't understand why good days always blew up into catastrophes, with my father slamming into his car and driving away, my mother weeping in her room, and my brother humming behind his closed door." As so many of our families do, the author's family responded to its crisis by splintering, and Swados was left to cope by herself.

Sometimes to help us manage we seek substitutes for our parents, but these don't always work much better. Advocacy groups like NAMI have begun promulgating support groups, and siblings who are also mental health professionals, such as Johnson, have made great efforts to connect us with one another. But these are still relatively new movements, born over the last decade, and the word is just beginning to spread. For those of us who grew up in the seventies and earlier, no such organizations existed, and our community's other resources could be painfully inadequate. Once her brother was finally hospitalized, Alice tried to find an adult to lean on. She went first to her ninth-grade guidance counselor, who told her that he could have her put in foster care, if she wanted. She then explained her situation to a favorite teacher. "He told me that his wife had had a nervous breakdown," she recalls. "And he hoped that I didn't also!" Although she was able to reach out, nobody gave her any help that she could use.

Such severe illness throws the entire family dynamic out of whack. The younger, smaller children in the house may be most affected by fear, as I was, while guilt may prey more heavily upon the older ones. Certainly, older children, even parents, may be victimized by a child's illness, threatened in the way that Zoe's mother was. But the continuous strain of dread seems less common among those who had independent lives, who had some physical parity with their ill siblings, or who had already been accustomed to seeing their siblings as more vulnerable, more needing of care, simply because they were younger.

In families with several children, responses may differ dramatically among siblings depending on their age and birth order in the family and when the brother or sister first developed psychotic behavior. And these differences place additional stress on the family as different reactions to the illness begin to separate the healthy siblings. Often, it appears, older children, who do not feel as threatened and who may not be living at home when their sibling breaks down, become protective and may step into a much more parental role. Siblings who follow the ill child in birth order, but who are older and more self-sufficient at the time of the breakdown, also seem to adopt some of this behavior. Many may follow Samuel's path of "becoming" the oldest child to the entire family, or simply fill in with smaller acts, as Rachel did when she guided her older sister home from school, and these shifts bring with them their own price of shock, grief, and fear. Younger children absorb some of this role changing. Although we cannot become practical parent substitutes, as our older peers may, we seek to appease the psychotic behavior and take on the job of cheering our parents. But, unlike our older siblings, who may feel more grief or even guilt at a sibling's breakdown, we younger children may be more motivated by fear.

As an adult who was the youngest child in my family, I have seen this dynamic at support-group meetings. I have heard oldest siblings lamenting their healthy younger siblings' lack of interest in the ill siblings' care. As one woman explained to me, "I tried yelling at my younger sister, saying, 'I'm not doing this all by myself. You have to help. You have to get involved.'" Her younger sister, three years the junior of their schizoaffective brother, replied by simply asking, "Do I have to? I feel bad." I suspect her burden is like mine and other younger children's; our view of the family is invariably different from the older children's. Likewise, our emotions may be so different that they prompt disparate reactions. I don't know if one side can understand the other. And thus the family splinters further.

There are so many ways we can end up alone, believing ourselves abandoned by our family and community. We have felt guilty about our siblings and responsible to our parents. To some extent, many of us experienced everything except our own most basic emotions. They were too raw, too sad, and too scary. Is it any wonder, then, that we withdrew into ourselves?

This process of disconnection is known as dissociation. Defined as a disruption in the usually integrated functions of consciousness, memory, identity, or perception, dissociation is a way of dealing with intense pain and stress. Simply put, we shelve it, we don't feel it. In these ways, many of us seem to have a form of what is now called post-traumatic stress disorder. First widely diagnosed among Vietnam War–era veterans, this disorder brings us from a period of hyperarousal—of being easily startled and very sensitive to our surroundings—through a constant reliving of our terror and, finally, into disconnection. Now, through the work of psychiatrist Judith Herman and her peers, this syndrome is recognized in survivors of rape and childhood abuse. And although no violence may have been intended, many of us with mentally ill siblings seem to show some of the same symptoms, particularly this estrangement from our own heart. It is there as we laugh nervously while recounting our most horrible memories, as we forget how scared we were while recalling the blood or the violence. And it is present when we look back on our own life as if viewing someone else's home movies, films that seem familiar but of little interest. Dissociation in its most extreme form is what causes "split" or "multiple" personalities, what is known now as dissociative-personality disorder. Ironically, this split personality is what most of the world thinks of as schizophrenia. For us, the healthy ones, dissociating from the pain and confusion of our daily life was normal, as sound a response as recoiling when we've brushed against a hot stove.

"I was frozen over in my gut" is how Lily describes the feeling that descended on her when her father told her that her brother was being moved out. As Jan explains it, the rupture in her family "has given me a feeling of isolation that goes right down to the root of my soul." Repeatedly, I hear phrases from siblings that echo how I felt, cut off and alone. And the worst part was recognizing how that childhood nightmare had, indeed, come true. The world as we knew it had ended, but somehow we were still standing there, looking around in the dark.

chapter three

INVENTING MYSELF

As my brother and sister receded from my daily life, as they left home and I became more involved with school and my friends, I wanted nothing more than to fit in. I wanted to be just like all the other girls in the neighborhood. I was vaguely aware of how my siblings' problems separated our family, but since our troubles had never been fully acknowledged, I assumed the internal rumblings I experienced were simply oddities of my nature. In some ways as I entered puberty, I still wanted to be the good girl and was very much still a child. For my twelfth birthday, among the presents I received was a diary. A little yellow book that could nearly be hidden between my hands, with two bluebirds on the cover and a lock and key to protect its secrets, the diary allowed me five lines for each day and presumably would last five years. Already enamored of secret places, I loved the idea of a locking book and inscribed on the inside cover, in rather timorous print: "I won't let anyone see this!" My first entry was simple: "Just got diary. Had party. Fun!"

From the start, I decided to consider the diary an imaginary friend. I named her Sue, possibly because that sounded so normal, and began each entry "Dear Sue," as if it were a letter. I had a real pen pal as well, Mercedes, a girl my age in Barcelona whose English was better than my first-year Spanish. The letters I wrote to her were full of facts about my pets and the kickball games I played with Debbie, a friend from around the corner, and Jeannie, whom I'd known most of my life. To Sue alone I wrote of my growing crushes on the boys in my class, of how cute Glen looked in his suit at our elementary school graduation, and of how given the opportunity I believed I would marry Stan, the drama counselor at camp.

But the good child I had affected to be was also a lonely one.

During the summer of my twelfth year, I met a girl at camp who would be closer to my heart than any previous friends and with whom I could share the intense feelings of adolescence. Joanne lived one town over, but we carried our friendship into the fall through nightly phone calls and frequent weekend visits. Both solitary bookworms, she and I began to share a vivid fantasy life—weaving worlds of talking animals and picturing futures that presented us as we desperately wished to be. Our friendship had all the intensity of my crushes, as often happens for girls at that age. As I started junior high school, having Joanne to talk with seemed a matter of survival.

Joanne was chubbier than I was and less compliant; she stood out socially where I could blend in. But the rejection she experienced at her new school struck close to home, and I'd blanch at her stories of standing her ground, pretending not to notice as the other girls in the lunchroom threw bits of food at her back and into her hair. I often wished she would placate these bullies, as I would have, or at least would have tried to. But she refused to be cowed. For a while, this difference didn't matter. When we were together, we were safe, and our friendship grew rapidly deeper. What we rarely talked about were our families, although her father's recent, unexpected death had disrupted her life in ways that went beyond my siblings' illness. Joanne's family had money problems, I gathered, and her mother wasn't coping too well without her husband. I know Joanne often started crying when she mentioned her father. On one level we were great together: sad girls escaping our family troubles in each other's fantasies. But something about her grief made me uneasy. Too visible, too raw, her pain embarrassed me.

I had no mode for such grieving. Even to my diary, I portrayed myself as a happy child, my days so full of fun and social events that I had to devise a grading system as shorthand for how my time was spent. "Had a fight with Shari," I would write, "but we made up." I gave the day an 89. "Jeannie slept over, 95." "I got a dress for Karen's bas mitzvah. I look pretty in it. Maybe she'll invite boys. 98." The year was 1974, and I was about to enter my teens.

I dutifully recorded lists of my favorite things on the inside cover of my diary. In my list of books, Narnia gave way to *Go Ask Alice* and *Rosemary's Baby,* both scary, both, in their way, more grown-up than my beloved C. S. Lewis fantasy. In the plastic cover of my diary I stuck a clipping, an item about George Harrison meeting President Ford at the White House, complete with photo, nestled next to my lists.

I also had my brother's high school graduation photo tucked in the cover, a three-quarter shot that shows how his entire face— cheeks, eyes, and all—could smile. It's a photographer's proof with only a number on the back. There is no other sign of his existence in my diary. Although I kept the diary for more than two years, I never wrote about my absent brother. His name is simply not mentioned. When I told my mother recently about this strange silence, she replied that Daniel wasn't home at that time. At twelve I seemed to be more involved with immediate concerns and with people physically present. I lacked the words for what had happened to my brother and sister, and could not explain what I felt about their changes.

Katherine appears in that diary, although briefly. Since she was twenty that year, she must have been in and out of the house several times by the time of the first entry. I recall that she had tried to move out two years earlier, but the move had not gone well. She had enrolled at local Adelphi University, commuting distance from our home, but she had wanted to live on her own. My folks helped her find a nearby apartment, a room close to the campus that seemed safe and quiet. But something hadn't worked, and she had come home. Perhaps she had felt unstable or insecure; perhaps she had been evicted. There were other attempts to launch her in an independent life, but the problems that had plagued Katherine in our house followed her. One apartment was the spare room of a family that had a teenage son. As she had with me, Katherine began sitting outside the son's room and talking to him for hours through the shut door. He began avoiding her, as I had. But when Katherine apparently lost it, swinging sticks and cracking them against a tree with great force, the landlady panicked. She told Katherine she would have to go and called us to pack her up and take her home.

Hoping that her older daughter would cope better in a less complicated environment, my mother found her a room with a couple who had no children living at home. This time my sister broke down completely. Although I had no idea at the time, I have since learned that my parents received a frantic call from Katherine's landlady. "Come pick up your daughter, immediately," she said. "You'll have to pay for the mattress." My mother didn't understand until she drove over. Katherine was standing on the lawn, screaming. And her landlady had placed her mattress, smelling of excrement, rolled up by the curb for trash collection. My mother gave the landlady some cash and immediately took my sister to the local psychiatric hospital. She wanted to commit her, but the social worker was resistant.

According to my mother, the social worker suspected that Katherine, who had become withdrawn in the aftermath of her frenzy, was an abused child. Katherine, with her delicate features and pretty hair, could still look sweet and demure to others, although not to me. I remember a way she had of pursing her lips, of fastidiously folding her hands and positioning her feet and any small items around her, as one of the warnings of approaching danger. With everything so specifically arranged, I knew, anything I did that would disrupt her perfect order could bring forth a rage. I learned to be wary of that prissy smile. But that same demure look, along with her now neat and tidy appearance, often won over strangers. My mother told the social worker about the first apartment, about the boy and the tree. She told her about the screaming and the mattress, about the fecal material Katherine had spread on its surface like finger paints. Katherine was admitted for a brief stay.

Although I must have been aware of strange happenings at the time, the only secrets entrusted to my diary were quite unrelated: "Haven't said so before, but *Jeff* sits next to me in Science." That little book, it seemed, chronicled a different, parallel life, a fantasy of what I wanted my days to be like. When Katherine came home from the hospital, she and I simply renewed the standoff of the past few years. I did not acknowledge her return with an official entry. One offhand comment was all I wrote: "Katherine is playing a beautiful song, must get the name of it."

When I think back on her playing the piano downstairs, my memory is of discordant, often furious pounding, the way she'd smash out chords of even the most subtly written passages. I realize now that I was writing for an audience or a censor, just the sort of thing I believed one ought to write about one's sister. Even in my most private diary I wouldn't admit that the song filtering up to my room wasn't so beautiful.

Despite the largely happy entries I recorded in my diary, I had no sense of my approaching teen years as possibly being fun. Adolescence, the example of my siblings had shown me, was a dangerous time. And all I remember wanting was not to go crazy as they had, which I defined as losing the ability to tell fantasy from reality. However, I also realized that I was daydreaming much more than I had a few years earlier and that my fantasies were entering new territory, and this made me worry that my own breakdown might have already started. With no model of what normal was, no way to tell for certain that I wasn't going to be just like my sister, I labored to keep my mind busy and my thoughts under control. I read late into the night, with a flashlight under the covers, until I could no longer keep awake. Even the quality of my fantasy life, when I allowed it, was intensified by my desire to be hypernormal. Instead of letting pleasant images flow, I engaged in a sort of compulsive mental activity, following trains of thought without rest (what if Rosemary had refused to feed her devil baby? how exactly did the Spanish words to *"Eres Tu"* go?), filling in the blanks of reality with well-ordered reverie. I did not let my mind wander at all. Where it would go if released wasn't a question I wanted to consider.

As a focus for all this compulsive thought, I developed a game plan to get myself through adolescence, and my fantasies took on a decidedly pragmatic character. I scoured celebrity bios and fan magazines for clues about the idiosyncrasies of adult life that I would have to deal with. How would I earn my own way, with time enough to enjoy the nightlife and other adventures I envisioned? How would I develop my career, whatever it was, and meet the people I'd want to spend time with? What would I wear to work or for dating? I wanted to fill in the intermediary steps, to start the future now. The new social world of junior high, I thought, offered the perfect setting in which to maneuver and to reinvent my life. No detail was too small. How should I look and talk? What could I do for a living? And, increasingly important, how would I deal with sex?

I was certainly as easily aroused as any other young adolescent, prone to crushes and hot climbing blushes that turned my neck and face dark red to the ears when a favorite teacher would call my name. God forbid my classmates should know about these feelings. I didn't believe any of them experienced anything remotely similar. If anyone but Joanne had asked me if I was in love with Mr. Silver, for example, I would have hotly denied it, the heat coming from my sense of secrecy, of shame and desire. But what seemed even more crucial to me was acquiring the knowledge I thought I needed to live as an adult. I would be ready, I would get through this current frightening period of my life as soon as possible. I had some problems with the concept of sexual intercourse—not only did I not have a great idea of how the mechanics worked, but I also wondered about morality. Was I bad or, worse, *damaged* for wanting sex? I didn't know.

I began to put more energy into becoming socially accepted and found myself drifting from Joanne. As much as I loved her, I had begun to pity her more. She was gaining more weight and began to tell me that boys didn't matter, although I knew her crushes were as strong as mine. I was glad we hadn't started the same junior high school. Engaged in the adolescent exercise of trying on roles, I, perhaps more than many of my peers, was set on leaving certain elements of my past behind. Although I shared much with Joanne, the part of a proud but grief-stricken loner wasn't a role I wanted. And as I observed the actions of the other kids in my classes, I was getting rather good at going along. As months wore on, it became more awkward to be seen with Joanne. I preferred to have everything flow smoothly.

In her place, I sought out the company of local girls, ones with "regular"—that is, complete—families. I was determined to bring the idealized world of my diary to life, and so I drew together a small band of friends. We made an informal gang: two classmates from my old school, two who had come from a different elementary school, and one somewhat worldlier girl whose family had recently moved out to East Meadow from Queens. Although we likely would have been friends anyway, I acted as catalyst and ringleader. We had nicknames, animal names—Kitty, Sparrow, Lamby for the gentle Bette, while I was Big Fish. We weren't the prettiest or the most athletic in the school. Junior high school being a tough time in the best of circumstances, we were probably considered losers by many of our peers. We had our own adventures, though, and we had fun.

As I was growing more involved with junior high school life, making friends and joining activities, I sometimes sabotaged myself. This was a period when social status could be determined by matters as trivial as whether you bought your lunch or brought one from home. And the correct answer could change week to week. Bright as I was in the classroom, I found myself missing many of the cues. I was heavy and tall for my age, which made the situation worse, but rather than try to conform, which is what I usually wanted with all my heart, I found myself compelled to accentuate my differences, much as Joanne had. I would make my unfashionable traits a point of pride and employed an in-your-face assertiveness when my temper flared. I was determined to turn our group's outsider status into a badge of pride as well. I wanted to redefine "weird" as "creative." I would change the world, I thought, through force of will.

One day in the lunchroom, for instance, my girlfriends and I were playing with the Chiquita stickers from the bananas. We stuck them on one another's faces and arms, laughing all the time. This was definitely uncool, the neighboring lunch tables let us know. But instead of beating a quick retreat—a fast rub to the forehead to erase any sign of the sticker, or a cowed blush—I felt something in me blaze up. I was sick of the stares and the sighs. I put one of those banana stickers right in the middle of my forehead and wore it through the rest of the day, haughtily staring down the disapproving looks from peers. And a month later when Ilene, a precocious flirt with a knack for getting attention, got into a fight with some of the older girls out by the school buses, I was the one who jumped in while she cried. I was the one who faced down the two ninth-graders, the one who got pushed down and who pushed back. As long as I had something to fight against, I knew I was alive.

I remember an intensity to my feelings, none of which is recorded in my childishly looping script, except through my nightmares. "Oh man, what a dream," I wrote on June 18, 1974, one month before my thirteenth birthday. "Sniper killed M&D [Mommy and Daddy] and they fell in water and drowned. They came and talked to me and I didn't know if they were ghosts or I was crazy . . . weird. (Try to analyze later.)" I gave the day a total of "80, but scared."

Everything else was depicted as mundane. Even when our cat James disappeared one night in a storm, I didn't record my fear for him. I only noted once, ten days after he had last been seen at home, that he was still missing. I remember calling for him, roaming the woods behind our house with an opened can of food in search of him. I remember how alone I felt, but I did not know how to communicate this sadness, even to myself.

The summer came, and I escaped again to camp, this time without Joanne. When I returned, eight weeks later, the conflict between my sister and mother had grown too obvious to be ignored. "I can't stand all this fighting," I scrawled in my diary on September 17, 1974. "It's getting to me."

The situation was growing worse, but that entry was the only acknowledgment I allowed myself. Once again, the years of denial, of working so hard at being what I thought I should be, at what I thought I wanted to be—a top student, socially active—kept most of my deeper fears at bay. I had turned thirteen, a ripe time for turmoil, but all I remember in place of panic or anger was a kind of slow boil. I couldn't understand how my mother could let my sister get to her. I couldn't understand how my sister could keep on screaming for as long as she did. Why couldn't my father moderate these disputes? Couldn't any of them, for one moment, step out of context, appraise the situation, and calm the other down? Why wasn't anyone besides me making this simple effort?

That's what I thought I was doing, trying so intently to make everything go smoothly: to get high grades, to keep the family entertained and happy. But while I remained proficient at calming my mother, soothing her after the fights if not preventing them, I wasn't faring quite as well in the rest of my life. In fact, outside my house, as far as I could tell, most of my efforts only worsened things. My forced gaiety, all that rage under wraps, didn't fit with my neighborhood playmates, and my self-consciousness made me stiff and hesitant. All the feelings that I could not identify just made life more awkward, prompted me to speak out when I wanted a low profile, urged me to snap at the kids I wanted to please. I didn't know why I was doing this. All I could see was that I seemed different from everybody. All I could foresee was that things could only get worse. I worried that I wasn't putting enough effort in or that I was missing some trick. And so I tried harder, but the harder I tried, the more I seemed to alienate myself from my peers.

At home, the fights got louder. My mother asked whether the man in my sister's life—whom we had never met, and who seemed available only on Wednesdays—was married. Katherine blew up at my mother, accusing her of jealousy and of wanting to destroy her happiness. She planned to leave home again, this time to stay for a while with Daniel, who was now living with a woman in a neighboring state. I marked the event in my diary: "Feb. 12, 1975: Got Denver's 'Rocky Mt. High' & Cat Stevens' *Tea for the Tillerman*. Rearranging room (blue ceiling perhaps?). Katherine moving out."

Only this time things were different. She wasn't coming home. While visiting Daniel, Katherine broke down again and was hospitalized. The hospital released her into a halfway-house placement. At no point did my parents fully explain what was happening, but even in the dissociated world of my diary, the pressure seemed to grow and threaten. I wanted so much to be normal, and as my fourteenth birthday grew near I had begun to fear that I never would be.

My diary entries began to fill with the words I didn't fully understand: "Do I daydream too much? I still have a crush on George! Maybe I'm schizophrenic! I hope not." Each entry was filled with such enthusiastic punctuation. "Tried to 'kill' daydreams the other day with reality but it hurt and I couldn't so I'm back to daydreaming again. Maybe I'm a schizophrenic."

In retrospect, I feel pity for the girl I was, the awkward thirteen-year-old adopting the clinical language spoken all around her in hushed tones to explain her emotional turmoil. Considering my circumstances, I thought my concern for my sanity was reasonable—both Katherine and Daniel had seemed normal until they hit adolescence and drifted off into their own world. What I remember from that time was an intensifying of emotions that scared me into a panic. I experienced forms of fear and a great seething rage as an almost physical pressure, a desire to push against something.

To their credit, my parents had said that if ever I wanted to talk to somebody, I could. I wished I could talk to them, but they meant a professional. One evening, after dinner, as I sat in my bedroom trying to sort out my share of problems, those that seemed natural to adolescence as well as those special to my family, I made up my mind. Screwing up my courage, I walked slowly down the tall staircase into the living room. I stood behind the brown corduroy sofa, holding on to its back for courage, and repeated what they had told me—that if I wanted to see someone, I could. I don't recall if they were surprised or worried, just that they responded. My mother made an appointment for me with her psychoanalyst, Dr. Esther Jahning, and told me that after we had met, she would be able to recommend a doctor of my own.

I remember Dr. Jahning's Austrian accent, her surprisingly small size in light of the authority in her voice and the weight she carried with my mother. I do not remember what we talked about, although on the night of that one session, I made note of it in what, for me, was great detail.

May 1, 1975: "Dr. Jahning told me to stand up for myself. I will. If I don't stand up for myself I'm nothing. Made appointment with Dr. Schaeffer, who sounds great. At first I was so scared I couldn't talk, but she was friendly, so I finally relaxed. She and Dr. S. were so helpful that I *know* I'm going to be an analyst. They *are* needed." As usual, I had deflected my current problems into a plan for the future, a decision to act that was directed toward others. I didn't want to deal with my own morass of emotions, but at least I had taken a step. I was two months shy of my fourteenth birthday.

On the basis of that first interview with Dr. Jahning, I began seeing Dr. Schaeffer one hour each week, visits I kept from my friends. A gentle, gangly man who, I noticed, often wore mismatched socks with his Earth shoes, Dr. Schaeffer was vaguely comforting, although not the magician I had hoped for. However, therapy with him did put some fears of mine to rest. Under his encouragement, I asked my parents specifically what was wrong with Daniel and Katherine. They provided diagnoses, and that gave specificity to the terms I had heard around the house: Daniel was schizophrenic, paranoid. Katherine seemed to have gone from having a borderline-personality disorder into schizophrenia. Armed with facts, I read up on these diseases, and after discussing them with Dr. Schaeffer, I became more assured that these were problems I did not have.

But therapy with Dr. Schaeffer didn't delve much deeper and never focused on the problems that I did have. I do remember him asking me about the poster beside his bookshelf: a detail of the Bayeux tapestry, a cartoonlike depiction of eleventh-century carnage. Did it scare me or make me angry? Did I want to be one of those simple knights lopping off heads and limbs, or see myself in the dismembered bodies falling beneath the horses' hooves? I was happy to discuss European history, but not my own, and Dr. S. didn't press. If he was waiting for me to discover my own killing fury, it wasn't going to happen in that office.

Instead what began to emerge was a new and tougher me, an angrier girl who hid her rage. I still pretended to be the well-brought-up, upper-middle-class student who joined the youth group and got good grades. I didn't think anyone saw this angry side, not even Dr. Schaeffer. And because of this deception, I couldn't totally accept his assurances of my normalcy. I knew there was a part of me he didn't see. I knew I wasn't like my friends. And since he seemed so calm and rational, so easily deceived, I didn't feel I could ever broach the disparity with him.

There was another patient, a cute and quiet boy about my age, whom I always saw in Dr. Schaeffer's waiting area. We talked occasionally in the few minutes between our appointments, and I sensed that he had a crush on me. After a month or two had gone by, he asked me out, and we spent an afternoon walking around the local college where his father taught. I liked him yet recognized with some sadness that he and I could never get together. He seemed sweet, but that very niceness kept me away. I saw his pleasant nature as a sign that he lived on a different planet from me, a sunnier one, while mine was clouded by dark rage, which I doubted he could understand. I brushed him off when he called again and avoided his gaze in the lounge for the next few weeks. I don't know if he brought me up in his sessions; I never mentioned him. I didn't see how I could tell Dr. Schaeffer that I felt I had no choice but to reject this boy. How could I tell him that it wasn't that my suitor wasn't fine, but that I was too full of darkness? I could see no way to explain this conviction to either my date or Dr. Schaeffer, and this, too, made me sad.

After about eight months, Dr. S. had done his job. If I was not convinced that I was entirely normal, at least I no longer believed that I was going insane in the way that Katherine and Daniel had, and I decided to end my sessions. However, there was still no stopping the powerful negative emotions that often washed over me, seemingly with little prompting. I fought against them late into the night by filling my mind with thoughts and plans. To fend off disarming sleep, I'd play the radio, tuning into the darker, heavier sounds of Black Sabbath and Aerosmith on the new FM stations that had begun to flourish in the midseventies. And, finally, in this music I began to find my release. Hard rock had replaced giddy pop on my radio, and in its amplified guitars, its evocative dissonance and wild, hard rhythms, I found an outlet for my own need to strike out, my own desire to roar and pummel something. In effect, this music created a second life for me, and I began copying lyrics into my diary in place of my own observations.

What therapy couldn't accomplish, rock and roll did, tapping into some of the pressure within, giving me, literally, the words with which to express my rage. My devotion was absolute: I wore the bands' T-shirts, bought their records, and listened to my favorite songs hundreds of times. But unlike many adolescents who crave the same release, who also define themselves through rebellion, I did not become an all-out rocker. I was careful to keep my peer groups separate but intact. Being the good child became my job.

By the time I turned fourteen, I had begun to patch an identity together out of the pieces. In retrospect, it only makes sense that I picked a loner like myself who had recently moved into our area for my first real boyfriend. Garry had already discovered the rock subculture and wanted to be a guitarist. I had played string bass in my school orchestra and now put down sixty dollars for a cherry-red electric. I faked ineptitude in algebra and kept bothering Garry for after-school help until he got the picture and asked me out. We became a couple and, soon after, formed a band.

My status as Garry's girlfriend won me a certain amount of acceptance, which helped my self-esteem in some ways. I kept my interest in books and my background secret enough to gain acceptance into his tougher, working-class crowd, but that seemed a reasonable sacrifice. My reading life had always been a private escape anyway, and I was happy to leave my family problems behind.

After a few months with Garry, I suggested that we have sex. Garry was certainly willing, despite my stipulation that he wear two condoms simultaneously. And so we planned our first encounter for a weekday afternoon on the sofa in his basement. The day came, and despite the double condoms we managed to do it, half-clothed and in a hurry. I felt little thrill. The magnitude of the act, of my decision, as well as the possibility of pregnancy, terrified me. What if anyone found out? I still squirmed with that early, acute embarrassment, confident that neither Bette nor Ilene nor any of my other girlfriends had even considered taking this step. But I knew I was different from them and wanted proof. In retrospect, I see that I needed acknowledgment of both my precocious emotional emancipation and my darker, self-destructive side. In so many ways at home I was expected to be an adult, and yet I was still openly considered a child. Sex would change that. And if the strong feelings evoked by sex didn't bury my rage and confusion, at least they gave these feelings an outlet. I could express myself, lose myself in this relationship, and mark myself as different from so many of my friends, all with one act.

At the time, I thought logic had led me to this conclusion, and although I accepted it, I did feel some trepidation. I wished a little that I had not yet felt it necessary to have sex, that I could tarry longer on the more pleasurable plateau of kissing and fondling. I had concluded that intercourse would be the quickest way to adulthood, but what if my calculations had been wrong? I went over my thoughts and could find no flaw in my reasoning: For now, this was something I had to do, and Garry's stale breath and sloppy kisses aside, I did. Less satisfying than our earlier necking, our sex life became a series of rushed and nervous couplings in his basement before his mother got home from work, or upstairs in my bedroom when my parents were out.

I stopped writing in my diary; I wanted no witness. From that point on, I thought, I had a real reason to believe I was different from my school friends—more advanced, which I wanted, and something else as well. I sometimes feared (and was secretly slightly thrilled with the idea) that I was damned. From where I had gone, there could be no return, and so I determined to remain as willfully independent as I could be, and sexually active as well, although increasingly Garry preferred getting high to making out.

With the rock crowd had come marijuana, and one day my mother went through my pockets in preparation for doing our laundry.

She waited for me outside the school that afternoon, the thin joint in her hand, much to my surprise. "I know what this is," she said. "It's a marijuana toke." I was terrified. I expected tears, lectures, and certainly punishment of some sort; I thought my entire double life would collapse. We drove home in silence. My father had come home from his office early, red-hot angry, and started in about the way he and my mother had raised me, the advantages and privileges I had. Finally he would around to that joint. "And this"—he held it out in front of him. "This! You won't do this anymore," he said. *"You won't do it anymore."* "He's wrong," I thought, as if a circuit had broken within me. My father was stating something as a fact, and I knew that his statement was incorrect. Had he lectured me on the dangers of drug use, or pleaded with me for my health, my safety, my future, or even the family name, I believe I would have been more responsive. Had he asked me why I was getting high, I might have broken down and cried. Instead, my feelings, even my free will, were negated by what he said. He didn't even ask me to respond, and so the only promise I made—to myself—was to be more careful next time.

I was never caught again, though as I passed from junior high to high school, my behavior grew more wild, and I replaced Garry with older boyfriends, men I never introduced to my parents or any of my friends. I had rejected the dictates of my family, but I let these young men guide my tastes and found my styles in music and clothing changing as I passed from boyfriend to boyfriend. Although I remained basically unaware of my own chameleon nature, I was growing suspicious that somehow all the men I chose were in some way lacking, and that I needed to give them my full allegiance as soon as we became involved in order to lend the relationship validity. I was the strong one, I sensed at some point with each new man, and it was necessary to use all my energy to hold each current boyfriend together, focusing always on his fractured life and needs instead of my own. What could I need?

Adolescence is rocky under the best circumstances. We lurch awkwardly into adulthood, trying on new roles, testing our new feelings and altered bodies, retreating occasionally to childhood ways and then lunging ahead again. In a perfect world, adolescence is the time when we prepare to leave our family home in order to start our own life, taking those first tentative steps before we are ready to be totally independent. In healthy families, there is a safe base from which to take those steps. However, in families where serious mental illness has already affected one child, we—as those children's siblings—do not have such security. We sense that our family has come close to breaking. We fear that our first steps out will upset its balance further. And so every move we make is shadowed by the anxiety that we may not, like other adolescents, have a safe place to return to. Unless we are much older than our ill sibling and safely past adolescence by the time of that sibling's breakdown, any change may seem too threatening to risk.

Sometimes the cause for anxiety is more personal. Many of us, particularly those who are younger than the sibling who has become ill, have more to fear than the usual changes of adolescence: Do our wide mood swings signal the onset of a mental illness? The odds seem against us. Siblings (who are not identical twins) of people with schizophrenia have approximately a 10 percent chance of developing the disease, a rate ten times greater than the general population. Those of us whose siblings have bipolar disorder may have as great as a 20 percent chance of developing that illness. For those of us who saw the decompensation and the beginning of psychotic behavior, observing changes in ourselves was particularly scary.

"Am I OK? Am I normal?" Jan remembers asking only a few years after her older brother broke down. "I wasn't like my friends. I knew in my soul I was a good little pup, but was I like my brother?" She shrugs. These days, happy in her career as a neurobiologist, she can be confident about her own sanity. At sixteen, she was not.

"Most siblings and children of individuals with schizophrenia are themselves haunted by a fear that they too will develop the disease," writes Dr. E. Fuller Torrey in *Surviving Schizophrenia.* Certainly, this fear is present whatever the mental illness in our family, especially as we enter what we consider the danger zone.

"All through adolescence there were times that I thought maybe I was going crazy or something," Rachel recalls of her high school years after her sister broke down. Rachel was a freshman when her sister became ill, and during the time when her sister was being examined and then institutionalized, Rachel saw her own grade average slip down to "just barely passing." Because she knew she was smart enough to be doing better in her high school courses, she wondered if another part of her mind was failing her.

"We have the same blood," Zoe remembers thinking as she neared the age at which her older brother broke down. "And I just wondered, How am I going to function? Am I going to stop functioning the way my brother did?"

So many of us did believe we might be getting ill—this, after all, was the trail our siblings had blazed. We learned that anything "off" could be the first sign of something very scary, and thus we constantly saw signs of emerging mental illness in ourselves.

Our fears were partially correct. Even if we were not as ill as our sibling, we might have been laboring under a load of anger or anxiety that did set us apart from our peers. Torrey and others note that heavy doses of shame, embarrassment, anger, jealousy, and depression are common to siblings of the mentally ill. These are powerful emotions, and the way they threatened to wrench us out of control was scary to experience. How easy it was, then, to confuse these feelings with incipient psychosis. And when we chose to suppress these feelings, we saw how much energy that took, and this fight scared us even more. In short, we found ourselves in a conflict we could not win. We were simultaneously afraid of giving in to our emotions, for fear we would lose control of our minds, and appalled by the battles we waged within ourselves in order to appear stable.

"I thought I was borderline psychotic," says Hillary. "I was aware that I had compulsive habits that I think are not signs of mental health. I counted words in sentences. I counted syllables. I counted letters in words." For Hillary, a slim, articulate woman, the uncertainties of adolescence were unbearable and exacerbated her counting habit, which had started around age ten, a few years after her brother became ill. "I felt it was not something I was in control of. It was something I had to do. I had this fear that I too could be a crazy person."

"I would get very absorbed with things in an obsessional way," agrees Sandra, a West Coast health professional whose younger sister June had been showing signs of encroaching illness for years. June first became psychotic during Sandra's freshman year at college, and Sandra reacted with controlling rituals. "When I couldn't sleep at night, I would go down from the eighth floor of the dorm to the basement and I would never take the elevator," she says. "And I would walk in a certain way."

In general, it is the younger siblings who share these sorts of fears. Younger siblings, after all, follow in the footsteps of their older brothers or sisters. Yet, as Sandra's case shows, even if we were older and had already passed the age of our sibling's breakdown, we still experienced doubt about our own health. We knew we were the same generation, knew we drew from the same genetic pool and had been, in a way, running on parallel tracks. Many siblings I spoke with expressed the idea "There but for the grace of God go I" and monitored themselves closely, always fearing on some level that if they relaxed their guard something horrible would happen. To fight back, we often reacted with a desire to control, with ritualized behavior, or by assuming an exaggerated appearance of what we deduced to be normalcy. Like the magical thinking of childhood—the "if I don't step on the sidewalk cracks, all will be well"—these rites gave us a feeling of control. But the environment we wanted to control was our own self, and the rituals that we felt compelled to repeat, the behaviors we desperately mimicked, only made us feel more afraid.

Despite her rituals Sandra knew that sense of barely contained panic well. "I knew more about something horrible in the world, or that I was more vulnerable or more dangerous or toxic in some way," she says. For her, knowledge, even curiosity, compounded the threat. "I had this idea that if I ever got in touch with the stuff that I was so terrified of, it would kill me. I would fall into a pit. I was afraid that there were things so painful, so horrible just about to happen or just about to be remembered that they would destroy me."

Many of us tried to control our world. Others wanted nothing more than to escape, to leave our childhood behind. If we could advance into a sphere that did not know our ill siblings, so much the better. Now a medical doctor in private practice, Jack graduated from high school at age sixteen and immediately went away to college. Jack's older brother, who had developed schizophrenia several years before, was living at home during Jack's high school years, and since he often refused to take his medication, the house was often wracked with the screaming of his psychotic rages. "I definitely had this feeling like, 'I want to get out of here while the getting's good,' " Jack says. "I've always been able to plan five years ahead. I've been able to fulfill a lot of plans. At the time it was happening, I was starting to feel burdened. I don't know if it was conscious. I know I was just really ready to be on my own and certainly able to do it. And the family was starting to feel more and more oppressive."

"The way I reinvented myself was 'enough of this childhood,' " says Hillary, who spent her teens in New York public schools, while her brother, who was later diagnosed with a mixed-personality disorder, attended a private school. "When I went to high school, it was a huge place and I had a boyfriend and nobody knew my brother. It was great. I was a grown-up."

"I became a wild animal," says Jan. She, too, went to a different high school than her older brother. "It was very freeing for me to not have him constantly over me anymore." Largely because of her brother's harassment, she had been a withdrawn child. But the quiet girl changed when she was out on her own. "In high school, I was a ringleader in the orchestra, and all of a sudden I was engaging with people."

For some of us, this social arena included the sexual. We were precocious in part because we believed ourselves, already, to be adult and because we were seeking something—affection, attention, normalcy—that we no longer found at home. Zoe, a petite and pretty woman, attracted men who were ten years older from her early teens on. Since her big brother, whose schizophrenia was at that point undiagnosed and untreated, was often physically and verbally abusive, she relished the opportunity to spend time away from home. "My social life was completely separate from my school life," says Zoe. "It was kind of my little secret. I was more or less pretending to be an adult, going to bars and clubs and looking for validation in, I guess, males. When I was sixteen probably the average age of the guys I was seeing was twenty-four, and I was kind of living this rock-and-roll lifestyle, experimenting with drugs and just looking for excitement."

"I was on the pill, I started sleeping with [my boyfriend] when I was fourteen," says Hillary. "I let myself be persuaded into a situation that seemed to make a lot of sense at the time. I loved his family. He had parents and sisters and a nice apartment. It was like a romance with his whole family, and if that's what I had to do to be a part of it, then it was reasonable."

Lily, whose older brother's sudden psychotic break monopolized her parents' attention, felt even more alone. "My parents never gave us enough emotional support, like hugging, or affection," she says. "So what I did was get drunk and sleep with guys just to be held."

For many of us, other aspects of typical adolescent acting out became exacerbated, perhaps more so for those of us who grew up in the 1970s and earlier, when dysfunction was less talked about and any discussion of mental illness was still largely taboo. We wanted to state our independent existence, but our family could not recognize the healthy nature of this growth. A family that has witnessed one child withdraw into catatonia, after all, will understandably panic when another one seems moody; parents who have seen their child whip about in a paranoid rage may want to clamp down on any display of anger in the next child, fearing that she, too, will go over the edge. In these homes, the norm can no longer bear even the most normal adolescent testing of limits; the elasticity has gone.

Given these constraints, how could we cry out in a healthy manner? By rights, our cries should have been deafening. We had been the good little ones, the careful children, and so as we became adolescents we felt even more reason than our peers to rebel. "I didn't want to have to take care of my mother and my brother," says Jack, looking back on his ill brother and the dependent mother who came to him, the smart one, the *good* one, to help her cope. " 'Who takes care of me,' you know? That's the childhood impulse that gets expressed sometimes in flirtations with being self-destructive."

But as Jack, who continued to be the good child by going from college to medical school, knows, we almost always reined ourselves in.

"Any sibling who must in some extraordinary way care for a brother or a sister has been to some extent abandoned by a parent," write Drs. Stephen Bank and Michael Kahn in *The Sibling Bond.* "The rage that the child, adolescent or young adult sibling feels toward that parent can be temporarily assuaged by a variety of defense mechanisms in the sibling relationship. One can wear a mask of responsibility . . . and thus deny that rage."

And so many of us went wild. But then we brought ourselves back in line, before we could truly test our family's limits, before we, like our ill brother or sister, could somehow fall out of favor. Most often, we contained our roiling emotions nearly entirely and continued to tread with care, trying not to shake anything up. As Diane Marsh points out in *Families and Mental Illness,* we denied ourselves "healthy opportunities for rebellion . . . to protect . . . already overburdened parents." We had lost so much already that we feared losing all the protection of our family. Most of all we took care not to further fracture the family structure that had proved to be so fragile.

Adolescence has probably never been easy in any culture, but for us it represented a tightrope walk over hell: We were set up to fall. Boiled down to its basic issue, the developmental task we must complete in this phase, according to the psychologist Erik H. Erikson, is that of consolidating our sense of ourselves and our sense of our place in the social world into one identity. This is our time to try out our wings, to see how we will function in a world larger than our family. But how, when our earlier growth was disrupted by trauma, are we to have developed a sense of who we are? How are we to leave our family when its needs seem so great? Our context has been largely one of crisis or denial, of obligation and guilt. In some ways we are younger than our more fortunate peers, less formed and complete. But we have also dealt with life-and-death issues, with crises that have aged us in ways others in our age group may never know.

chapter four

OUT OF SIGHT, OUT OF MIND

Once Katherine was out of the house permanently, our home quieted down. And while the lack of screaming was a blessing, the peace that replaced it remained uneasy. We had no closure, no final calamity that would allow us to mourn. And so, without knowing how to heal, my parents and I cultivated the harmony between us, as if to say to the world, "See, this is how we were meant to be." As I proceeded through my teens, my parents and I developed into a most civilized threesome. Over dinner each evening we talked about art and music, about people we knew. Our conversations rambled pleasantly, with each of us bringing more detail into the weave but rarely dissenting from what would develop as a family line on any topic, and I believe we all took comfort in this. By unspoken agreement, we rarely mentioned Daniel or Katherine. Only recently have I filled in what was going on in my siblings' lives during these years.

As I had recognized at the time, Katherine had been getting worse after her high school graduation, and each of her successive attempts to live independently ended with more trauma. I later learned that when she had gone to visit Daniel and his girlfriend Ellen, my mother had called to warn them of Katherine's penchant for hurting small creatures, since Ellen had recently had a baby. Although Daniel wanted to welcome his sister with open arms, Ellen would only let Katherine visit, refusing to let her stay with them. Nor could she be left unsupervised with their baby.

Katherine found a room near them, it seems, and soon became extremely psychotic, screaming with rage and throwing furniture about. The police came and had her hospitalized. When she was to be released, someone at the hospital recommended a halfway house, a place that would give her some freedom and some responsibility but that had a trained health care worker living on the premises. Although there was a vacancy in such a house nearby, there were also many applicants. She would have to decide quickly. Katherine wanted to be on her own yet was willing to accept this kind of halfway situation, at least for a while, and moved directly from the hospital into Suffolk House. My parents were relieved. Katherine was twenty-one, legally an adult, but she was also their child. If the hospital had released her to their care, she would have likely come home to East Meadow. The cycle of moves, of emergency calls and screaming fights, would have started again.

As it was, she seemed gone for good. Although at thirteen I was only dimly aware that this latest move by Katherine had a better chance of lasting than any of the previous ones, the atmosphere in our house seemed immediately more calm. Certainly, as the peace continued, everything seemed more final. My mother set up her free-standing Singer with its multiple bobbins in Katherine's room, turning it into the "sewing room." Down the hall, Daniel's room was renamed the "blue room." To further distance these rooms from their former occupants, it seemed important that we occupy them, and both served as corollary reading rooms. Following my mother's lead, I used the sewing room as a workroom. I took over Katherine's rolltop desk, keeping my notebooks and folders of poetry in its three big drawers. Daniel's room soon collected my father's books on sailing and nature, as well as a paperback collection of the complete works of Sigmund Freud. It was there I'd sack out, on the blue corduroy cover of Daniel's old bed, and read, working my way through Freud's case histories, starting with the story of the "Wolfman," while my mother sketched. She still has a watercolor of me from this period, reclining in a red nightshirt, feet and head propped up on the corduroy bolsters, a book in my lap.

This charade worked when either of my parents was around. When I was alone, the rooms took on a different atmosphere. Often I would get up from my poetry and look through Katherine's windows at her view over our woods. I would finger the white eyelet lace that Katherine had chosen as curtains years before; the cloth seemed so delicate and feminine. The room down the hall held a different kind of mystery: For so long I had seen only the outside of this room, as

Daniel had become withdrawn and hidden behind his closed door. Now, with the pot smoke, the Bob Dylan poster, and my brother gone, I found myself poking around a space I barely remembered, looking for clues. As I had when younger, I would open the drawers of the long, low bureau that had held his clothing and examine the plastic drawer dividers that had cupped paper clips, safety pins, and memorabilia from his years as a Boy Scout. These drawers were empty now, and I remember running my hand over the wood grain inside, half hoping to find a letter that he had left behind or a secret panel that would open at my touch. I explored his closet with the same sense of expectation and awe. Like the closet under the stairs below, it had an L shape, with a space to the left of the door that continued for a bit under an eave. I sensed a kind of kinship with this cavelike space and knew that if I were a few years younger I would want to crouch down in there, my back to the wall, and invent a whole world around me. I wondered if Daniel had ever done that, in younger and happier days, or later, when he had been tormented by the voices in his head.

The only thing left in the closet was a yellow terry cloth bathrobe, which I found hanging on a peg. I took it, and wore it until time and our washing machine shredded the soft cloth into fringes. It seemed, after a while, to be a legacy, the kind of casual hand-me-down a young girl would want from her dashing brother away at college, and my parents didn't question my choice. When I first saw the robe hanging there, though, I don't recall feeling either comforted or connected. Instead, I was startled, almost embarrassed, as if a figure from one of my dreams had exposed itself in the daylight world, for everyone to see.

Soon after I turned fourteen, my father asked if I wanted to join him and my mother on a visit to Daniel and Ellen. He might as well have been talking about a trip to Mars. My brother must have been twenty-four at the time, and he hadn't lived at home for about five years. The first two or three of those he had primarily spent in hospitals or wandering around the country. Over the past few years, however, Daniel seemed to have settled into a more structured life; he appeared to be taking his medication and making a go at a stable relationship, and so my parents wanted to reach out to him. I hadn't seen Daniel since I was nine. I agreed to go, having no idea what to expect or what I would say to him.

Our visit grew increasingly complicated. Ellen, it seems, had at least a little paranoia. She and Daniel had met at one of the outpatient programs Daniel attended, where he got his injections of antipsychotic drugs and some counseling. She seemed the more grounded of the couple, but when my parents tried to finalize our plans to visit, she grew suspicious. My parents, she decided, did not think she and my brother were fit parents. They were going to try to steal her baby, who by then had grown into a rambunctious toddler named Rebecca. To some extent, her perception was accurate—on the rare occasions that they mentioned Daniel's child, their grandchild, my parents sighed heavily. They did not think anything good could come of the relationship and worried about Rebecca's future. But Ellen's major fear was delusional. My parents had no desire to adopt their grandchild. I suspect they would have been happiest if the little girl was taken by the state's social services division and put up for adoption, but they would not interfere.

Ultimately, Ellen refused to meet us. I have little recollection of that lunch, except for trivial things. I could describe in detail the wood-toned booths of the dimly lit dining room, the paper place mat printed with "fun" historical facts, and the heavyset waitress who hovered three booths away, waiting for us to finish our soup, our seafood salad, and then our coffee. But I can barely picture what Daniel actually looked like as he sat there, except that he was tall and a little skinny and that his red, curly hair had started to fade. And I felt polite as a stranger, answering my brother's questions by rote when he asked me about school, friends, and the cat that had replaced James. He sounded relatively healthy, very connected, as he talked— more to my parents than to me—about his current program of monthly injections, of the church he and Ellen attended regularly, of how it gave them both support and a sense of community. Although I can't recall any exact phrase, I believe Daniel was trying to show my parents how well he was doing. I think he said he was going to try to go back to school, part-time, and that he would like to get off Social Security and be a real father, supporting his family. My father began to caution him at that, I remember, and Daniel humbly backed down. He knew it would be hard. One step at a time. But, he said with humility, he was ready to try. He wanted very much to try.

I recall watching Daniel as he spoke, trying to picture the hero I had once seen in my older brother. He resembled somebody I knew, a version of Daniel, but hearing his deep, somewhat husky voice—the same voice that had told me stories years before—made me feel as if he were lost to me. The entire day assumed the surreal quality of a nightmare in which real and comfortable elements pop up in bizarre and unsettling situations. We drove back to Long Island after lunch, listening to tapes of Debussy, subdued and not talking much. Soon afterward, Daniel sent me a brief letter. He said that Ellen was sorry she hadn't met me and thought that maybe sometime in the future we could try again. Rebecca, he had told her, looked a lot like I had at that age. She was growing almost visibly, he said, and seemed to be smart as a whip. He enclosed a picture of her that I still keep.

Not long after that, things began to break down for Daniel again. He thought he was better, that his mind was healing and that he could make do without his medications. Of course, as he missed appointments the paranoia came back and he began to suspect harmful intent behind his monthly shots. They were mind control; the drugs were suppressing his natural brilliance, his intuition and instincts. Ellen, I found out later, tolerated his changed behavior for as long as she could. But when he flat out refused to go for his medications and became increasingly delusional, she feared for herself and for Rebecca and left their apartment. He moved out soon after, and a long time passed before my parents heard from him again. I haven't seen or heard about my niece since.

My parents and I rarely if ever talked about that visit, and in many ways life was better. I wanted them to know their youngest child was still their good child, though I was growing older. One of the carry-overs from my childhood was that my parents always made a big deal out of my birthday, and as I neared sixteen they began to ask me how I wanted to celebrate. I hadn't had a bas mitzvah, as had many of my classmates, and so my parents suggested we throw a sweet sixteen and told me I could make it any kind of party I desired.

Katherine had had her own sweet sixteen, I recalled. My folks had taken her and some of her friends to a dinner-theater production of *Gypsy* somewhere out on the Island. I remember the songs and, even more, being allowed to dress up and stay with the older girls, at least for a time. I still kept the white porcelain candy dish she had given her guests as favors. In gold script along the little dish's fitted top it said "Katherine's Sweet Sixteen" and gave the date, eight years earlier. Mine had a chip in its lid, and sometime in the intervening years I had broken off one of its legs. Still, it was a pretty thing.

Katherine had enjoyed the idea of such a delicate favor, much as she enjoyed most feminine flourishes: the gold engraving, the floral centerpieces, a bit of lace in her room and on her dresses. And she loved sweets. After she left home, candy was one of the few things my parents sent her. She never responded to the care packages delivered to her at the halfway house. But my parents continued to mail her presents of candy and money. They had stopped celebrating Daniel's birthday years before, when he had, once again, been out of touch. But each May, when both Daniel's and Katherine's birthdays came around, they would send Katherine the treats they thought she'd like. As she turned twenty-three and then twenty-four, they bought her a big pastel-colored box of petits fours, which had been her favorite as a child. They had the box special-delivered, along with a birthday check, and would keep the receipt as proof that their gift had arrived.

I too loved sweets, but candy dishes were not my style. Such a girlish celebration seemed foreign to my more liberated image of myself. Still, I welcomed a retreat to my girlfriends and to the safety of my parents' more innocent vision of me as well after having been recently dumped by one of my more inappropriate boyfriends. A sweet sixteen seemed like a lovely idea.

The party was a success, the reward of frenetic planning and production. My father and I had strung lanterns around our backyard from the driveway back into the woods, to provide lit strolling areas. We plotted the placement of citronella candles in groupings around the lawn for mood and atmosphere. My mother and I cooked for three days beforehand, laboring over recipes that I had chosen from the party cookbooks she had brought home: veal Marengo, chicken Kiev, pasta, salad, punch, and cake. More than thirty of my classmates came to wish me a happy birthday, and we had dancing on the lawn and later, when the night turned buggy and damp, in the playroom of the house. The core gang stayed past two, Bette and Ilene and Laurie and I, piled on the sofa, bare feet up on the tables, talking about the future. My mother and I had overcalculated the food, of course, and we ate veal Marengo for days.

Sixteen seemed a watershed. This was the age that I remembered Katherine at best, when she and her friends would try on different lipsticks and practice dancing with each other in front of the mirror. Katherine's side of our shared bathroom had overflowed with cosmetics, skin creams, and foundations. Her brightly colored clothes held great importance in her life, and the careful setting of her long, straight hair assumed the sacred importance of a ritual. Her illness began to manifest itself as early as fifteen and certainly had affected her behavior by the time she was sixteen. But I still associated her with the bright pop of the era, the emphasis on the unique and optimistic teenage subculture that was blossoming at that time.

Once the spark of my sweet sixteen party wore off, my actual sixteenth year, in contrast, was dark. Over the intervening eight years between my sister's sixteenth birthday and mine, Katherine's mod fashions had been superseded by the "natural" look of the midseventies, flowers and wild colors replaced by worn denim and leather. Where Katherine had set her hair for a flip, I believed I had to let mine hang loose to have integrity. Natural, in my mind, was ugly, but at least it was real, which mattered to me. Over that year, I lost any interest in being a teenager and began to find the role confining, if not downright embarrassing. I did not want to be a child, but I did not want to be a teenager either. As do many adolescents who want to be taken seriously as young adults, I found the category trivializing, a catchall used by elders to dismiss our issues. And along with this traditional discomfort, I had my experience of Daniel's and Katherine's adolescence. Because of them, I knew that this stage of life could also be dangerous.

I needed to make some sense of this murky period and tried, at one point, to communicate with Katherine. Although I had stopped seeing Dr. Schaeffer the year before, I followed up on a suggestion he had made and wrote my sister a letter. When my mother gave me

Katherine's address, she warned me that my sister had never responded to any of her letters or gifts and that I might be similarly ignored. I thought the risk worth taking. My first letter was in the tentative, falsely cheery voice I used at home, full of news about my classes and the books I had read. To my parents' surprise, she responded. Her letter reawakened some of my fear. She had found Jesus, she wrote in an imperious tone. She had taken refuge, figuratively speaking, in the church and now she was one of the chosen. She was glad to write to me because I was her blood relative, her only sister, and she could reach out to me, offer me my only chance of salvation. I could accept Jesus and be like her, be saved—or I could be damned. I wrote back, this time in a more personal tone, and told her that organized religion was not important to me, that I believed in some form of guiding spiritual presence but not anything specific. As I rarely had in my diary, I wrote honestly of ordinary things, hoping to turn her back into a sister. I received one more letter like the first, full of warning and damnation, and that time I didn't write back.

Katherine never responded to my parents, never called after getting their cards or presents. All the contact was born out of crisis, as when the police found her wandering, disoriented, in Oregon and called our house. My parents were able to put them in touch with her halfway house, which still had room for her, provided she stayed on her medications. They arranged for her to fly back to the East Coast and then tried to visit her, but she refused to see them. Soon after that, my mother stopped sending gifts of candy and money.

By the autumn of my sixteenth year, my brother and sister might as well have been ghosts for all the acknowledgment they received in our house. Although I gather now that my parents maintained some contact with the social workers and doctors who worked with Daniel and Katherine, they were never mentioned, and I knew better than to bring them up myself. They seemed to carry some kind of terrible contamination, a pollution that threatened to cover us if we ever invoked their names.

I had just started my junior year of high school and was beginning to think about college when, for the first time, my mother actually lied about my siblings. I had requested information about

Harvard and was invited with other local high school juniors and seniors to a picnic given by the local alumni association. It was a fairly low-key affair, a chance for the alumni to dispel any lingering fears that an Ivy League school would be stocked with stuffy geniuses. But, of course, it gave alumni a chance to check out the next crop of prospective applicants, and all of us guests worried that our college career depended on making a favorable impression. My mother and I sweated for days over what I would wear. I seesawed, I recall, between thinking I should dress conservatively and wanting to be outrageous, to state my independence and dare the world to come to terms with me. I think I compromised, leaning toward the former.

The afternoon spent on Long Island's ritzier North Shore began as pleasantly as possible, given the loaded situation. And then I remember someone asking my mother if I had any brothers or sisters, an innocent question from an idle stranger trying to start up a conversation. But it frightened my mother. "Oh no!" she said. "Clea is our only child." I couldn't be sure what was at stake, and so I didn't contradict her. I had heard her on previous occasions say with a note of finality, "Our other daughter is away" or "Our son lives out of state." My father never elaborated on these half-truths, letting her take on the full burden of deflecting unwanted questions. But this was a different denial, a complete abnegation, and I was stunned that she could erase their lives so swiftly. "It's just easier than explaining," she said to me when I confronted her later in the car. She looked tired and beaten down as we pulled away, and I forgave her. There was so much at that point that she had already been blamed for. Now that she was trying to launch me into life, why should I be tarred with my siblings' craziness? Why should she subject herself to the automatic censure of stangers; why should any of us?

But with that lie came the threat of exposure and the attendant pressures of maintaining the facade. I wanted it to be over and began to view college as a ticket out. Although I had never stopped being an honors student, as I progressed through my junior year, I began to really apply myself. Up until then, I had cruised along on my love of books and had, with my parents' prodding, taken the PSAT, which served as a qualifier for National Merit Scholarships, the year before.

But I had taken it with a hangover and a muzzy head after a night out drinking and getting high. Now I was ready to get serious. This would be my chance, I told myself, unconsciously taking my cue from my mother's denial. Once I got away to college I could reinvent my entire past, without the rash moves and mistakes of high school. Just as my brother and sister could be polished out of our preferred family image like the tarnish off silver, I could erase my own failures. My awkwardness at school, my social failings, even the tauntings of the neighborhood boys who knew of my sexual exploits through the high school grapevine, could be left behind as if none of it had ever happened, as if I were not in some way marked.

I was also afraid of leaving home, afraid that it might not exist for me to come back to if I needed a breather or if I was unable to make the transition. I worried about leaving my friends, my current boyfriend, and the complex high school society that I had only just started to figure out. But I was anxious to prove some of them wrong, to show myself successful at getting away, at moving up in the world—to an Ivy League college, to another city in another state. I wanted a new life, a second chance at getting everything right. And I believed I was going to get that.

The next spring, I knew I'd been right. I'd already gotten into my "safety schools" and confirmed my place on Yale's waiting list. Then, one morning, I heard my father hooting and saw him running up the driveway toward the house. He had stopped his car on the way to the office when he saw our postman come by with some letters. And, with the engine running, he had leafed through the stack of mail until he found it. I remember him, car door open wide, as he whooped and called to us, waving one arm while the other held a fat white package from Harvard. My life was finally moving forward.

One night later that spring we got a call from Daniel. We'd been out on the porch, drinking iced tea after dinner, enjoying one of those blossomy nights that begin to feel like summer. I was thinking that I could nearly reach into the damp air and mold anything I wanted from it when we heard the ring through the open window. My father went in to answer it, and when he didn't return my mother and I followed to see what was up. He was talking to Daniel, a good talk, about Daniel's current treatment and the new girlfriend he had met. He must have been taking his medications, because my father was able to speak with him for more than a few minutes. I recall the tense set of my father's face, and while that did not ease, at least it did not worsen as the conversation stretched on and my mother brought us more tea.

"Clea? She's doing fine, just fine." My father and I made eye contact, and I motioned that I would pick up a nearby extension.

"She must be nearly grown up by now." I hadn't heard Daniel's voice in so long it sounded out of place in our comfortable evening, like a dream come to life.

"Yes, she's seventeen now." My father wasn't offering much information.

"So is she going to college soon?"

"Yes. She'll be starting off at Nassau Community, so she'll be with us here for a few more years." I didn't contradict his lie.

"That's so funny." I heard Daniel puzzling it out. "I was so sure she'd be going to Harvard, also."

"Well, things don't always turn out like one expects," my father countered. "But she's a good girl, and we're proud of her."

"Is she around?" my brother asked. I nodded and my father said he'd put me on the line.

"Hi!"

"Hi."

"So you're doing OK?"

"Yeah." I was afraid to ask him the same question. And there wasn't much more to say. He told me about his new program and soon after we all said our good-byes and went back out on the porch. By now the late twilight had turned to full night.

"We'd discussed what to tell him if he asked," my mother said to me. "We didn't want him showing up on your doorstep in Cambridge."

"That's fine. That makes sense," I said. "I'm glad." We stayed out a little longer, emptying our glasses despite the first mosquitoes. I remember thinking they had made the right decision. I certainly didn't want to worry about dealing with Daniel alone, and I was somewhat relieved that they hadn't shared their plan with me earlier.

But hearing his voice made me long again for the big brother of ten years earlier. I'd wanted so much to brag to him, to be his pet. In my own way, I badly wanted the last ten years not to be true.

The brittle peace that ruled my house, with its underpinnings of silence and denial, was not unusual. Families with mentally ill children, after all, have weathered almost more than can be borne. Family structures are often destabilized by the great amount of effort needed to cope with such diseases, to work through recognition and find treatment, to reinvent family patterns and reconfigure shared hopes and goals. And often, as can be the case in homes with a physically ill child, the sheer energy required by the day-to-day management of the disease has exhausted our parents, leaving little for themselves or for any healthy children. In reaction the family may freeze up. Roles that are normally mutable may become rigid as each member fears making the one move that will cause other loved ones to shatter. Add to these factors the apparent hopelessness of the disease, aggravated by its stigma, and it becomes understandable how normal growth and flexibility can be replaced by denial and a certain anxious holding of breath. In this tension many parents of the mentally ill do as mine did, and perform a sort of triage. Since nothing seems to make the ill sibling better, they divert their resources to the healthy one. Sometimes that means cutting our ill sibling out of the family entirely.

"I remember my dad telling us not to say anything to people," says Lily, whose older brother developed schizophrenia when he was in his late teens. "He said, 'Well, you're the oldest now.' I was like, 'I'm not the oldest, my older brother is.'"

She recalls this abrupt severing of ties with pain, but such a split is not uncommon. And although she remembers wanting to disagree with her father, she did not dare say anything to contradict his fiction. Julie Tallard Johnson says she sees many such cases in her practice counseling family members of the mentally ill. Families are "enshrouded by silence," she says. "There's a lot of guilt, a lot of confusion."

Often this split with a family member has been suggested by mental health professionals, social workers, or other caregivers. Sometimes these professionals may have underestimated the severity of the illness and, thus, overestimated the ability of our sibling to function independently. Sometimes they believed such a drastic move was necessary to save other family members. With increased awareness and more treatment and support options, a prescription to cut off a family member no longer seems to be the norm, but many young adults still recall receiving just such a prescription.

"When my sister was admitted to the hospital, after three days the doctor told my parents, 'She's schizophrenic; she'll never be well,' " recalls Sandra, whose younger sister does indeed have schizophrenia but now manages to live independently with the help of drug therapy. "He said, 'She can't go back to college and you should just find a long-term hospital to put her in.' "

"The professionals insisted that my parents should basically just kick him out," another sibling remembers. "Make him survive on his own. And so he ended up homeless."

For me, perhaps because the split was more subtle, the chill of my parents' rejection came with a frisson of guilty pleasure. Once Daniel and Katherine were out of the house, I received all the attention. I could do so little, and yet garner so much praise, simply by being apparently stable. This phenomenon has been noted by Drs. Stephen Bank and Michael Kahn in *The Sibling Bond*. "A well sibling derives a distinct and satisfying subidentity from having a deviant brother or sister," say the authors, noting that "the parents play a crucial role in assigning these contrasting identities." We are, once more, the good child, but the price of being loved seems to be our willingness to contribute to the family denial. As Diane Marsh notes in *Families and Mental Illness,* siblings "may join other family members in retreating from the anguish and pain, as the family invests heavily in a facade of normalcy."

In *The Four of Us,* Elizabeth Swados describes how she maintained such a facade, even as she saw her family "break and shatter apart" after her brother's diagnosis of schizophrenia. "My mother went into a severe depression. My father ran all over the country claiming he had business, and my mother accused him of having affairs. I drank, did drugs, drove fast, and took up residence at my best friend's house several times. Once when my mother was very ill, a social worker came to my room and tried to get me to talk. I knew my job was to prove to her how healthy and happy I was. I spoke very little. The family chaos was a secret I'd learned to keep very well."

This outward calm may also be maintained by a reverse kind of denial. In these cases the family downplays the severity of the illness at the expense of the well child. Hillary recalls her family "jumping through hoops" to accommodate her brother. As some families do, her parents began to sacrifice Hillary to keep the fiction of her brother's stability alive. She tells of coming home from elementary school with a perfect grade on a spelling test, which her mother posted on the family bulletin board—that is, until her brother came home with "a barely passing grade on some very messy paper. And my spelling test went in the garbage. Because we wouldn't want to have mine up there to make him feel bad."

"When I tried to suggest to my parents that they get help for my sister, they told me I was overreacting," recalls Lou. Although his older sister has never been diagnosed, she suffers from paranoia and various phobias that have at times kept her housebound for several years. "They told me, 'That's just the way she is.' They said I was making too big a deal out of it just because she wasn't like me."

Even when the family does not ignore the illness, the parents may keep their balance by similarly favoring the ill child. Sometimes that means expressing hostility toward the healthy sibling; sometimes it simply means neglect. Lincoln remembers how his mother would visit his psychotic brother when he was in jail or the hospital. "She would leave us for three or four days straight to spend time with him," he says. He was not even ten years old at the time. "Our fifteen-year-old sister would baby-sit all of us."

"I didn't get any parenting as such," recalls Jeffrey, whose sister became ill when they were both in their teens. "The roles reversed almost entirely, and I took care of everyone."

From the safety of adulthood, Rachel now feels able to describe an extremely painful period of about a year and a half when her older sister Callie first developed schizophrenia. Rachel was going through her freshman year in high school when Callie first broke down, and between her sister's illness and the pressures of adolescence she had some difficulties coping. But her mother devoted herself solely to Callie's care. "I would frequently leave at eleven at night and go to a friend's house to sleep over," Rachel remembers. "It was intolerable. My mother was spending all her time with my sister. I'd say, 'Mummy, I need you,' and she'd say, 'I know you need me, but Callie needs me more.' "

Sometimes our parents became so caught up in caring for our siblings that they did not realize they were ignoring us. Lou remembers feeling entirely invisible at the family dinner table with his parents and ill sister. "My parents would get all caught up in trying to talk with her or start arguing with her about the outlandish things she would say. And so I would just slip away from the table," he recalls. "Then I would sit in my room and time how long it took for them to notice I was gone."

One forty-year-old woman whose older brother has been ill from an early age still recalls stopping at a scenic overlook on a family trip when both she and her brother were quite young. "My brother, who was ten, was held up to see the view," she remembers. "I remember my father holding Doug's legs so he could stand on a stone wall and Doug was taking pictures, and there was all this talk about this fabulous, wonderful, beautiful view. Then the next thing I remember is that we drove away.

"I never got to see it," she recalls. Although she was the smaller one, only seven at the time, she was clearly healthier, and her parents assumed she could cope even at this early age. Because she did not know how to ask for a lift, for her parents' steadying hands—basically because she usually seemed so competent—she was neglected.

While we were often extremely mature and capable, at least in comparison with our ill siblings, this self-same competence sometimes robbed us of the attention that we craved and that, as children, we needed. Our parents may have had little choice. "Having a psychotic kid in the house is such a drain in every way," says Dr. Edward Shapiro of the Austen Riggs Center. He points out that when they become adults, healthy siblings often realize in retrospect how great their parents' burden was. "People are surprised at how little they noticed how much their parents needed to take care of the [ill] kid, because they were so resentful about the parents' lack of availability." Our parents did have to exert their energy where they believed it was the most crucial. But it nonetheless amounted to a form of abandonment, and that often left us insecure and angry at best.

Such a split in our parents' care of us may not be universal, but it is common. And whichever side our family chose, no matter what the degree of abandonment or overprotection, it carried the same message: Family ties could not be trusted. They could, in fact, be dismissed in a moment. Many of us reacted as I did to this lesson. If we saw our sibling rejected, witnessed his or her existence erased, we felt a wild desire to prove how different we were from our brother or sister. We feared being rejected ourselves and instead worked on demonstrating how acceptable, how lovable we were. If we were ignored because our parents considered us capable and independent, we may have lashed out. But ultimately, even those of us who felt abandoned knew that our place in the family—tenuous though it seemed—depended on our fulfilling the role of the competent child, the one who did not need attention. And we, too, spent our energy trying to be what we thought we should be.

Psychological literature has many references to overcompensating children and adolescents, the ones who act more mature than their age, who "help" their families at a great price. Dr. David Shore, of the National Institute of Mental Health, calls such children "survivors" who may be "supernormal," their good behavior often emanating from unhealthy roots. In his doctoral thesis for the University of Hartford, Dr. Keith Roeder studied healthy adolescent siblings of adolescent psychiatric patients. These "well" siblings, Roeder wrote, "cannot progress to higher levels of ego development because they cannot, or are not allowed to, recognize, integrate and make sense of contradictory experience. By role definition, they cannot give validation to the 'good' and 'bad' aspects of themselves. They must blot out, repress, or hide those contradictory aspects because they do not fit with their concept of who they are." As Bank and Kahn describe the syndrome in *The Sibling Bond*, "Well siblings must balance two divergent identifications: identification with the parent and identification with the disturbed sibling."

For me the decision was simple: Not only did my sister scare me, but my parents had seemed to reject both of my siblings. Given a choice between joining enemies in exile or remaining in a loving home, I threw my lot in with my parents. In opposition to my brother's teenage isolation and my sister's adolescent rages, I became the one who specialized in civil discourse. And I was rewarded by membership in my parents' acceptable, if compromised, world. However, even those of us who remained "good children" believed on some level that our parents' care was contingent on our remaining happy and well behaved. We, too, could be abandoned should we cross some unseen boundary. And so to preserve our place in the newly fragile family, we had to actively set ourselves apart from our siblings. We, too, had to reject them.

Some separation from all our family members is a healthy and expected part of identity development. The psychiatrist Frances Fuchs Schachter has coined the word "deidentification" for the process by which siblings set themselves apart from each other. Such a process, she says, helps balance sibling rivalry and secure separate roles in the family in a normal, formative way. But for us, as siblings of the mentally ill, it became a critical and pressured obligation. As Bank and Kahn explain in *The Sibling Bond,* "Where the family engaged in denial or avoidance," well siblings may focus on "scapegoating" and "differentiation, rather than the commonalities of identity."

For those of us who felt that we had been defined in terms of our ill sibling, we often saw the chance to break away as a positive move, almost as our salvation. For Jan, now a highly respected scientist and avid skier, high school gave her a chance to break away from the pattern set by her brilliant but increasingly withdrawn older brother. Ultimately diagnosed with schizophrenia, he was sent to a private school the year Jan started at the local public high. Not following in her brother's footsteps for the first time, she strove to create an identity that was the opposite of his. "I dove into sports that he didn't care about. I dove into music which he didn't care about, and I dove into an entire different group of people."

But those of us who had been neglected in favor of our siblings could never make up for the parental attention we missed. We knew we were different but suspected that "different" meant inferior or not lovable. Rachel describes how she felt ugly in comparison to the schizophrenic sister who had all her parents' attention. "Callie was thin and blond and, in my eyes, beautiful. I was heavy and dark and, I thought, ugly. I felt I wasn't part of the family."

Some of us, perhaps the luckiest, saw the very real gaps that the illness had opened between us and our siblings and realized that we didn't have to exacerbate the difference. How our parents reacted, as Kahn points out, may make a crucial difference. "If it's an acknowledged problem, where clearly Mom and Dad may be saying, 'Your brother is not as fortunate as you are,' that may easily permit the well sibling to be a helper, with dignity."

Such balance is rare, however, and most of us saw our parents put more energy and time into one side or another, and as a result we skewed our own behavior. Whether or not we felt we could express it, we were often terrified of abandonment and thus also filled with anger. As the NIMH's Shore puts it, "When the ill child tends to get all the attention of the parents, often of necessity, the healthy sibling will vacillate between feeling angry and deprived and feeling guilty about being angry at someone who is ill through no fault of their own."

"I used to feel like a bad person for being mad at my sister," says Debbie, whose sister has a borderline-personality disorder. "I would think, 'She needs the support. I should feel lucky that I'm not going through the same thing.'"

Zoe remembers a friend finding her crying. "I had just talked to my father." She had been working every summer since she was fourteen to save for college. "And my father had said to me, 'You know, if your brother wasn't sick, I could give more.' And I was livid. How dare he make me be angry [at my brother] for being sick? And that just hit me with a wallop."

We feel such hurt and anger from this kind of emotional abandonment that we often don't know what to do with it. Sal recalls visiting from college during the period when her youngest sister was in and out of hospitals because of her schizophrenia. "It would make me so jealous when I would come home for holiday weekends and we'd wind up taking her to the emergency room," she recalls. "I was supposed to be the child returning home for the holidays, and she got all the attention."

In her rage, Rachel turned on her sister, rejecting her and her heritage. "I didn't want to talk about it. I didn't want to acknowledge having a sister. I didn't acknowledge being Jewish. I wanted nothing to do with my family." The wound of her own rejection fueled her anger, and witnessing her parents continue to care for her sister as they did not care for her made it worse. "Part of it was seeing my mother with her: It infuriated me. She'd put her hands on my sister's and say, 'Don't worry, when you get out of the hospital I'll stop working and I'll be there for you.' And it infuriated me." Of course, her mother had ceased to "be there" for her healthy, younger daughter.

Jan experienced this rivalry with her brother as a fight for survival. "I wanted to kill him," she now says. "When you feel like you're fighting for your life, you *are* fighting for your life." And so we struggled through our teens and through another formative process. Most of us kept our mental health. But we also assumed the twin burdens of anger and deep guilt. We wondered how much we were responsible for our parents' rejection—of us, or of our siblings. And, with this baggage, we proceeded into the adult world.

chapter five

For those of us whose siblings cannot make a successful transition to adulthood, the time comes sooner or later when we pass them by. Just by surviving we become more mature than our older siblings, or, with the passage of time, watch our younger siblings pass birthdays without the achievements we had attained at their age. We finally see that we are more successful, more competent at relationships, at school, and at work than they may ever be. And with time these differences increase. Unlike many of our siblings, we pass through our trials instead of being overwhelmed by them on the road to leading full and independent lives. But one question remains for which we have no good answer: Why have we been allowed to develop when they have not? Our health and their illness seem arbitrary. We often feel that we are subverting nature, that we are overturning some basic order simply by living. We sense that nature will exact a toll, a sacrifice to set the order straight. We fail to see that in our guilt and our alienation from our own emotions, we will, at some point, make the sacrifice ourselves.

College—specifically, the experience of living with other young people—was so intoxicating, so marvelous for me, that at first I felt as if I were breathing pure oxygen. There were no visible conflicts during that first flush of freshman joy as my parents helped me pack and we drove up to Cambridge. I was following in my father's footsteps, and my parents were as thrilled as I was. I was retracing Daniel's steps, too, but nobody mentioned that. My parents, I'm sure, did not want to scare me by introducing thoughts of failure and illness on the eve of my great adventure. They couldn't know that I had already played through every possibility for my own decline into schizophrenia. I, in turn, did not want to disturb them by bringing up such a sad topic as my brother. We all wanted the day to be gay; we all silently agreed that any mention of Daniel or Katherine could break the spell.

Our magic seemed to be working. Even the coincidence of my first-year dorm placement—I'd be living on the fourth floor of Thayer Hall, in the south entry—seemed like serendipity. My father had lived in Thayer North, the other end of the brick block that stood hard by Memorial Church. True, when he moved into this freshman dorm, forty years earlier, it had no female occupants, and now we took up every other floor. But the building looked the same, and even the traditional rivalry he had told me about with Holworthy, the dorm across the green, still existed. My father and I felt a tie, a meeting across the decades. I don't think I ever knew what freshman dorm Daniel had lived in.

This was not Daniel's Harvard, and soon not even my father's. After breakfast together the next morning and many hugs and kisses, my parents left, and Harvard was mine: the great lawn out my window studded with trees, the church and library with all their history, and a new world's worth of peers living across the hall or just downstairs. I remember being surprised and then thrilled when I realized that the people in my freshman dorm were more or less like me, that they, too, were trying on roles in search of a cohesive identity. For so many of us, the odd ones, the ones with a troubled family life, college was where we could finally fit in, and it felt like coming home to a place we didn't know existed. What mattered for me was that it was territory I had never shared with my siblings. I had no memories, no reminders of Daniel here, no thoughts of Katherine's sudden outbursts; I thought I really was free.

In such a heady environment, I went wild at first, hitting every party, staying up all night with my newfound friends, talking until the Freshman Union opened for breakfast. But my adventure had an air of unreality. What right had I to be here? During orientation much had been made of freshman insecurity. "You're *not* the one admissions department mistake," we were reassured constantly, openly, and with humor. But the cracks in my confidence ran deeper than most. My brother had been admitted to Harvard, just as I had, and he had not made it. He had been brilliant and charming, much more competent, at least in my memory, than I felt. What chance did I have?

His memory shadowed my first few weeks, but as I learned my way around the campus and began to make my own associations with its libraries and dorms, his image faded. To all outward appearances, after all, I was doing well. By the end of September, I had made the by-now familiar swap, trading in my high school boyfriend for a junior, a tall, blond premed from the Deep South. I wasn't positive I wanted to be locked into a relationship my first semester at school, but Reggie had picked me out of the freshman pack and seemed so sure of himself that I felt unable to resist. That set the pattern for our entire relationship. He quickly grew more domineering, drawing on his age and status as an upperclassman, and I never voiced my objections as he told me what to read, which classes to sign up for, and even whom I should make my friends. His rigorous tutelage took me from my partying to a serious study schedule, and my midterm grades reflected my efforts. But increasingly, that autumn, as I tried so hard to mold myself into the sober, studious girlfriend he wanted, I had no sense of what role my feelings could or should play in any social interaction.

This year should have been so fine. Here was the opportunity I had desperately desired, the chance to remake myself without the shadows of my brother and sister hanging over me, and yet I wasn't. I was away from home, finally, free. But what did that mean? While part of me—the healthiest part, perhaps—understood that this year was a time to experiment and to begin to build a life that would reflect not only my innate skills but also my tastes, I lacked the sure sense of myself to discern those preferences. So deeply buried were such feelings that I could not have told anyone that year what I truly liked, what gave me pleasure or what caused me to fear. I felt rootless and numb, and looked to others to define me. I could not yet see the true cause of my lack of connection: My brother's breakdown had taught me that every nightmare was possible, but I did not yet attach my fleeting memories of him to my own insecurity. All I knew was that somehow I was drifting, and that after years in a household where the only peace was a facade and where memories of volatile behavior still lingered, I tended to wander into situations where instability and even danger were the norm.

No inner alarm went off, for example, the night two of my male classmates, virtual strangers, invited me to drink with them. I cannot recall being thrilled when they showed up at my dorm room with a jug full of green limeade and rum. But I do remember that I had been fighting with my boyfriend and that I was feeling hopeless and unlovable when they knocked. Any distraction, any request for my time and attention, seemed preferable to that loneliness, and I ignored any warning signals that I might otherwise have noticed. And so when I woke up later that night to find one of them on top of me, our bodies nude and sweaty, I felt nauseated and foolish, but not angry. How could I feel violated when I had no boundaries to begin with?

The next summer, back in East Meadow, my isolation and sense of unworthiness continued to build on each other. I arrived home with no plans, no energy, and no desire to do much more than sit around listening to music. However, my parents were wary of such idleness. Ever since I had ceased attending summer camp four summers before, they had told me that I would have to find jobs to fill my free time, and I always had. Although I could have used some time to reflect on the past year, I didn't see any sign of the house rules bending. If anything, they had become more rigid. But I hadn't questioned my parents when they chose to cut off my brother and sister. I had wanted peace then, and the order that had ruled our house since reminded me constantly of my collusion in this denial. Dinner was at six, phone calls should be limited to twenty minutes. And Daniel and Katherine were never, never mentioned.

I did not see how this summer could be any fun, and so, when I was offered a two-month placement in the billing office for a group of anesthesiologists, I jumped at it. My assignment was to help out the three women who had full-time jobs there, adding up accounts and sending out bill after bill to insurance companies and clients. The office was windowless, and the only distraction from the numbers and the lists was gossip about celebrities, makeup, and boyfriends. I never tried to join their confidences. They were not fundamentally unkind women, but I felt excluded from their lunches at the corner deli and their Friday-afternoon beer. I was the college girl. We all believed that I was different.

For me, the job was a kind of dull torture, an exaggeration of the quarantine atmosphere of my home. In truth, the office felt like a tomb. Although I couldn't put my finger on what seemed so poisonous, I sensed that somehow I had contributed to this unnatural stillness. In it, I became even more aware of the pressures building in me, more forceful and more complicated than they had been even the year before.

One of my freshman friends came through for me. Gay and increasingly flamboyant, Phillip was as eager to leave his Long Island suburb behind as I was. Together, we explored the New York City scene every night we could: discos, video clubs—even, finally, punk clubs such as CBGB's and Max's. I loved the deserted Bowery streets that led up to CBGB's, and the constant rattle of night people and street people in the park outside Max's. It was there I found the music that kept me going, and every chance I could I would take my mother's car to the nearest train station and ride the commuter rail in. My parents did not like my late hours, but since I was obeying the rules of our house, they agreed that my free time was my own. In a way, they appeared to envy me my freedom and my friends. Our home had grown so sad and stagnant, and we seemed to broach every conversation gingerly, as if mention of Daniel or Katherine might somehow sneak in. Looking back, I suspect that unconsciously they wanted me around for a diversion, hoping I would fill the role of the happy one, the part that I had assumed through much of the last few years. But after my own difficult nine months at school, I couldn't fill the house with cheer. The quiet tension and depression felt suffocating, and I fled as often as I could. This added another layer of guilt—not only had I let my siblings go, but I was abandoning my parents as well.

I was rarely in much before dawn. Weekends, the last train back to the Merrick station left at 3:15 A.M., which meant I could stay in the clubs until 2:45 and still catch that forty-five-minute late-night run. Every now and then, I would miss that train and wait on the bench near my track, dozing and oblivious, until the electronic address system announced the 5:20 milk run out to the Island. Although I had no curfew, my mother always seemed to know when I had gotten home. No matter how quiet I was, I'd always hear a little rustling soon after I locked the front door behind me, and I knew she'd soon poke her head out of her room to say good night. I always hoped I wasn't waking her, but the thought that she'd stayed up waiting was worse.

Fall brought me back to the freedom of college, and I jumped into the social flurry of Dunster, my upperclass house, with a vengeance. We were a unit, a family to ourselves. My new roommate, Dana, started seeing one of Reggie's friends, and the boys' large senior suite became a second home for us. Even when Reggie and I started to drift and I took up with another of their crew, the resulting turmoil seemed minor. Finally, I had a crowd. I fit in. The stultifying silence of East Meadow was banished, and I shared that sense of freedom with Dana, who came from a strict Japanese-American family. We talked about our parents a lot, and how their expectations differed from ours. Dana was an only child, and I let her think I was the same, somehow never mentioning my brother or my sister to her. There was enough to complain about without them, I told myself when I realized what I was doing. I wonder whom I thought I was protecting: Would I have scared my friends off if I told them about my siblings? Would they have looked at me differently? That was a risk I didn't want to take. Dana and I had already agreed to share a sublet in town that summer. There was so much at home we both needed to leave behind.

Summer in Cambridge promised to be a different world. I landed a job at a university press and soon discovered that many of my classmates had stayed behind as well. But once again, just as I was poised for independence, I fell into that same familiar pattern with another boyfriend whom I quickly let dominate my life. Jesse had a girlfriend who had gone home to Maryland for the summer, but I didn't let that stop me from getting involved. One morning at breakfast, several weeks after we had started going out, I told Jesse that I thought I loved him. He looked down at the floor and said in a flat voice, "Oh, that's not good," and then he finished buttering his toast. We both went off to work without saying anything else about it. He never did mention it, although I stayed awake each night after our lovemaking, waiting for him to respond.

I greatly feared what would happen if I let Jesse out of my sight. But he had tickets back to Minnesota at the summer's end. And so, as August ended, I also decided to head home. I needed the break, I was exhausted by my obsession with Jesse, but all I could think about on the train ride home was how I would get him back. This was a breather, a strategy-planning session only. I'll spend the week dieting and exercising and come back irresistible, I told myself. My train pulled into Manhattan, and I changed for the commuter rail to the Merrick station, where my mother was waiting.

On the drive to East Meadow, I was barely listening when my mother told me she had bad news. "I'm afraid Tara is dead," she said, and told me how my cat had been ill that spring and never quite recovered. She had seemed slower, less energetic, and finally her for-merly quick reflexes had betrayed her—she'd tried to slip under the garage door one night as it closed, a habit she'd had since we got her, but this time she didn't make it. "I knew you'd look for her as soon as we arrived," my mother continued, "and I wanted you to know." How horrible, I thought, and how fitting for the way my life was going.

I tried to put it from my mind as we drove home, but once there I felt too tired to take my bag upstairs. I poured myself a diet soda and sat at the kitchen table; my mother began making dinner prepa-rations, both of us deep in our own thoughts. Soon after, my father got home. We hugged and then he sat at the table next to me. My mother sat down, too.

"I'm afraid we have some bad news," he began. He doesn't know that she told me about Tara, I thought. And then, in the same even tone, he told me, "Daniel is dead."

Between them, they mapped out a story of what had happened. Apparently, Daniel had been the victim of a hit-and-run accident in Connecticut. The state troopers had called them. This had all happened close to two weeks earlier, but they knew I was dealing with my own problems and hadn't wanted to break the news over the phone. Having told me this, they fell silent again, as if waiting for me to respond. Is there anything else I should know? I thought, but didn't say. Daniel, Tara, anybody want to go for three? I couldn't really answer, and so I thanked them for telling me. I said I wasn't surprised, that we could hardly have expected Daniel to live to a comfortable old age. I didn't ask about Katherine, about whether she had been told or when. I did not ask about funeral services, assuming (correctly, as I found out later) that my parents had held none. I simply acknowledged that I had understood. Then I excused myself and walked up to my old room. There, on my bed, where I had been used to finding Tara curled into a neat circle, I lay down. I'm going to miss her so much, I thought.

One week later I was back at school but the magic wasn't. I told no one about Daniel, partly because I felt embarrassed, partly because I didn't want to have to explain. How could I now introduce a brother I had never spoken of? And how would I explain why we hadn't had a funeral? Daniel's death, like his life, became a nonevent, and instead I focused all my thoughts on Jesse. He didn't break up with me, but he wouldn't commit to our relationship either. Between his hemming and hawing, and my own growing desperation to have him, I began to obsess about my weight, my skin, and even my tone of voice when I talked to him. Was I sounding pushy? Was I controlling my fear? I felt that I had no choices in my relationship with Jesse, but also that I could not free myself from him. I could talk of nothing else, do nothing but worry about where he was, if he wasn't with me, or about what our future would be, if he was.

The tension was unbearable, and I began showing up at parties in the hope of running into him. Sometimes I did, and we would go home together. Other times he would be with his old girlfriend. On those occasions, I would force myself into the frenzy of the evening, drinking too much and staying until even the hosts began to crash out. Sometimes when Jesse didn't show up, I found myself making out with other men. I would do so ostentatiously, on somebody's sofa or framed in a doorway, hoping that word would get back to Jesse. I didn't know if I wanted to hurt him or to lure him back through jealousy; I know I had no interest in the men who took his place. I was simply lashing out.

Finally there was a night when, after yet another round of parties and drinking, an acquaintance walked me home and invited himself in. I had no desire for him, yet didn't have the energy to reject him either when he pulled me onto his lap. I was tired but didn't want an argument, and so I took him to the bedroom to speed things along. Afterward he excused himself, saying he couldn't spend the night because his girlfriend would worry. I felt relieved to be alone, glad to hear the suite door close behind him. But later, brushing my teeth, I saw in the mirror my hair hanging limp and greasy around my face, and I realized I hadn't washed it in a week, hadn't thought about it. I had been so preoccupied, so busy hunting Jesse, that I had stopped taking care of my own life. I had finally let myself go, as I had feared I would all through my years at home. And although I knew I was not going crazy, I recognized that my life was veering horribly off course. In some way that I had not envisioned even in my nightmares, I was losing control.

When I look back on my college years I see, among all the usual adventures of a young woman away from home for the first time, two disturbing developments that fed on each other. The first, which had begun earlier and would grow more pronounced in years to come, was a disconnection from my own emotions that left me vulnerable to certain kinds of exploitation. I distrusted my own instincts and had little sense of who I was or what I wanted. The second development was a deep and pervading sense of guilt that made me doubt whether I really deserved anything good at all.

The guilt came from two connected sources: my success and my siblings' failures, which I felt I had been complicit in. Along with my parents, I had denied my siblings' existence and cut our familial ties. I had then made it into college and, unlike either my brother or my sister, survived my first year without breaking down. By the beginning of my junior year, I had outlived my older brother. Since I hadn't done anything special to deserve uninterrupted progress, and had perhaps done something awful, I felt an overwhelming sense of guilt.

This kind of guilt has been documented in the survivors of all sorts of trauma. "To be spared oneself," writes Judith Herman in *Trauma and Recovery*, "in the knowledge that others have met a worse fate, creates a severe burden of conscience. Survivors of disaster and war are haunted by images of the dying whom they could not rescue. They feel guilty for not risking their lives to save others, or for failing to fulfill the request of a dying person."

Because of this burden, for me the relative freedom of college, of moving on, came at a high price. And like many of us who have trouble accepting our relatively benign fortune, I tried to equalize the situation by sabotaging myself. We may have many reasons for hurting ourselves. Partly it serves as a distraction: It's easier to worry about a boyfriend than a brother's lost life. Partly we suspect that we deserve to be punished, and we seek some element of control over our future, even if this control is manifested in a negative fashion. Sometimes, that is, we plan on ruining our own chances of happiness just to get the inevitable over with, as if by making such sacrifices we control exactly how and when disaster will strike. Partly we may fear that our guilt is a signal that we should take responsibility for our ill sibling or our entire family. And so we punish ourselves, set ourselves back developmentally and at the cost of our own happiness, to avoid this responsibility. In other words, we try to purchase an extension of our unhappy childhood, we choose to face repeated terror and failure rather than what we fear may be the burdens of adulthood. No matter how we interpret our motivation, the results are the same. As mental health experts explain it, family members of the mentally ill commonly express such guilt through "difficulty in coming to terms with success, or accepting it," says Dr. Ed Shapiro. "People get in their own way to preclude success."

In my own life, particularly during my years at Harvard, I see the evidence of this everywhere. Whenever there was a more difficult path, I felt obligated to take it. Throughout my freshman year I avoided joining the school newspaper and literary magazines, where I thought I would find kindred spirits, in order to please my exacting boyfriend. Relationships that could have been uncomplicated and comfortable didn't interest me. Romances in which I would probably be hurt or rejected captivated me. Much of this drama can be put down to my age. When we are younger, we expect all passions to be feverish, and we fail to recognize the romance to be found in friendly, comfortable love. Experimenting is healthy, but I was acting out without any regard whatsoever to my own vulnerabilities, my own needs. Intensity and turmoil were the only emotions I could recognize. Whenever there was a problem, I was to blame. Whenever things were going well, I felt uneasy and distrustful of fate.

This intimation of a reckoning, this dread, is common to many of us with ill siblings. We are fledged, while they are not. No matter what our families have sacrificed for them, no matter at whose expense, we are the ones who have learned to fly. We are the ones who will live fully.

In the most blatant ways, we try to redress the balance, pulling ourselves down if we cannot push our siblings ahead. Rachel, now a social worker and the younger sister of a schizophrenic woman, recalls sabotaging herself in the face of so much guilt. "In high school I started off with a very high average, and that went down." She then attended three different colleges and "dropped out, flunked out, and got kicked out" of each in turn. Although Rachel now holds two master's degrees, she could not stand achieving once her older sister became hospitalized. For her, that meant not letting herself enjoy a smooth course through college. "It took me fourteen years to get my bachelor's. Part of my difficulty in getting a degree was that she had finished high school, but getting a college degree was going beyond her."

Sometimes, our adoption of this behavior can be surprisingly quick. "Earlier I was able to kind of do what I wanted," says Samuel, referring to the time before his older brother became psychotic and his younger brother entered his first manic period. "I was very optimistic and things kind of came my way." In this first blossoming of early adulthood, Samuel worked through college and graduate school with ease, aiming for a career in engineering. "Then, after I got my master's degree and everybody had become mentally ill, it was kind of like I couldn't do anything right." After all his successful preparations, he sank into a depression and didn't work for several years.

For me, the sabotage was more subtle. I still clung to the role of good student, of overachiever, and I was able to graduate in four years with high honors and my parents' approval. Instead, I poisoned my personal life with abusive men and chance encounters I could have avoided. I chose not to listen to my best inner voices. Ultimately, these betrayals of myself came back to haunt me, lowering my opinion of myself and compromising my mental health.

In others' stories, I have heard similar denials of our instincts, sometimes of our entire emotional nature. In Hillary's family, her older brother, who has a mixed-personality disorder, was always very expressive, usually of pain or rage. She got stuck being the "rational" one, although her insomnia and, later, clinical depression revealed the toll of this control. "I had to be self-contained. I didn't have feelings," Hillary says, describing her sacrifices to guilt and fear. "Feelings were what my brother had."

Older siblings face a less obvious reversal. They are, in chronological age, already ahead of their sibling. However, many report that they too avoided success in various ways.

"For a while I tried to step in and help my sister, save my sister," recalls Sandra. But as her sister became increasingly ill, Sandra sabotaged her own college career and self-image. "I started breaking into the [college] dining room. I'd take ice cream out—they had buckets of ice cream—and I'd just sit in the kitchen in the middle of the night and eat ice cream." She laughs about it now, about how she coped with her fear and loneliness. "I gained twenty pounds, and I focused on being obsessed about my weight."

The differences in how we play out our guilt may be subtle. Older siblings, as Shapiro points out, may have already escaped the family, although they may feel guilty about "leaving a mess" for their parents. Some older siblings deal with that guilt by becoming surrogate parents. Helle Thorning, of the Schizophrenia Research Unit of the New York State Psychiatric Institute, recalls one man with two younger brothers, the younger of whom had developed schizophrenia. "His middle brother had gotten married and had children, but the older brother believed it was inconceivable for him to have a relationship like that. He felt he needed to be there for his ill youngest brother. And he felt he couldn't ask his middle brother to be more involved because the middle brother should be happy. So he took on the responsibility for everybody's happiness." For this particular sibling, that meant deciding that he could never marry or have children, never have a life of his own. He saw these as selfish desires that he had no right to hope for, not when the youngest brother was ill.

Such cases of near-total self-sacrifice are dramatic and may be fairly rare. More often, we blur the lines while making smaller offerings to appease our guilt. If we are older, especially if we assume some form of parental role, we may avoid recognizing our younger siblings' full limitations for years. We allow our traditional roles—the guiding older brother or motherly older sister—to obscure the fact that our sibling is not progressing as we wish he or she could, is not successfully leaving the nest. We allow them to be helpless, to be younger, for as long as possible, so we don't have to see the truth. In these cases, the age difference helps our denial.

Stan, now a doctor, found it difficult to believe for many years that his younger brother had schizophrenia. Their sister, who is also a doctor, had confirmed the diagnosis and told Stan about their brother's medication, but Stan still saw his "kid brother" as just that, a child. "I really had doubts how sick he was because I didn't have much contact with him," says Stan. Now he admits that he was refusing to let go of the healthy image and was pretending that his younger brother's withdrawal and inability to function were because of his immaturity. "My memory of him was quite different from what she was describing. I thought he was just a normal kid," says Stan. "He just hadn't gotten on with life."

Even when we accept that mental illness has in some ways incapacitated our siblings' life, those of us who are older may respond by assuming more responsibility. In a way, the guilt of the older child is the guilt of not being able to provide proper care. We may feel less as if we are subverting the natural order and more as if we have failed in some way.

"Being the oldest child, the most educated person in the family and the one who's been to school longest, there was a sense of responsibility," says Sal, whose youngest sister has schizophrenia. Her other younger siblings, the healthy ones in her big farming family, have stayed close to home, while Sal, a mathematician, is the one who went out in the world. In addition, she has channeled her classic older-sister feelings of responsibility into her work as an activist for her regional branch of the National Alliance for the Mentally Ill. "There's a responsibility to get the knowledge and take it back to the family," she says.

"I've had to modify my own savior complex," says Rick. Now a health care professional, Rick was such a doting big brother that he still talks about how his younger sister ran for vice president of her high school class just before she became ill fifteen years ago. He recognizes in himself the desire to "make everything all right" for his schizophrenic younger sister. Now, since they live close to each other in the Pacific Northwest, he is able to see her fairly regularly and discuss the guilt he felt during those first few years. These days, that guilt has been transformed into simple grief. "She was popular and doing well at school. So just thinking about what her life could have been, I feel really sad."

As family members of the mentally ill so often point out, we have mourning without resolution. When our sibling actually dies, our issues—including grief and guilt—become more complicated. Often we have longed for this kind of resolution; we were so angry and guilty, so weighed down, how could we not wish for an end of some sort? I was certainly relieved not to have to worry about Daniel showing up on my doorstep. Of course, this wish brings its own load of guilt, and I hated myself for savoring this relief. Another sibling recalls her healthy sister saying, "I think this thing could end just one way, and that's probably suicide." She objected to her sister's thoughts aloud, but secretly agreed. "I thought he would kill himself just to get out of his misery," she says. "And I felt awful."

Shapiro explains, "One of the least permissible responses is the wish to kill the ill family member. It's an inevitable aspect of the range of feeling. And so, people who feel this have to defend themselves against it, or feel guilty about it, and manage it in some way."

If we are honest, we recognize that, at least at times, we almost all see death as a preferable resolution. For many of us, it is a secret, shameful wish. And, for many of us, it may come true. Suicide, according to Richard Keefe and Philip Harvey, is the number-one cause of premature death among people with schizophrenia. In *Understanding Schizophrenia,* these New York-based researchers point out that between 10 and 13 percent of people diagnosed with schizophrenia do end their own life; at least 50 percent attempt it. The rate is equally high for people with serious depression. In *Surviving Schizophrenia,* Dr. E. Fuller Torrey estimates the rate of suicide among schizophrenics as at least 10 percent greater than among the general population.

Other risks contribute to premature death among the mentally ill. Self-medicating with alcohol or with illegal drugs may contribute to health problems, as well as legal concerns. Acting on the prompting of delusions can also be dangerous, even if the action is not consciously suicidal. For example, a woman who believes her house is on fire and jumps from an upper story is trying to save herself, not hurt herself. But the result is the same. People with mental illness are, of course, prone to the same diseases and physical weaknesses that affect the rest of the population. Often they have trouble navigating through the bureaucracies of hospitals and insurance plans to obtain proper health care. In addition, Torrey points out, our siblings' mental illness may make health care providers less likely to take self-reported symptoms seriously. All these problems are exacerbated when the mentally ill person is jobless or homeless. As Torrey writes in *Surviving Schizophrenia,* "I predict that when we finally do a careful study of mortality rates among homeless individuals with schizophrenia in the United States, the results will be shocking."

Even in the best possible living situation, where there is a home and proper care, sometimes death comes early. Stan's brother, for example, died before his fiftieth birthday of cancer, as do several million other Americans each year. The difference, for Stan, is the regret about the brother who was lost to him even before cancer claimed his body; it's the regret for the loss of potential, for even the possibility of resolution, of reconciliation, if not for a cure. "I think if

I had been living around him more I might have been able to work something out," Stan tells himself now, and lives with that guilt.

Still, even with full foreknowledge, we often cannot do anything. Rikki's older brother tried to kill himself several times, including one attempt that broke his back, before he finally succeeded a few days shy of his thirtieth birthday. His determination left her with a strong sense that she, too, had an obligation to die at twenty-nine. "I figured that my fate would have to be like his," she says. "Only worse. Maybe I'd have a drug overdose, or maybe I'd be murdered. I just assumed I would die young in a horrible accident at the same age that he did."

Jeffrey's sister, who had schizophrenia, planned her suicide long before it took place. "She told me on many occasions that her goal in life was to kill herself," he recalls. Jeffrey now talks about feeling "responsible, guilty and angry," a situation intensified by his professional capacity as a psychiatrist. Once his younger sister broke down, the family—including his younger sister—expected him to take care of her. She killed herself, finally, during a week when he was out of town with his own patients, a group of people with mental illnesses whom he regularly takes on a camplike retreat. His sister, because she was not his patient, was not invited. "I felt and continue to feel guilty. I could have probably prevented her from killing herself that week if I had been more attentive, perhaps, before I left town."

Facing this kind of guilt, we siblings may find self-sabotage a small price to pay for relief. Unless, that is, we can find some strong, external confirmation of our innocence. In fact, the few siblings who report not having problems with guilt tell of health professionals and caretakers who specifically talked to them about their responsibility and who made a point of addressing the possibility of guilt. "The whole time my sister was sick and when she killed herself, my mom would say, 'Don't think that this is your fault. This isn't something you've done,'" one young woman remembers. "I think that was why I was able to just chug along in life."

"I remember thinking that I survived and he didn't," reports Nancy, recalling the time, thirty years ago, when the chronic nature of her brother's schizophrenia became clear. He had been the star of the family, the bright child who was going to college before he was hospitalized, while she went to finishing school. "I had gone to visit him at the VA hospital and was talking to the doctor, and she said, 'Just go and lead your own life. There is nothing you can do.' It freed me."

I think, now, that my parents tried to give me that relief. But in their efforts to spare me, and themselves, from unpleasant topics, too much was left unspoken. In their silence I assumed the worst. I felt guilty about surpassing both Daniel and Katherine. And I felt complicit in their downfall—in his death and her repeated hospitalizations—because I had let my parents separate me from their care. I loved the freedom of being without them. I thrived initially in the space to experiment and reinvent myself, but I did not believe that I deserved such bounty. What will I have to pay? I wondered throughout those first few years at school. When would the ax fall?

I would never find out. To avoid a reckoning, I brought it down on myself. Years before, I had stood silently by while my parents gave up on Daniel and Katherine. And just as they had been abandoned, I was abandoning myself. The only difference, I realized that dark day when I saw my competence crumbling, was that I didn't even have an illness as an excuse.

chapter six

In the summer of 1983 I turned twenty-two; the month before, I had graduated from Harvard. Finally, I was free, or so I thought. Like thousands of young people who graduate every spring, I was set loose to find my place in the world. As so many of my peers did, I stayed near school, away from my family and all supervision. And like many of them, I floundered a bit, not sure how to proceed independently after sixteen years of school discipline, not sure, even, what I was worth outside of the structure of grades and tests. But I knew that I wanted the same thing I had wanted all along: a life of my own, as different as possible from the stifling rigidity of my family's life on Long Island, our reaction to the turmoil of my siblings' breakdown and all the denial that weighed on us afterward. With this goal, I sought to develop relationships that would feel spontaneous and intelligent and to build a career that held some challenge and creativity. But somehow, even while I worked toward these goals, I saw them recede as I found myself dragged down by forces I could not comprehend.

Soon after I graduated, I began to have a recurring dream. It was too calm to be termed a nightmare, but it frightened me nonetheless. What I remember most explicitly about it was the silence. The backdrop was pure black space, infinite space, falling away in every direction, and broken only by an array of stars with no comprehensible patterns or boundaries. Then, in the middle of the darkness, an astronaut would appear outside a spacecraft. He would be lumbering around in his clumsy white suit, working on the outside of the craft. In a deliberate fashion, his hands passed slowly over panels while his feet, in a countermotion, swung slightly away. He made no noise, but somehow the astronaut would be cut loose. His safety line would break, and the slow recoil of the snapping line would send him tumbling over backward. Without any ground for him to fall on, no gravity to pull him down, his backward fall simply continued, rolling him away in slow-motion somersaults. He was moving so slowly through space that it seemed that one touch would stop his spin. But there was nobody there to help. I never saw his face through his glass helmet as he slowly and inexorably tumbled off to his doom. But I sensed that he was alive and conscious of his fate. I think, maybe, if I had seen his face I would have seen my own, and I knew I couldn't stand that sight.

My dream stole shamelessly from *2001: A Space Odyssey,* and it probably defied several laws of physics. But this recurring vision nonetheless packed a wallop every time it came to me during those first few years out of school. At the time I had no idea what the dream meant. Now I can look back and point out the obvious. Perhaps Daniel was the astronaut, the one who lost his equilibrium, the one we couldn't save. As a child of the sixties, I would forever link growing up to the NASA space program, but those years would also be marked by my siblings' breakdown. The dream also seemed to link my early years to the present. In 1983, fresh from college, I had broken free from my family. And like the astronaut who tumbled endlessly into infinite and silent space, I had made no connection to anything or anyone else. Paradoxically, this lack of contact weighed on me considerably. I had left home, but now I was lost. "One small step," indeed.

On the one hand, I felt I had come so far when I looked back at high school, only four years earlier. I was determined never to go home again, apart from the holidays. Not that I didn't love my parents, but I knew enough to realize I never wanted to live in our old house; the burden of being the healthy, happy daughter was too great. Similarly, I no longer could cope with being caged by anybody else's expectations. I missed Dunster House a little; it hurt to see my friends go off to jobs and graduate schools around the country. But I told myself my turn would come soon. Something would happen—I would make something happen. I wouldn't be left behind.

I knew I could pick myself up. After all, I had survived my horrible junior year. My tailspin didn't even seem that bad to me just one year later. As a senior, I had started concentrating on my school-work again, and my grades had quickly recovered. And with the aid of a university health services counselor, I had even confronted my parents about keeping Daniel's death from me. Whatever their reasons, I was angry at them for this deception, I told them when they came up for the day. I half expected them to yell at me for bringing up the topic and was a little afraid, as well, that they would crumble. But they did neither. They apologized, and for the first time in years, I saw their grief. My father cried. My mother looked grim and talked about all the mourning she had already done, ever since Daniel's first hospitalization, and about how burned out she felt about Katherine. They drove home the next day, and she called me on their arrival to tell me that she had dreamt of Daniel the night before. She said that dream made her realize she too was mourning again, or perhaps mourning still, for his lost life.

That brief but important interaction helped me begin to sort out the end of my time at Harvard. I started to see how my obsession with Jesse was connected to my brother's unexpected death, how my preoccupation with my lover was helping me avoid and deny this tragedy, and I even heard myself begin to open up about my family, my siblings' illness, and my early life. But then the school year ended, and my counselor went on leave.

During my senior year, I tried another therapist, a man this time, and with him I finally broached the subject of sex. My new boyfriend didn't interest me sexually, and I had trouble understanding why, since I so much enjoyed talking to him. I realize now that I had split myself in two when it came to men and my own sexuality. I wasn't turned on for long by men who made me feel safe. Instead, I craved the intensity and danger of men, like my brother, who were unstable and ultimately unreliable. But as graduation rolled around, the best insight my therapist could offer was that possibly my boyfriend was a substitute for himself. On hearing that, I concluded therapy wasn't the answer at all. I just needed a different boyfriend.

At night, in the clubs, potential lovers were in ready supply. And as I left my college circle behind I began to see a sequence of men who were all eerily reminiscent of Daniel. Although I never consciously chose men with serious emotional problems and never became involved with anyone who had to be hospitalized—at least while I was with them—I found myself repeatedly being drawn into obsessive relationships with marginal men. Each time, I thought I was making a change, but within a month or two, I would realize that once again I was the one who was holding together not only the relationship, but the man I claimed to love.

There was Hank, for example, a local boy who'd gone through college on an athletic scholarship. At twenty-four, he lived at home with his divorced mother, with whom he was always fighting, but none of this mattered to me. The sex was great, and I had someone to hear music with. We went out almost every night, rarely returning to my place before three, and often I found myself napping in my chair at work. I had gotten a job as a secretary, while Hank worked as a disc jockey. I envied the easy one-on-one banter he maintained with so many club staffers. Still, I was usually the one with money and kept bailing Hank out of trouble during the year and a half we were together, paying the speeding tickets that threatened his license, picking up the dinner tab when he found himself short.

After a few months, even our sex life began to falter, and I began to suspect that his increasing difficulties weren't due to the muscle relaxants he took for his bum knee, as he had once told me. But I still found it hard to accept when a girlfriend told me she thought he was freebasing in the station's studio and that he was seen escorting his young intern around town. Could I have been that wrong about him? I never knew. Soon after, Hank called me from his office to tell me he wanted his freedom. "It isn't working" was all he said, and I wondered where I had failed.

In my typical pattern, I did not know how to let go, not until I found another man to take his place. I kept hounding Hank, drawing him back into a series of desperate one-night stands, until the day I met Stephen at a friend's wedding. We flirted throughout the reception, and suddenly Hank was gone from my mind. Stephen and I had connected, and now he became the focus of my life.

My first date with Stephen lasted through the weekend, as would every date with him throughout the next few months. During our time together, we rarely left his apartment, the small, dingy studio that was all he could afford as a freelance photographer, largely because he was strangely phobic about clubs and parties and all the other social events I had previously enjoyed. For Stephen, I surrendered them freely. And I no longer gave a damn about Hank, refusing even to answer his occasional phone call.

I was terrified without a boyfriend by my side. But as soon as I had a new man, I could see how imperfect the previous one had been, and I could discard him without a second thought. The individual never mattered as much as that one recurring challenge: I was always looking for the key that would make the unreliable one stay or, as I see now, make the unstable man healthy.

Of course, once I had settled in with Stephen I told myself that the failure of my relationship with Hank had been entirely my fault. I had chased him away with my constant crowding and my possessiveness. With Stephen, I would be smarter. I never asked whom he spent his weeknights with or how he managed to drink so much, and I always made a show of waiting outside his room when he played back his answering machine tape, although I could clearly hear the voices of his other women. I kept the few clothes I took with me on Friday in a plastic shopping bag in his closet, my contact lens solution and an extra toothbrush pushed far to one side of his dresser. Even after we had been together half a year, I made plans with him only gingerly, suggesting that I might want to go to a dinner at a friend's the following weekend, or that I had heard of a concert and thought of buying tickets. Only if he responded positively would I assume that we would function that night as a couple, and I used this kind of vague invitation as the months wore on to introduce myself into more of his life, suggesting Thursday-night dinners and Wednesday movies as a way to insinuate myself into his time. Never did I question this imbalance, and when the relationship was over, I prided myself on the length of time I had managed to keep him, as if he were an unbroken horse I had ridden in a rodeo.

Looking back, what I recall is how fragile everything about these relationships felt. I remember how carefully I believed I had to coddle these men, remaining alert for their particular unspoken rules and taboos. I was always willing to negate my own needs in favor of their demands and constantly reworked myself. I wonder now if I ever showed them any part of my real personality at all.

Another pattern I failed to recognize at the time was how the ones who seemed to be the most fragile were invariably the most cruel, and how these were the men I could not ignore. The most needy and terrible was Tom, a man who seemed to melt away from normal while I looked on, becoming sicker and more withdrawn during the course of our eighteen months together. We met at the laundromat, which seemed a good omen to me: daylight, no drugs or alcohol in sight. He wasn't in my rock world, the circle that had given me enough Hanks for a lifetime. He even had a real job, testing software for one of the larger computer firms, and he owned his own home, a neat little condo with a roof deck. Granted, he didn't share my wild side, didn't, in fact, like rock and roll at all. But he attended the symphony regularly and prided himself on his knowledge of dance. So this was my chance, I told myself, to make up for the opportunity I had missed so many years ago, with the kind, shy boy who waited with me at Dr. Schaeffer's. Tom would be that boy, and I would not run away.

Tom was not that boy. In time I realized that he combined much of the paranoia and possessiveness of my earlier lovers, though his behavior initially appeared completely different. At first, I enjoyed his taking our relationship seriously. Here was one who wouldn't pick up my replacement at a party. But for Tom, "serious" meant sacred, and with him I entered into a world of rituals and hidden meaning. He saved wrapping paper, for example, and ticket stubs from every event, no matter what its importance. He expected me to do the same and would become furious if I had discarded anything he gave me, including its packaging. His obsessions, however, alternated with neglect, and his mood could flip so fast I often wasn't sure what had happened. Soon he was picking fights with all our friends, refusing to socialize with even his oldest buddies in the neighborhood. And increasingly often when I let myself into his place on Friday evenings, he would be sitting in his underwear in a darkened, stuffy room, watching TV. Those nights, he wouldn't talk to me until, bored and uncomfortable, I would make moves to leave. "Where are you going?" he would ask. I rarely told him how restless I was, or that I found his housebound life unsettling. Instead, I would stick to the facts: I was going to get some Chinese food. I had a book at home I had meant to start. Sometimes I said that I was going to call a girlfriend. "When will you be back?" he'd ask, looking first angry, then as sad as a child. "Don't leave. Don't go." He would whine and pout, only to be distracted by the television the next moment. "Come back soon, will you?" he'd implore me, though still facing his TV. "Bring me something." Walking away from his house, I would tell myself that I'd had my fill of his insular world. I would call a friend and make plans. I would see a movie by myself or read, uninterrupted, at home alone. I would break up with Tom.

In truth, I rarely called anyone or made other plans. Mostly I went for walks, long fast ones, swinging my arms until my breath came heavy as a way to relieve tension. I'd postpone my return as long as I dared, knowing that he might still be distracted but would likely be sulking whenever I returned. No matter how far I walked, I felt the string reeling me back in to Tom's house. My freedom was an illusion, but I wasn't sure why that was. All I could think was that Tom had changed and that I didn't know how to change him back. Looking back, I now believe that Tom at the age of thirty was breaking down with a late-onset mental illness. All the signs were there: the withdrawal, the paranoia, the increasing reliance on a magical world of signs and rituals. But after he and I split up, he forbade me to contact him ever again. And he seemed so angry that I never dared to break this one final rule.

I found it difficult to function without a boyfriend partly because I needed company and I never had an easy time making close female friends. Too often, the women I chose to get close to scared me and dominated me. With them, I would feel trapped and in some way culpable, as if I should have known what to expect and had no right to ask for anything better. Although I could not see it at the time, just as I was replicating my relationship with Daniel in my affairs with men, I repeatedly restaged many of my scenarios with Katherine with other women. And as happened with my romances, although I recognized the basic pattern, I could not place its source and could not avoid its traps.

Almost as if I were consciously replaying the triangle that had formed between my brother, my sister, and myself, I often drew the women I knew into my romances with an obsessive fervor. I always thought I was simply looking for a confidante, as in the case of Sara. She had introduced me to one of my more abusive boyfriends and served as my sounding board for that uneasy relationship during the years we roomed together after college. She didn't seem to mind going over and over everything he said and did, scrutinizing his behavior with me for clues to how I could secure his affections. Then, one day, everything changed.

I don't know what triggered it, but that evening when I returned to our apartment after work I found the place in turmoil. Our little black-and-white television had been knocked off the deep windowsill and lay facedown on the carpet. One chair was turned over, and the Indian bedspread covering the raggedy couch had been ripped off and dumped in a corner. My first thought was that we had been robbed, but then I stepped into the kitchen. All over the refrigerator, in large dark letters, were curses and expressions of hate. "Enough of this boy-shit, blah! blah! blah!" read one caption above an angry face drawn with an extra-thick Magic Marker. "Shut the fuck up!" ran another, overlapping smaller scrawled epithets. The handwriting was clearly Sara's, and the hostility obviously directed at me.

At first, I felt terrified. To read those declarations of rage shook me as much as if they had been yelled in my face. It was terrifying to see how much she had been holding back without my having a clue. I wondered if there had been signals that I should have picked up, things I could have done to diffuse her anger. I reasoned to myself that there must have been, and that I had been lazy and careless to miss her growing discontent. Never mind that Sara had not come out and told me that she was sick of my obsessive behavior. It didn't matter to me that she had never said aloud that she had had enough. I felt that I was to blame for mishandling the situation. I felt responsible for her anger and for putting myself in a position where I could be attacked. And I slipped back into the mode of coping that had gotten me through my years with Katherine: I would learn better how not to offend. I would make myself inconspicuous. I would do my best not to incite such a reaction again.

My initial shock caused me to overestimate the actual damage, I told myself as I started to clean. The chairs just need to be picked up,

I said to myself as I readjusted the cover on our couch. The TV, once I had reattached the antenna, still worked. This wasn't that bad. There was nothing I could do about the refrigerator, though, and as I passed into the kitchen, the anger on it shook me anew. My automatic distancing faltered, and I retreated to my bedroom. Much later that night I heard Sara's key in the lock. I had been afraid to turn my stereo on.

"Hi." I stood in the doorway of my bedroom, waiting to see how she would be.

"Good evening!" She sounded so formal that I couldn't tell if she'd been drinking and trying to cover it up, or if she was really furious. She made an elaborate show of hanging her coat up, brushing the shoulders and straightening the collar in a fastidious way.

"I'm sorry," I said. "I've been such a jerk. I guess you were really angry." I felt I had to apologize quickly, to preempt her rage. I was grateful that she hadn't attacked me or even turned to face me yet.

"Oh, it's nothing," she said, her words falling into a singsong parody of her normal voice. "Things were just getting to me, you know. Men!" She scrunched up her face in a mock grimace and opened the refrigerator to take out some juice. She seemed not to notice the furious graffiti all over the door. "Do you want some?"

"Yeah." I sighed in relief. I couldn't believe she was letting me off the hook. I knew at some level that her actions—the trashing of the room—had been irrational. But at the time I couldn't make the connection between my reaction to her fury and my fear of Katherine. The damage, I told myself, wasn't that severe. No furniture was broken, and the old refrigerator had already had several generations of stickers and decorations on it. Sara had simply gone further than I would have because of her extreme anger, I rationalized, and that anger was my fault. From then on, I vowed, I would treat her with care, and we began a period of exaggerated solicitousness. I sensed rage under her polite manners, however, and I never relaxed in my efforts to please her. When our lease expired and Sara chose to move out, I felt relief, but also a deep sense of failure. Once again I had failed to find a better way to resolve this kind of relationship.

Again and again, the women I became close to tended toward

irrational behavior and great anger, and yet I always believed that I had provoked them. I had answered an ad for a third-floor apartment and remember dressing with great care for the interview, determined to have the two current housemates, Trish and Shari, like me. Both slightly older than me, they were eager for a third to split the rent for their sprawling apartment. I looked at the spacious kitchen, the workroom, the porch, and the cozy den and fell in love. Everything seemed so homey. The women themselves seemed nice enough. And they told me I could move in.

At first, things were going well, but soon enough little things started to annoy them. My printer made too much noise. I offered to print out only during the afternoons, when neither of them was home. My music magazines were cluttering up the living room, as were my books. Why had I thought they or any of their friends would have any interest in *Rolling Stone?* Why did I leave my copy of *Musician* about? In the face of Trish's attack, I crumbled. I started apologizing. As she stalked around the living room, pointing out my mess, I gathered up periodicals, a book, two throw pillows that I thought had matched the color scheme. While they both looked on, I carried my possessions back into my bedroom and stayed there, once more afraid to turn on my music or computer, afraid of making noise. I read until I thought they would be asleep, only after midnight venturing out to use the bathroom and to brush my teeth. This was their house, never mind that I was paying one third of the rent.

From then on, our pattern was fixed: Trish attacked and I retreated. My hours, Trish decided, somehow denoted laziness. Never mind that reviewing late-night club shows was a regular part of my freelance work; if I wasn't awake by eight in the morning I would hear about it. On Saturdays, the vacuum cleaner would ram against my bedroom door. And on Sundays, I would be awakened by loud knocking—the house finances, from phone bills to electricity, suddenly became an early-morning concern.

I was miserable. I told myself that Shari and Trish had never given me a chance, but in my heart I once again believed that I was to blame for the breakdown in relations. Somehow, I hadn't figured out the rules, and now I was paying the price. I would not have been surprised if one of them had started yelling, in Katherine's voice,

"You're giving me a dirty look!" I walked around the apartment with my eyes on the floor. I needed to get out, and after six months I gave them notice.

Even my moving day, when it finally came, was full of anxiety. As I eased down the stairs with my last box of books, I saw Trish in the foyer. She was crossing out my identification on the mailbox with a black ballpoint pen, obscuring my name with a furious scribble. She didn't acknowledge me as I lumbered past. Sweating from the work, hoping that I had not left anything behind, I shoved the box in the back of the rented van and slammed the door. As I pulled away from the curb and drove down the street, I realized I'd been holding my breath. Instead of feeling angry at how I had been treated or disappointed that such a promising living situation had become untenable, I felt that familiar sense of humiliation accompanied by relief, as if I had escaped great danger.

That same overlay of fear and guilt followed me to work, coloring a series of jobs that I held through my twenties. Right after college, finding an entry into journalism was difficult. My hopes of glamour, of a writing position at a New York glossy, fell through quickly enough. The one position I interviewed for there quickly lost its luster when I realized that the pay would not enable me to live on my own. If I got that job, I would have to return home and commute. I was waiting to hear, but not with much glee. Then, back in Cambridge, my alumni magazine offered me an entry-level job, editorial secretary, at a salary I could live on, and I took it. I would spend my days filling out the paperwork allowing other magazines permission to reprint our authors, and I would read my classmates' notes, checking their letters for facts or errors against our large file of sourcebooks. It was a start.

Somehow, I lasted a year. The people at the magazine were kind, as idiosyncratic as most book lovers and writers, but I didn't see myself as the editorial secretary of a small, exclusive bimonthly and felt trapped in a horribly square world. Already, by the age of twenty-two, I had spent too long feeling like an outsider to let myself be welcomed in, and I kept myself aloof. Although my work suffered, I felt it a badge of pride to be out till the bars closed on work nights. I began freelancing stories to a local weekly, mostly out of a need to let these people know I wasn't like them and never could quite relax in that quiet, cozy space.

In fact, I rarely connected. For my first seven or eight years out of school, I held only one position for longer than a year, and that was a part-time secretarial job. Basically, I considered myself a freelance writer, a rock critic at large, beholden to no one company. I contributed to one of the big dailies for a few years and would waltz in, most afternoons, with my copy. It was fairly steady work, and I valued having a forum in which I could tell people, a lot of people, what I thought. I even liked my editors, enjoyed the few hours each week when I would chat with them, as much about our lives as upcoming assignments. But ultimately I was grateful that I did not have to put myself in their hands. With them, as with the alumni magazine, I held myself distant, afraid and diffident in the face of this big organization.

I suspected that I was running, but to all outward appearances I was still the good child, the successful one who would make up for all my siblings' failings. I might not have a steady job, but, I pointed out to my parents, I was building a name for myself in a competitive field, carving out a local niche for my writing and contributing occasionally to bigger publications. If they noticed my fatigue on my occasional weekend visits, or the short, ragged fingernails I had worried till they bled, they never commented. I was publishing in national magazines that they had heard of, and they were proud of me. More important, I now suspect, I presented myself as happy, busy, and on the go, and they no more wanted to question the validity of my pose than I did.

When I did finally commit to a staff position, I told myself that the publication was more my type. I had been recruited to join a new monthly magazine; it had just published its first two issues before I decided to take the leap. The title of arts editor was exciting, something I could tell my parents about with pride, but I didn't take the job for its prestige. Something about this situation already felt comfortably familiar. It was smaller than the big daily paper, I reasoned, more challenging than the alumni magazine. And I could do so much there. It would be many years before I realized that what drew me to this new job was the extent to which it re-created my family life. In this job, I was once again thrust into the role of the good girl, the hardworking wunderkind who would save the day.

Signing on with the magazine was like joining a team, I thought at first, because we ran as much on spirit as on money. We were a start-up, but that was fun. Any gains we made were wins, any discoveries ours to claim. Sure, sometimes our paychecks bounced and we had to make do in novel ways, but I appointed myself the staff cheerleader as well as its arts editor and soon found myself doing much more than my original job description had outlined. There was so much to do, so many gaps to fill in, particularly as our publisher began firing other staffers for assumed disloyalty. My job grew: I solicited publicity shots to use as stock footage, hired nonwriters to compose columns on their specialty (money, law, and real estate), which I would later rewrite. The magazine made up for low fees, and late fees, by giving out trade scrip, free meals at restaurants that had paid for their ads with gift certificates rather than cash. When my check didn't clear one week, I ate softshell crab and duck confit each night. With so much effort invested, I felt a strong allegiance to the magazine and would defend it to detractors who pointed out its ad-based features, its poor record of payment. We were trying so hard, I said. And I, it now seems obvious, was going to save everyone at the magazine to make up for letting my brother and sister go.

I fared no better with this job than I did with my family, and our creditors closed in. When the money problems became inescapable I was finally forced to jump ship. Rather than return to freelancing, I accepted a job at a branch of a weekly newspaper. I had a small crew and was entrusted with making this latest outpost work, but I had no set budget and a lot of undefined responsibility. By the end of a year, I again saw my job collapsing. I had thought that this paper would offer structure and stability but found myself working in a situation where the rules changed regularly. Now I can see that the edition had not been well planned and that all the changes could have been expected. All I knew at the time was that I was exhausted, completely overworked, and run-down. I did not know where else to turn and went home for the weekend. There, I told my parents about my multiple job duties, the battles between my superiors, and my ever-changing budget.

Until this point, I had held them at arm's length from my independent postcollege life, assuring them that all my job changes were normal for journalism and publishing, and they tried to believe me. They had never seen one of their children begin an adult life before and seemed to be working hard at accepting and respecting my moves. My father had even taken to calling my first few jobs my "internship and residency," likening them to his first few years after medical school. I, of course, suspected that my path was not so well marked, but in a continuation of my childhood behavior had willingly shown them only the positive side.

Now I complained that the pressure at work was affecting how I did my basic tasks, my writing and my editing. I explained that because I had agreed to do this job without properly examining it, I believed I had no right, now, to object. This was my job, and my problem was figuring out how to make it all work. I felt trapped and grew weepy as I talked about the infighting and my own conflicting loyalties. As I talked, my father grew visibly agitated, frowning and tapping his chair's armrest as I related my troubles. I thought he was angry for me and looked forward to what I expected would be an impassioned defense. I talked until I had told them all, and then he blurted out, "When are you going to stop being a good girl and start being a smart woman?"

I didn't know what to say. I was stunned and went up to my room without comment. On some level I knew my father was correct: Instead of seeing myself as a skilled junior editor who had a right to expect professional treatment, I was assuming the role of den mother, trying to make everyone happy at any price. But I had come to him, in part, to tell him that I was being a good girl. I was trying as hard as I could. To be rebuffed and then chided for being the very thing my parents had always exacted from me was too confusing and awakened anxieties that I did not want to examine. If I was not to be the obedient and smiling child, then what place would I have in the family? Was it now my turn to be cast out, as both my brother and sister had been? I had sought comfort and confirmation but left in tears.

A month later I was called into the newspaper's Boston office: I could resign or be fired. If I chose to resign, I would save face and be given two weeks' severance pay. If, instead, I insisted on being fired, I could collect unemployment. I didn't think I had any reputation left to lose, so I chose the latter and spent the next few months in a daze, doing very little but drinking coffee and trying to make sense of the past few years. I felt alone and rejected. I had thrown myself into an undoable job under untenable circumstances and been afraid to leave. I felt victimized by abusive bosses and ridiculous demands. I suspected a pattern but could not see it. I did not recognize how I had chosen positions that I then believed I could not leave. I know I told myself each time that my boss had great faith in me, and that he— always a he—really believed I was capable of pulling his publication out of the fire, that I was the only one who could. But most of all I always told myself that I was missing something, that if I could only master some very basic skill, then I would be able to do the job, and I would be a good girl. Of course, I never could. And then I would feel very ill used. I rarely walked away from these jobs, but when I was finally drummed out, pushed out, or fired, I thought myself victimized. It wasn't until I admitted my deeper fears to myself that I found I had expected to be a failure all along.

Sometimes in those first few years out of college, I felt like a pinball. Time and again, I found myself ricocheting off the same bumpers of uncaring men and scary women. I saw myself falling into the same ruts, drawn to the same situations repeatedly and seemingly against my will, and I didn't know how to stop these painful replays. Maybe I didn't entirely want to—the knocks I took hurt, the lows were depressing, but at least these bumps and grooves were familiar. When I wasn't stuck somehow, I was careening wildly about in a way that used a lot of energy and served to distract me from the other aspects of my life.

To some extent, I think, I had fallen into a common predicament, one that new graduates face every year. As happens with so many young adults, I felt alone. My college community had been mostly dispersed, our lives now focused on separate concerns. Even though I first moved from my dorm into a group home with four classmates, we were not like college roommates. We all had either jobs or graduate programs to think about. Our days were full, and our Porter Square house was simply a place to eat and sleep. Usually, we didn't see one another after the morning rush until late in the night.

Surely this isolation is common, whether it happens to us after college or during some other transitional period. We have moved away from the places where we grew up, separated from our families, and transferred our allegiance to our college or training group, to something that is by nature temporary. Then we are released into the world, and we lose our social system in the process.

Some of us know how to rebuild our network of contacts and connections. We join alumni clubs or gyms, gather with our new workplace colleagues at local bars, or return to our childhood homes to renew older friendships. These new alliances lead to others, and to our own families and adult friends. But what about those among us who have good reasons to want no old ties? What if we do not know how to make new connections? For me, the first years out of college were incredibly disorienting. I had no practical models from my family for how to build continuity in life. I wasn't sure how to act, and I looked for one answer, one thing to complete me—either a man or a job.

When I look at the series of screwed-up relationships and work patterns that dominated my first years out of college, I see how I chose badly in many ways, and how I made these choices worse by my reactions. Most of us have probably had frustrating jobs and some amount of heartache, particularly when we were first starting out. However, what I see in my consistent inability to find any meaningful connection is another manifestation of the unresolved turmoil of my family.

Even at the time, I sensed that something was off. Although I could not yet trace the roots of my unhealthy patterns, after each breakup the similarities between this lover and his predecessors would become clear to me. After each job failure, I would see the same things, and this repetition filled me with anxiety. Sometime during my early twenties my fear of losing control had been replaced by a subtler one: I became convinced that I was damaged and unable to interact meaningfully with other people. This suspicion made me fearful of closer examination of my life and made me afraid to seek help. I didn't want to know the worst. Underneath this anxiety, I can now see another dynamic at work. I was not damaged, but I had left too many earlier relationships unfinished. I, like many other siblings of the mentally ill, was re-creating my family's patterns in my dealings with the outside world.

In her work with siblings of the mentally ill, Julie Tallard Johnson sees these patterns repeatedly. "However we have learned to respond to the mental illness, in the family and the effects it had on the family, we take that into all of our relationships," she says.

We want so much to start anew, and yet over and over we replay the scenes that marked our life. We manage each situation in the ways we have learned even when the roles we had earlier adopted, such as being the good child, may no longer prove useful. Our fear made us rigid; our family's trauma has cramped our ability to grow and change. Looking back over my own twenties, I see how impossible it seemed to ask my parents' advice or aid. To do so would have felt like an admission of my own confusion and human weakness, emotions I had been encouraged to hide. And so I resisted going to them until that one job reached crisis proportions. In part, my parents' unquestioning attitude, their careful acceptance of all my excuses, played into this petrification of our roles. We all treated each other as gingerly as if we might at any moment break. And so when my father's pragmatic nature finally came through, when he told me with exasperation and a touch of despair to grow up, I did not know how to respond. He was no longer following the script that he had helped write.

Debbie, whose younger sister has a borderline-personality disorder, recalls a similar period of disorientation. She was in her midtwenties when her old role failed her. "My mother was always saying, 'Oh, you are doing so well. We really appreciate the fact that you have your life so together.' So when my marriage fell apart I couldn't tell anyone. All I could think was that I wasn't the good person anymore."

It may be in our search for adult relationships that we pay the most for our incomplete adolescence, for our incomplete separation from our parents. Years before, we didn't get to learn that we could step away from our families and still be loved. We never dared to discover if we could leave home without destroying it. Now, the stakes have grown too high to risk it. Those of us who have grown up with mental illness, Johnson explains, "fear that if they separate from a person at all, it will be a total and permanent separation. And we think the person who has been cut off will die without us."

This fear, Johnson says, contributes to a general lack of autonomy for many siblings. "There is hopelessness and helplessness, a sense of not having choices and alternatives." After all, without this separation, we cannot be confident about where our life ends and others' begin. And without a good sense of personal boundaries, of who we are as people, no real adult closeness can be achieved. We cannot be fulfilled adults if we are still trying desperately to be good children.

"I am the child that stayed," says Grace, whose only sibling, a brother, has been diagnosed with schizophrenia. "I am the child that will look after them. I could not go my own way."

For Rachel, the desire to be a good child caused her to sabotage her one long-term relationship. She was able to fall in love, she notes, during a period in which she lived in Israel, far from her family. But when her parents came for a visit, she began to pick the relationship apart. "He was from India and somehow I felt my parents would not approve," she says. "When my parents came to visit I broke up with him. I just couldn't be with him. As soon as my parents left I got back together with him." She now wonders how much her ambivalence cost. "He wanted very much to get married. I loved him dearly, but I just felt I couldn't marry him, and I never married."

To say that all the men I became involved with were Daniel and that I wanted to save them but somehow couldn't would be simplistic though in many ways true. Likewise, my encounters with women, particularly angry, confrontational women, replicated my relationship with Katherine. And since I continuously found myself in dead-end jobs, situations that perhaps others would have avoided or bailed out of much sooner, I can only interpret my persistence in trying to salvage these situations as a renewed, and futile, desire to save my family.

Time and again other siblings told me stories of how they stayed with unsuitable mates, trying to "save" them. When we couldn't help the mate or salvage the relationship, we blamed ourselves. "I think the longest relationship I've had was about eight or nine months," says Zoe, who began dating several years after her older brother's breakdown and is now in her midtwenties. "The first two weeks would always be great. And then the next two weeks I'd try to figure out what was going wrong, thinking, 'I must be doing something wrong,'" she recalls. "Then things would kind of settle down, and then die out."

Maria, now in her late thirties, can look back on a decade of "mean and nasty and crazy guys," as she puts it. She now wonders if her younger brother's schizophrenia has influenced her choice of men. She was in her twenties when his illness became apparent, and she responded by "moving in with a jerk." Now a licensed therapist, Maria finds that "the recent ones are the more upsetting ones, because I have enough knowledge that I should have walked away. There was a psychotherapist that I dated who was violent," she says. "He was a really scary guy, and I noticed it pretty early on, but I stayed with him for four months until I was totally scared of him. The guy after that was really emotionally unstable and abusive. I knew before I got involved with him exactly what he was like, and I did it anyway.

"I always think, 'I should be open to this,'" she explains. A buoyant and sparklingly pretty woman, Maria usually has her choice of lovers. "I think, 'Maybe we're all flawed and I shouldn't judge them,'" she says. "'I should be with them and we can help each other.' But that's not the way it works."

So often we try to give ourselves entirely to the mates we chose, with an obsessiveness that Johnson describes as common: "You vacate and let the other person dominate."

Although women may more commonly adopt this behavior, men are not immune to it. Richard, who has two mentally ill siblings, often finds himself replaying his older-brother role with girlfriends who have some form of mental illness or who have ill family members. "I'm attracted emotionally to people that come from that situation. In all these relationships I feel like I don't get anything. I feel like I'm always giving, but I don't get anything."

This behavior also overlaps into nonsexual relationships. As Zoe points out, "I've always taken care of my friends. I've been the one who had the car who drove around when we were young. If somebody needed ten dollars, I'd be there to loan it to them."

In her book *Hidden Victims, Hidden Healers,* Johnson identifies this pervasive but dangerous practice as becoming a caretaker. This role, she explains, is an extension of the behavior we learned at home. We made life tolerable for ourselves by being the ones who did things, who somehow modified the environment. This becomes our way of coping, even, Johnson writes, "during noncrisis times." Her studies show that those of us who adopt the caretaker role are likely to neglect our own needs while we rescue others, and to foster unnecessary and unhealthy dependence in our friends and intimates. This makes us feel like we have close relationships, but they are not satisfying ones. We do not know how to set healthy limits to the amount of responsibility we assume. We do not know how to say no.

The other trend siblings adopt, Johnson has found, is exactly the opposite, retreating from responsibility and becoming what she calls an "escape artist." If opting out provided some relief, we made a habit of it, later choosing to withdraw whenever we were anxious or faced with unpleasant situations. We learned to avoid anything that might hurt us.

Sometimes the escape is emotional, a flight from commitment. Often, we say, our relationships with our ill siblings have shown us that intimacy is "impossible." Lou's sister, who is seven years his senior, used to tell him their family was cursed. "She used to say that we were all alike, but that nobody else was like us," he remembers. Her paranoia convinced him for many years that he could not have a healthy, lasting relationship. "She would say we were doomed not to marry or have children, and since I could see how she wasn't dating or likely to become involved with anyone, for a long time I thought she was right about me, too."

"In a long-term relationship, you need to want to fight to hold it together even if it's killing you. I just don't have that attitude," says Jan, who believes that her brother's schizophrenia has influenced her decision to remain single. "From my brother, I learned that the way two people perceive the same situation can be totally opposite, and I don't want to go commit myself to making something like that work."

Many siblings also put physical distance between themselves and their families as soon as they can. Carol's sister was willful and cruel to her parents. Eventually she was diagnosed with schizophrenia, and her parents moved the family from California to Vermont, seeking a simpler lifestyle to accommodate their ill daughter. But by then Carol was old enough to break free. "The way I chose to deal with it was to move three thousand miles away—to Vancouver."

Samuel's entire family has reacted in a similar fashion. "All of us [healthy] children wanted to get out of the Midwest," he says. "Nobody wants to live away from the water, because somehow the one closest inland is gonna be responsible for the family situation." One brother lives, like him, on the West Coast, and their sister has moved to the East Coast, while the brother with schizophrenia remains at home near Chicago. "We were all trying to flee a bad situation."

Often the roles are blended, with the desire to be the good child, the caretaker, alternating with a blind urge to run away. Jack, for example, admits, "I have a lot of ambivalence about my role as my brother's caretaker." Since Jack is the only doctor in his family, the responsibility seemed natural to him at first. "I want to be there for him, but I find oftentimes that it's easy for me to disappear, be inconsistent and shift the burden to my mother."

Our wavering is not always conscious, especially when we extend it to our relationships outside of the family, the ones we may have unknowingly patterned on our earlier lives. For example, Nancy, now in her sixties, married an alcoholic, a man who could become violent when he was drinking. "I was afraid of him," she recalls, using almost the same words she chooses to describe her feelings about her older brother, who had schizophrenia and could be dangerously aggressive. "I was afraid of his being out of control," she says about her husband. "It just triggered things in me."

Although Nancy is not convinced that she was drawn to her former husband because of her schizophrenic brother, she can tick off all the similarities: Like her older brother, her husband was very bright, "bordering on genius," and mechanically oriented. Like her older brother, her husband was rather controlling, even before he was drinking. Nancy may be classified as a caretaker, re-creating the family situation but this time "saving" her ill brother by caring for her brilliant but troubled husband. But, in classic escape-artist mode, Nancy also talks about how she ran from the relationship. Leaving her husband probably made sense by any standards, although twenty years ago divorce was much less accepted. However, Nancy sees that split as symptomatic of the way she now treats all troublesome relationships: "I don't adapt, I cut loose."

All these reactions, no matter how different they seem, serve to hurt us both because they tend to be extreme and because they are often not appropriate to the current situation. As was true earlier in our adolescence, we are really worried about leaving our family. We are also shying away from new intimacy because of how badly we have been hurt. We continue in some ways to re-create our family, or we continue to evade them. Either way, our lives are defined by our reactions to our ill siblings, which blind us to other options. We choose badly, we run, we overreact, and we find ourselves even further from the warmth we crave.

Samuel, aware of encroaching age, fears he may never find a mate. "I always felt that I would fall in love and have children. But here I am, forty-eight, and I haven't. It's kind of a mystery to me. I don't think there's been a deep love in my life," he says. Rachel, now in her fifties, expresses a similar loss of hope. "I have always selected men who were in some way or another unavailable," she says. "And it's not that I never wanted to get married. I wanted desperately to get married and have children."

We have many hindrances to healthy relationships. From the start, we have harmful patterns to overcome. We create mirror images of our unhappy family, because that is what we have learned. We fear closeness that leaves our heart vulnerable to incredible loss, and this gives us further incentive to sabotage ourselves and our closest relationships. With repeated failure we become more afraid of trying anything new, of trusting anyone or any pattern that seems healthy, and so we set up unfulfilling futures for ourselves. We do not see ourselves doing it; we simply discover time and again, painfully, what we have done. We are caught in the traps of our past just when we thought we were free, and our struggles only wear away what strength we have left.

chapter seven

SEEKING HELP

In those first years after college, my life took on a treadmill-like quality, as if I were on some awful machine on which I ran harder by the minute simply to hold my place. And I began to realize that I could not continue. At the moment of recognition, I had little hope, only a stubborn belief that things had at some point been different and that things could again be different. That spark saved me from despair and propelled me into therapy. There I found the only way to make any forward progress was to take the time to finally face the demons of the past. And some of the hardest to face, some of the biggest demons—even in a family in which horrible things happened—were the ones I had created myself.

This showdown, when it came, was long and wearying. But in some ways I had a head start. Because of my family's history, those long-ago days when my parents had told me that I "could see someone," I didn't have any great fear or shame about therapy. My job at the alumni magazine had excellent health insurance, covering more than half the cost of private counseling. And because the magazine was part of Harvard, I was familiar with the health service's mental health program. On one side, I had nothing going on in my life, nothing but a deep sense of loss and building agitation. On the other, I had moderately good memories of my first therapy experiences with Dr. Schaeffer and with the Harvard counselor who had later gone on leave. She had, after all, helped me confront my parents. She had let me cry for many hours over Jesse and over Daniel. If she hadn't helped me change my life, she had at least listened to me. In some ways, the decision made itself.

I called that original therapist for an appointment. She wasn't taking any new patients, she told me, but she would meet with me and make some referrals. I took her earliest available hour and on that day spent my lunch break telling her how alone and disconnected I felt. I told her of the horrible fear I had that I was doing something wrong, that I was missing some trick. Everyone else was moving forward, I explained, while I expended all my energy to stay in place. And I was wearing down.

I could hear the despair in my own voice. I sounded panicked. That was partly because my terror ran deeper than even I could explain. It took me years to admit, even to myself, that I wasn't afraid of merely being off track. I secretly suspected that my problem was deeper, that I was not like other people. Somehow I felt I was doomed to be isolated, to be set apart always in a more exaggerated form of what I had felt on Long Island and in my home. This fear played itself out in every social arena: I became clumsy when talking to the people I met in the clubs and reasoned to myself that I really didn't belong there. I was better educated and more refined than they were, I told myself, although in fact I was meeting many sharp young college graduates, women in particular, with a taste for bohemian life, just like me. At work, my older, more settled colleagues appeared dull, seemed to be living only half a life—a daytime life—and I dismissed them too. As I had for years, I moved between worlds. But since I had left home the cost of my double life had risen. I no longer simply wanted a way to express my deepest rages and fears. I wanted an integrated life. I wanted to share these and other intimate parts of myself with other people, but the walls I built had solidified.

The awkwardness of my advances as much as what I had to say made connection seem nearly impossible. I even felt stymied by the casual banter of office conversations. Once, when people were talking about various anniversaries, I mentioned that we were close to the date of my brother's death. My colleagues looked disturbed by my revelation, which sent a wave of embarrassment through me. They must see me as a freak, I thought. It was years ago, I stammered, feeling suddenly exposed. An accident. He and I weren't close. He was mentally ill, I said in a tone that did not invite further inquiry, and then turned away. This was the first time they had heard of my brother. Many of my close friends did not even know of his existence or of my sister. Years before I had cut off my siblings, and with them part of myself. I felt awkward, ashamed, and now completely alienated from the social interaction around me, as if I were some sort of hybrid, not quite human.

My former therapist gave me three names. The first, a social worker, had her office nearby, so I called her for an appointment that afternoon. She smiled when I came in, which reassured me, and her office looked comfortable, full of bright colors and children's drawings. She asked if I minded if she put her feet up and if I would feel comfortable calling her Ann, and then she invited me to begin talking. My story was beginning to sound rote, but it still made me tear up. I told her about my desperation to get my life moving, and her face grew serious. I told her I wanted feedback, that I needed something to happen soon, and she discussed her willingness to interact with me, to use various forms of therapy as the situation arose. I asked if she thought we could work together, and she offered her cheery assent. Her optimism warmed me. I liked her and felt comfortable with her style. But being my father's daughter, I wasn't sure about her qualifications. She wasn't an M.D. or even a Ph.D.

The next day I made an appointment with the second name on my list, a woman with a doctorate and an office downtown. I took the subway and arrived late and a little breathless. She buzzed her door open and was sitting behind her desk when I came in. In a tailored suit with her hair in a tight bun, she looked more like a personnel manager than a doctor, and her questions supported my impression. Why did I want to see a therapist? What did I expect to get out of it? As I ran down my list of woes—aimlessness, a sense of being off track, loneliness, some concern about my increased drinking—she murmured her acknowledgment, as if checking off items on a list. Then I got to the end of my story and paused. The office was silent. I knew enough about the procedure to understand that she was giving me room to continue as I wished, allowing me to direct the conversation. But I also remembered that I was auditioning her. I asked her whether she thought I could benefit by seeing her. She was silent a moment longer and then told me that she believed I could benefit from psychotherapy and that she would be willing to take me on as a patient. The decision, however, had to be mine, she added. I had to be willing to make the commitment. I looked at her, in her business suit and severe hair, and made my choice. I wouldn't even bother with the third name on my list. I would go back to Ann, the social worker.

We set up a schedule of twice-weekly visits and got down to work. I had thought the process of therapy would be intellectual, that I would recognize patterns and precedents in a rational way and thus free myself. But somehow time changed in therapy. Sessions became a perpetual present tense that made my early childhood as current as the day outside, and often I would leave the office in a daze. I lived for these appointments, week in and week out, and saw the time between as filler. I felt as if each session were a vine in a jungle and I were swinging from one to another, afraid to drop, always looking for the next lifeline to grab.

Twice a week during those first few years I would come in to talk and end up crying. Often without apparent reason, I would say a word or Ann would ask a question and my eyes would fill up. Sometimes I would be doubled over sobbing; often I didn't know why. Within the safe harbor of Ann's office, all my defenses crumbled. All the pain I had been holding inside came out. Sometimes I thought I would never stop crying.

A few months in, the dreams started—not useful, comprehensible dreams that illustrated the points we had been discussing, but wildly terrifying nightmares. Many of them were dreams of transformation, in which something that seemed solid would melt away. Sometimes I was in a room, an ordinary room, I would think, until I saw the walls begin to move and blur. Sometimes there was paneling that began to crack apart; sometimes a pattern in the paint began to come alive, and suddenly the wall would become animated, moving yet not sentient. I was surrounded not by solid walls at all, but by giant masses of twisting grubs or crawling swarms of roaches, oblivious to me, but horrible.

Sometimes the dreams involved bodies or body parts. Again those same walls might fade away to reveal decaying corpses hidden inside, a la Edgar Allan Poe. Or the grubs would part to reveal red, angry flesh. And sometimes I was immersed in a filthy sea, along with these writhing horrors and this mutilated flesh. Too often, as the months passed, I spent my nights floating in such stagnant oily water with nameless dead things brushing against me and mindless moving things swimming around me and beneath me, where I could not see them but could feel their passing. I began to wake up regularly before dawn, tense and sweating, and either unable or unwilling to sleep again until light.

By day, looking at the robin's-egg blue of Ann's walls, I tried to explain the horror of those nights in terms of their emotional content. Clearly, there was disgust, for I was in a world of bugs and bodies. And there was loneliness, because although many things swarmed and crawled in these dreams, I was the only thinking creature there. There was also the horror of sensing some presence I could not see or name, as I felt hard wings brush against my face and tentacles pass beneath my feet as I swam. I stared at the walls of Ann's office, as if the painted paneling would crack open to reveal something. I did not see how these nightmares connected to the memories we also talked about.

After months of these nights of terrifying dreams I was exhausted, shadows making my eyes look bruised. That's when Ann finally brought up the possibility of taking Elavil, an antidepressant that suppresses REM, the dreaming cycle of sleep. She wanted to put me on a low dosage so I could rest. If the drug also helped me get some of these terrors out of my system, so much the better. On her recommendation, I went to another doctor, a psychiatrist, who prescribed the drug. I started taking it that night and fell asleep within an hour of swallowing the little pill. Over two weeks I worked up to the dosage he had prescribed, and I began to sleep through the night. Any dreams I had on Elavil I did not remember.

Whether I was now rested sufficiently to unclench my jaw and to speak, or whether the drug was having an antidepressant effect despite the low dosage, I don't know, but I began to make connections where I had previously been blocked. I talked a lot more easily now, but mainly I still cried. In my sessions, I returned to my childhood. I went over the killing of Honeybun, and the fights, the screaming fights, as my world—like those nightmare walls—crumbled, as those closest to me became crawling, scary things or became dead. I choked as I talked because I was crying so hard. I sucked at the air between words, desperate to talk more, to get all the horror out. By the session's end my nose would be stuffed and my eyes streaming. In Ann's office, I was six years old again and confused. I was eight and terrified.

By that time, I had left the alumni magazine and was working freelance. Sometimes after my sessions I wandered around Harvard Square, finding it a comfort to walk among people and see daylight. I must have looked a fright, my eyes swollen and my nose all red, but I didn't really care. After a while I could go home and wash my face. I could call my editor and figure out that night's assignment.

A few months later, with Ann's support, I tapered off the Elavil and began to dream again. Still scary, but less horrible, these new nightmares seemed more composed. Sometimes I saw Daniel, but he had become a rubber man. In these dreams, I was often in the backseat of the car and he was in the front, but in the magical way of dreams his neck stretched somehow to bring his face right up to mine. He would be grimacing, his face too close to mine, frightening me. There was something wrong with this proximity, I knew, even before I awoke. I began to dream also of a small animal that jumped around and vomited and then expired. And I began to wonder how often Daniel must have masturbated in front of me. I wondered if he ever rubbed himself against me, lay on top of me, pressed himself too close for comfort. I remembered the night my mother yelled at him for walking down our hallway nude with an erection, and I asked her during one awkward, painful phone conversation if this had happened more than once, if she knew of any other sexual behavior toward me. She said she didn't have any proof, but that she had worried about what Daniel might do and had tried to stay on the alert without scaring me. I suspected that her fears were well founded and began to believe then that my brother had been, at least, sexually inappropriate. I didn't know if I would ever know more, but as Ann and I discussed the possibilities, the dreams receded.

After the Daniel dreams subsided, my nightmares began to focus on enormous images. These images changed but their size stayed constant. The proportion alone was terrifying. In one version, I was looking out of a picture window into a vast sea, as if I were in an ocean liner with an oversize porthole, when a gigantic whale swam by. It was so huge that, even far away, it filled the entire window and obviously extended far beyond it. Even my peripheral vision could not detect its edges. The ship and I were totally dwarfed, and although the creature was passing us, soundless and oblivious, I would wake chilled with fear.

Sometimes the dream placed me on a dark and polluted beach, where I stood among wreckage and the shadows of pilings. At some point I would look out and see that the horizon had been filled by a huge wave. Sometimes, as in the older nightmare, there were parts of cadavers, hair and rotting limbs, in the wave that towered over me. Then I would be disgusted as well as terrified. It never crashed, this wave, and the giant whale never ate me or sank my ship. My dread came not from such a threat of violence as from the size of the thing, from the impossibility of escape. There was an inevitability of doom in these dreams that made them dreadful but also imbued them with calm. They scared me in a new way that seemed particularly chilling.

By this time, more than five years of therapy had passed. I'd return to my office at the magazine after our sessions, shutting my door for a few minutes and readjusting to the working world. But often this world felt less real than the one I was exploring with Ann. Neither my job as editor of the magazine nor the one that followed at the newspaper would last as long as my therapy. Although I wasn't aware of it during those early years, I was building, for perhaps the first time in my life, a consistent relationship. I was learning to trust. Here was a relationship that did not depend on my being good or happy or successful, as I felt I needed to be for my parents all those years at home. Here I could test the boundaries by indulging my most sullen mood or simply sobbing and not worry about upsetting the family balance or being judged. My parents were not here to reject me, and I began to accept myself.

"What would happen," my therapist asked me one day, "if the wave were to come crashing down?"

"It would destroy everything," I answered immediately. "It's so high, it would even drag the moon under. Foul, filthy water would cover everything, and the impact would be so great that nothing would live."

I hadn't thought, before she asked, of what could happen. I'd been living with just the threat of the nightmare image, but I found I could easily draw the scenario out. And, I discovered, I liked to elaborate on my picture of ruin. Horrible as it was, the sweep of images had some appeal. I warmed to the idea of total destruction. I was sick of fear and waiting. I realized perhaps for the first time that I was angry.

The wave, it seemed, wasn't just the sense of impending doom I remembered from childhood and then, in a different form, from adolescence. Yes, I had sensed my brother and sister, our whole family structure really, falling apart long before it finally happened. Yes, I had felt their illness to be looming over me as well, all through the years when I waited for schizophrenia to crash through my life and wash me away. These interpretations rang true, and we had been discussing them since the dreams started, but now I had to face another option. I had to accept that something else terrifying had been building and threatening, something so ferocious it could destroy the world. Whatever else it might be, the giant wave of my nightmares was also all the rage that I had suppressed from early childhood on. All the years when I had been the good child, never screaming when Daniel scared me or crying out when Katherine threatened my pets, never railing at my parents for their failure to protect me; all the tantrums I hadn't had because I wanted to be praised for my good behavior—these had been building up. It didn't matter that my brother and sister couldn't help themselves. It didn't matter that my parents had coped as well as they knew how. I had been hurt, scared, shamed, and ignored, and I was furious.

Connecting the giant wave of my nightmares to the anger inside me felt right, as if some internal recognition had clicked in. My repressed rage terrified me, but Ann's solicitude and real empathy helped get me through many painful sessions. We had a more free interaction than any I had known in counseling. Once I asked her why she thought I should be so afraid of myself, and she in turn asked me what it would mean to me to be angry.

"I could destroy the world," I said without pausing to examine my reasoning. "If I ever really let my feelings out, I'd blow everybody away." I pictured my anger rushing out like a personal hurricane, literally leveling houses, trees, and people, or like that giant wave.

"And what would be wrong with that?" she asked.

"I would be a bad person," I replied before I had time to think. That's when I realized how uncomfortable I was with my anger. I could handle the sadness and the fear; I felt safe with those emotions. But the violent, suspicious, and aggressive emotions were harder to release because they didn't fit into my image of myself. I had gone from being the golden child to the high-achieving student to the tough and independent career builder, at least as far as my family knew, as far as report cards and job titles represented me. And the picture I had given my parents was, in truth, what I wanted to believe about myself. At some level, I had incorporated my family's black-and-white paradigm for life: People were healthy or mad, good or bad, in or out of our house. I had so wanted to be loved, to be accepted, that I swallowed every negative emotion, turning all my rage and anger inward.

With this insight, I could feel myself becoming a whole person again, albeit racked by wildly conflicting emotions. I started sobbing fiercely, breathlessly, in Ann's office when it hit me and wandered around dazed for hours afterward.

I had so much healing to do, so many years of emotions to sort through. In a way, my unhappy work life was a blessing. Soon after this revelation, I was fired by the weekly paper. Even as it happened, I was wondering: "Am I angry? How angry? Was I expressing rage inappropriately all along? Did I bring this down on my own head somehow?"

I might not have wanted such a good reason to be mad, but the firing served me well. Afterward, I felt threadbare and exhausted. I managed, the week after my dismissal, to apply for unemployment benefits and then sank into a months-long daze. Great sadness and fury filled me; alternating with bouts of extreme fatigue. All the unbearable years had caught up with me; the energy that had kept me going had run out. All I could do each day was wake up and pull on my leggings and a sweatshirt. I would meet a friend for coffee and wander around downtown. The unemployment benefits barely paid my rent, and I was running up large balances on my credit cards, using them for cash advances, but I could not do more. I needed the time to pull together all these emotions and memories. I needed the time to heal.

During these quiet months I called my parents often and began finally to tell them everything I had left unsaid. I talked about the pressure I had felt to appear happy and about how scared I really was. I told them how angry I was that they hadn't been able to protect me from Daniel and Katherine, and my mother broke down in tears. She talked about her dilemma, about the horrible triage she had felt forced to perform. My father tried to comfort us both, reassuring her that she had done what was necessary and telling me how he had always known I was different, had never doubted that I was healthy. Hearing their concern, hearing at last the reactions they had hidden from me for all those years, I began to relax.

By that winter, I felt much calmer—also more concerned about my financial situation—and I began job hunting in earnest. I took the first position offered, writing promotional copy, but soon grew frustrated and bored. Several months later, I was able to quit for a position on a daily paper, and the change exhilarated me. I felt alive, thrilled to be editing news stories on the five-till-midnight shift. Only the excitement never settled down. Two months in, I was still not sleeping regularly, still never relaxing. I worried, too, about things I said, casual comments thrown into the newsroom banter. Did I seem silly? Stupid? Had I been insulting to anyone in any way?

Once more, I started to brood about my behavior, afraid that yet again I was going to bring one of my earlier traumas into the workplace. Ann saw my agitation as a manifestation of depression and asked if I thought antidepressants might help me again. I said no, my previous experience had been a one-time crutch to get me through a crisis. I didn't want to be the sort of person who had to take antidepressants—it struck too close to home. What if I had, in some milder form than Daniel or Katherine, an incurable mental illness? What if I had to remain on antidepressants my entire life in order to function?

"How do you feel about your contact lenses?" she asked me. Every day since the third grade I had had to wear glasses or contact lenses, as she well knew. "Do you consider putting lenses in shameful? Is being nearsighted a failure of will?"

Of course, I didn't think so. I simply needed them to function. That, she concluded, was her point exactly. I might simply need antidepressants. But the issue wasn't so easily resolved. For so many years I had feared mental illness, and defined myself as the one who was healthy, that I had great trouble getting my mind around the idea that I might have some kind of permanent psychological disability. Ann dropped the idea when I grew too agitated, only to bring it up a month later. This time I became angry, accusing her of laziness, of not wanting to help me find the real, historical causes for my mood swings and for my near panic. She countered that we could use more than one tool.

Her persistence dovetailed with my problems at work. My self-consciousness in the office was beginning to border on panic, and I had trouble making the most simple decisions. This was 1990, when Prozac was being hailed as a miracle drug. It had just made the cover of *Newsweek,* and people at the paper were openly debating its benefits. I brought it up in conversation and soon found that two of the other night editors were taking the little green-and-yellow capsules. Both, in private conversations, urged me to try it. A new year would be starting soon, I told myself—might as well try for a new life. I met with the same doctor who had given me Elavil years before and got a prescription for the so-called wonder drug.

Over the next year and a half, I spent most of my time on the drug and saw much of my depression recede. I still would begin to worry, after the fact, about things I had said earlier in the day. But I learned that I could let them go, quickly and completely if I chose to. When I quit taking Prozac my obsessiveness returned, so I went back on the drug for an immediate improvement. I still fell into dark moods, usually at times when I wasn't seeing anyone or my job security seemed uncertain. At those times I'd imagine that there were no options for me and no hope. On those dark days, my life was going down. But with Ann's help I usually felt as if I were learning to swim again. If I didn't tense up, I could float, and life became less threatening. In early 1992, I went off the drug again, after promising both myself and Ann that I would go back on if the dark downward-spiraling came back.

I had learned to trust life more and begun to believe that even if I could not take care of every detail, the world as I knew it would not necessarily crash and burn. Ann called this "taking a trust fall," after the exercise actors use in ensemble work. In this exercise, each actor must fall backward into the arms of her partner, without clenching or breaking the fall. Each must believe that the other will catch her. Ann was asking me to do that with life, to relax and to unclench. I had learned that I could survive great sadness and live. I had come to accept that I could be less than a golden girl and still be allowed some happiness. Now I had to learn that once I had done all I could do, I had to let go. I had to stop trying so hard. Until I did, life could not meet me halfway.

In some ways, I was progressing well. My work and my writing were more fluid; I was letting myself take some risks and no longer obsessing about small details or imagined gaffes. Then I received a blow that threatened my newfound equilibrium. My father was diagnosed with terminal cancer. I still remember the message he left on my answering machine. Just the fact of his calling signaled something out of the ordinary; my mother had always been the one to handle most of our communication. But his message summoned me home. The afternoon he told me, I just hugged him and cried. In the weeks after his announcement, more complex reactions shook me. Some days I wanted to be his golden child again, to chuck the growing honesty of our relationship for my old role. He had already begun to look weak and gray, and I sought to reassure him that I would be all right, that I was doing well and really would take better care of myself in my current job and in my current relationship. Other days I wanted to freeze time, and got him talking about his past, about growing up in Brooklyn. He loved to reminisce about his college years, about the day he arrived in Boston by train only to be confused by a native's directions to take the "Park Street under" to Harvard Square. But he didn't want to talk about our early years, about the son or daughter he no longer saw. I felt torn, desperate to know what he was feeling, what he regretted about the way our family had forgotten Daniel and shucked off Katherine. I was very aware that my time for such queries was limited. He was getting thinner rapidly, growing sad and frail, and his obvious decline stopped my questions. All I wanted, finally, was to make him happy, to make everything good again.

But the strain of his illness and of my own regression left me shocked and unbalanced, panicky at work and weak in my dealings with my then-boyfriend Tom. Ann suggested going back on Prozac, concerned that I was relapsing into my old depressive habits as a way of coping with my father's illness. I suspected she was right, but I was resistant. I thought of it as "going down for a third time," as if this would be my third strike at bat. I didn't want to think of myself as indelibly depressed. I also thought that I was caught on some lump of fear. Knowing that my father was dying made me feel particularly vulnerable, and we spent our next few sessions talking about old emotions. Some sessions I would close my eyes and curl up into a ball, trying to dredge up the panic of being very young and of having Daniel wander into my room. I remembered how I held my breath when Katherine would knock at my door. I dreamt again of Daniel leaning over my bed, of his face too close to mine.

A few years earlier, when I had been at the magazine, I had written a feature story about a new type of self-defense course called Model Mugging. The class was distinguished by its emphasis on physical contact. In five intense five-hour sessions, women learned to defend themselves by fighting real people, male instructors who (in protective padding) acted as "model muggers." Women learned how to use the particular strengths of a female body—our strong legs and hips, as opposed to fists—to escape being raped or mugged. The class taught women how to work through surprise and panic, how to keep fighting even after being thrown to the ground. And each meeting rehearsed these techniques over and over until the actions became automatic. At the time I was researching the piece, one of our art staffers had taken the course and returned exhilarated after each session. She had urged us all to sign up, and I had actually put down a deposit. But I had chickened out before the first meeting. My interviews with the course founders had been fascinating, my talks with the instructors had been encouraging, but the course itself just seemed more than I could handle. Now I thought of it again. Perhaps my father's illness drove home the reality that I could no longer entertain the fantasy of my daddy's protecting me forever. Perhaps anger was working through my grief, making me admit that he never had. The number was still listed as across the river in Brighton, and I found out that a class would be starting soon.

The next few weeks raced by, and before I knew it, I was in the gymlike Brighton studio, sitting with a dozen other women on the edge of a mat. That first night we started by telling a little about ourselves and then proceeded into breathing exercises. You cannot fight, our instructor told us, if you are not breathing. Conversely, no matter how afraid, how frozen you feel, if you remember to breathe, everything else will follow. What we would start with, she explained, would be the first part of an attack. Each of us would take our turn standing on the mat, waiting for the "mugger" to grab us. Our only responsibility, that first exercise, would be to remember to keep breathing.

It sounded simple enough. I'd watched my classmates go through this exercise. I knew we wouldn't be thrown to the ground or hoisted into the air. But the first time I was to be grabbed from behind, my mind seized up. Our instructor stood in front of me, trying to calm me as I waited for the grab. But that moment of waiting undid me. Suddenly I was back in my bedroom, praying for Katherine to walk by my door. I wanted to be invisible. I held my breath until spots bounced before my eyes. And then I heard my teacher, coaching me, reminding me she was there to help me, asking me just for now only to breathe.

And that was only the first class. Later in the course, I would remember to keep breathing, but I cried more than once during a scenario in which I was surprised, supposedly asleep in bed, by a would-be rapist. Several times, I was able to lie still only by silently repeating, "This isn't real. This is just a class." How horrible it felt to lie once more in wait for a tormentor, how difficult to keep still and not run from the room each time my turn came around. But how liberating finally to kick out, to thrust the intruder off me, to yell loudly from the gut, "No! Get back! No!"

More than once during those five-hour sessions I repeated an aphorism about therapy that Ann had shared with me years earlier: "That which we most fear has already happened." This was old fear, much of it, dating back to my childhood. I was an adult woman now. And I was learning to fight back.

Then I did something I had never dreamed possible: I initiated the breakup with my current boyfriend. Until then, I had held on to whatever man was in my life, desperate for the show of security and validation. Although I had known Tom wasn't right for me almost as soon as we started dating, I didn't have enough sense of my own power to break it off. But after returning from my third session, feeling newly in control, I called Tom to tell him I could no longer see him.

Fifteen minutes later, there was a pounding on my apartment door. As I walked toward it, I heard my deadbolt sliding open. Tom came in.

"I want my house keys back right now," he said. His voice sounded deeper and more menacing than I had ever heard it.

The keyring was in my hands. I'd been addressing an envelope to put it in, and I simply handed it over. He didn't leave.

"You know," he said, his voice low but frightening, "you can't just make this decision by yourself. We will have to discuss it."

"If I want to leave, I can." I gathered some courage from my own words. "And I am."

"We will continue this conversation tomorrow." I shrugged, and he turned to leave. I realized, then, that the balance was off.

"Tom, I need my keys." He looked back at me. "The keys you just used to open my door." He scowled and stepped toward me. Although he had never been physically violent, I realized then just how imposing he was—taller than I by several inches and undoubtedly stronger. I started to shrink back when a novel thought came into my head: *I know what to do. I could protect myself.*

The fear left me. I stood still and held out my hand. "Give me my keys," I said. He stopped approaching and looked suddenly confused. And then he placed the ring with both my building and apartment keys in my open hand, turned, and walked out the door.

As I slipped the bolt behind him, I felt the blood rush through me, making me tremble and blush at my own audacity. And then the euphoria hit me. I had done it. I had taken my own life back.

In many ways, I consider the self-defense course a continuation of the therapy I had started nearly nine years before. It served several of the same purposes, most notably giving me the tools to change the patterns of my life, patterns that had been delineated largely by my desire to avoid conflict and my conviction that any showdown would be dangerous.

Our reasons for seeking help are as varied as our experiences. Very few of us, however, seem to have identified our issues with our siblings as reasons to seek counseling. If anything, we thought the problems came from something in ourselves.

Rachel, for example, first sought counseling when she was just eighteen. A bright and eager student in high school, she found college intolerable, largely, she now believes, because her brilliant older sister had broken down during her last year of high school. At the time, all Rachel knew was that she couldn't concentrate and couldn't behave.

"When I went into therapy, it wasn't my sister per se," she remembers now, more than thirty years later. "I could not handle being in school. I got kicked out for wearing pants, and I also flunked all my courses. I thought, 'There's something wrong here. I need help.'" In counseling, she realized that she was sabotaging herself because she felt guilty surpassing her sister. With time she was able to return to school and earn two graduate degrees.

Sandra recalls how her depression set in gradually, until one day its depth scared her. "I have never been suicidal, but I remember standing and watching the trains go by one day and thinking it wouldn't be that bad to die." At the time, Sandra, now a happily married mother and a doctor, didn't connect this vague unhappiness with her schizophrenic younger sister. However, she knew that her thoughts could be dangerous. "And I finally started to get some good help at that time," she says. "It made all the difference. I learned that I was allowed to be happy."

"I was despairing and looking for something," explains Kyra, "some kind of resolution to the pain I was feeling." Kyra's oldest sister, Lucy, had been diagnosed with schizophrenia many years before. Because of the fifteen-year age difference between the two sisters, Kyra had grown up regarding Lucy as a second mother. Then, when Kyra was fourteen, a tall, shy girl just entering high school, Lucy moved back home. Kyra's gregarious older sister had become so withdrawn that she couldn't hold a job, but once she moved back to the family home her psychosis expressed itself in screaming rages.

Although Lucy eventually married and Kyra went off to college and then to a job several hundred miles away, the pain of that period stayed with her and began surfacing in her postcollege years. "I would get just completely drunk," she now recalls. "Not often, but on occasion, and like there was something I just knew I couldn't talk with people about that I was internalizing." Another sister, who had also lived at home during Lucy's breakdown, urged Kyra to get help. "She just let me talk," says Kyra of her therapist, "and when I kept talking the real me started to enter in. The inside, the part I had suppressed."

For Terry, marital problems provided the impetus. "My husband and I had therapy for a year and a half to save our marriage," she says. "And I ended up really talking about life and my brother." Her brother is autistic and has very particular obsessions. Growing up, for example, Terry learned never to bring anything red into the house, never to do anything in a sequence of three, and never, on any grounds, to confront her older sibling, although they were only five years apart. She knew the reason; she had seen him become so angry that he would bite his hand clear through to the bone. Nevertheless, having spent her childhood around his rules, Terry experienced both shame and the loss of her parents' attention. These issues surfaced years later in fights with her husband.

Terry, like so many of us with mentally ill siblings, didn't always know what was going wrong, but could tell that some part of life had gone off track. She, as many of us are, was lucky; in therapy we found out what we had lost. Often simply expressing the negative feelings we felt compelled to hide served to bring us back to a full and more fulfilling range of feeling.

Recognition can be adequate compensation. Terry found a therapist whom she describes as "very compassionate." This therapist,

Terry says, "gave me a lot of the love I was deprived of. Love that should have gone to me as a child in a family when it all had to go to my brother. And she gave me the opportunity to complain, which I was never allowed to do."

For those of us who grew up in the shadows of our siblings' illness, the thought of individual or group psychotherapy can be daunting, especially if we defined ourselves as the healthy child. However, we must accept the reality: Few of us remain unscathed if our family has experienced the trauma of a family member's breakdown. In groups, particularly self-help and sibling-oriented support programs, we may find the companionship and support of those who have lived through similar trauma. This can aid healing, in part, because it directly addresses the isolation that so many of us have experienced. "The restoration of social bonds," writes Judith Herman in *Trauma and Recovery,* "begins with the discovery that one is not alone."

Support groups may be the best way of getting through a crisis, and for many, they offer an excellent introduction to the idea that help is available.

"Most people coming into the group have no friends," says Julie Tallard Johnson, who has designed a system of support groups for people whose siblings have mental illnesses. "That is a big issue—no community. You can't heal in isolation, so you need a community even if it is just starting out with a therapist or a minister."

For Debbie, the community of a group provided confirmation that her emotions were valid. "I used to feel like a bad person for being mad at my sister. To talk to these people showed me it's OK to be mad. Sometimes being mad, actually allowing myself to get angry and talk about it, has made me feel so much better."

"It's really comforting for me to get together with other people who have lived through this," adds Kyra, who has attended sibling support groups in addition to her individual therapy.

Some prefer this community approach to therapy with a leader. Rex Dickens, who is very active in the National Alliance for the Mentally Ill, has a brother with schizophrenia and another who has been diagnosed as bipolar. He organized his own sibling support group in the early eighties as an alternative to traditional therapy.

The mental health profession, he says, "feels they should have certain training. You don't need that. It is healing simply to be around others."

Grace, who survived violent abuse at the hands of her schizophrenic brother, has also found support groups to be more comforting than traditional therapy, which to her felt invasive. "I found the meetings were really good because they were only once a month," she says, "and because you could say all this stuff and nobody would ask you a stupid question, like, 'Well, how come you don't try this, or what about . . . ?' "

Siblings have to keep in mind, however, that groups, like therapists, differ greatly. Some focus on education as opposed to therapy. The program called Journey of Hope, for example, starts with basic information and encourages family members to accept their feelings. This twelve-week-long course relies on what founder Joyce Burland calls the innate strength of people, rather than on the guidance of mental health professionals, to foster healing. Burland, a clinical psychologist, thinks that this nontherapy, group-style meeting works best because "family members will often not talk about pain," she says; many actively avoid mental health professionals for fear "their pain will be misinterpreted as causing the illness" in their family member.

Burland very clearly emphasizes that Journey of Hope is not therapy. Yet this kind of course can have the same beneficial effect for family members that advocacy work for groups like the NAMI and its various counterparts may provide. Other groups, usually with more personal, internal goals, employ methods garnered from various traditional therapies. The groups Julie Tallard Johnson leads, as described in her book *Hidden Victims, Hidden Healers,* follow an eight-stage group process (loosely patterned on the famous twelve-step programs for addiction) in which members work through steps of awareness, validation, acceptance, challenge, releasing guilt, forgiveness, self-esteem, and growth.

Sometimes the goal, as was true in my self-defense class, is to conquer a specific fear. By choosing to take a self-defense course, I was unknowingly following the steps outlined in Judith Herman's

Trauma and Recovery. Herman, a clinical psychiatrist, presents such courses as a useful way of working through trauma. "Like reenactment," she writes, "this choice is an attempt to master the traumatic experience; unlike reenactment, however, it is undertaken consciously, in a planned and methodical manner, and is therefore far more likely to succeed." For Herman, the group is a natural follow-up to individual psychotherapy.

Kyra augmented her one-on-one therapy with a weekend est-type program called the Forum. Not focused specifically on survivors of trauma, this somewhat controversial program consists of intensive self-examination and aims at helping people grow partly by encouraging them to confront their fears. For Kyra, that meant calling her oldest sister, Lucy. Kyra hadn't spoken to Lucy in four years. "One of the assignments was to do something you would not normally do that is very difficult," she says. "So I called this sister. That was the most difficult thing I could think of. My sister answered the phone and I said, 'Hi, this is Kyra.' Lucy just heaved a big sigh and she went, 'Yeah, what do you want?' "

While her sister's reaction was disappointing, Kyra learned that her fears had no real power over her. "I felt good that I faced her," Kyra now says.

"Back in the early eighties, nobody even thought that the siblings or children of the mentally ill were affected," remarks Samuel, who has two brothers with mental illness. Samuel knew that he was feeling despondent and that he was letting his work slide after the brother who developed schizophrenia committed suicide, but he found that his traditional therapy did not help him connect these feelings to his brother's illness. "I tried seeing a couple of people," he says. "I knew things weren't working, and I thought maybe they could solve it, but sadly, I learned that this was wrong."

Psychotherapy is probably as much an art as a science, a large investment with no guaranteed results. One-on-one therapy, particularly, is long and expensive; groups, as well, can continue for years. Sometimes such therapy feels aimless, "a waste of time," in Samuel's words. In addition, abuse of trust does exist. We want to trust our therapist and, if we are to gain anything from the interaction, we need to. However, we must also keep in mind that we are consumers. We needn't stay with any therapist or group if we are not getting the help we need.

Siblings should also be aware that many of the support and advocacy groups for family members were started by and for parents. While these may be helpful, they may also feel like a continuation of our home situation. "Sibling pain is different. It is qualitatively different," Burland stresses. "But sibling groups that are restricted to siblings can do some awfully good work. I was really gaga about what they were able to do with each other, what they couldn't do in the larger group when all the family members were there."

But some groups, no matter how focused, may also unintentionally encourage their members to continue their denial of their emotional needs. One sibling support group I visited, for example, spent the entire ninety-minute session talking about current problems with treatment in local hospitals. Perhaps this discussion disseminated some useful information. However, it was totally focused on the ill siblings. This, for me and possibly other attendees, simply reinforced the message of our youth: that we could cope, that our family members needed the attention, and that our own problems were not worth discussing—even in a format specifically advertised as being for our support.

Johnson recommends using a facilitator. "Groups need a trained facilitator or a therapist for ten weeks at least, someone who can go in being able to be autonomous. It can't be one of the members; they need to be separate so they can really come in and say, 'OK, here's what's working, here's what's not,' " she says. "Because everybody comes to a group with their family issues. Everybody needs and deserves a group leader who isn't going to be caught up in that and who can facilitate the group in a way that gives them options and has them take a look at what's going on and what's working."

Sometimes, of course, therapy doesn't work. After all, we buried our fear and anger for good reasons, usually for our own or our family's survival. And we got as far as we have—into at least a nominally functional adulthood—by continuing the behaviors, the defense mechanisms, we learned at home. Letting go of these tried and true ways of life must now be incredibly threatening. These patterns we learned were what helped us survive.

"I just couldn't get into it then." Rikki recalls her first attempt at group therapy, made before she was ready to confront the issues that had sprung up around her brother's schizophrenia. "I was denying my brother's existence for a good amount of time. As much as I could manage it, he didn't exist for me. And the fact of going there and purposely discussing it just turned me off."

"I had formed my identity around this sense of sorrow," says Alice, whose older brother became rapidly, and seemingly permanently, psychotic when they were both in their teens. "That sadness had just been a real core part of who I was." Sorrow, she continues, "is this uncontrollable thing, and part of the fear was that that sorrow had become almost like my foundation."

Burland explains that often she sees people who just are not ready to let go. "They will say, 'I think this is a little too much for me,' " she says. " 'I don't want to know all this.' We say, 'You just do what you have to do and then when you are ready for it, you come back.' "

Partly through the solace she found by joining a church, Alice began to accept her older brother's schizophrenia and to let go of her unhealthy definition of herself. "I started to realize that I could be joyful. And that I didn't have to go into the grief process in order to feel real or to have deep feelings." Of course, letting go of this immediate, incapacitating grief also meant moving further away from her brother emotionally, which brought with it a lot of guilt. Now in her midthirties, Alice has finally discovered that although her brother is ill, she is very healthy. "I learned that I was grieving for him and not for me. I've started to find some boundaries I didn't have before," she says. "I've really started to separate out my identity from my brother's."

Ceasing to define ourselves in terms of our siblings may be tricky. As siblings of people with mental illnesses, we have lived with a chance of developing such disorders ourselves. If, as mentioned earlier, the disease in our family is schizophrenia, we had an 8 to 10 percent chance of developing it; if the disease is bipolar disorder, we had higher odds. Although other illnesses, such as autism or the nonspecific personality disorders, may not have such clear numbers, we may safely assume that we share a genetic loading for them as well.

What many of us now may have to consider is that we may have a trace of our sibling's disorder. We may be mildly depressed because of our childhood environments, or because we have a genetic tendency toward mood disorders, or perhaps both. And we may never be sure exactly what is affecting us. Can we still see ourselves as good and as lovable even if we are not entirely "healthy"?

Many of us may fear any kind of therapy, but particularly treatment with drugs, as proof that we are truly, organically ill. Lily, for example, was diagnosed as being clinically depressed when she entered therapy. She had barely slept for two weeks before she decided to seek help. Now she recognizes that she has some kind of chemical imbalance. Although she does not know if her depression is somehow related to her brother's schizophrenia, she now accepts the fact that her illness, like his, may best be treated by drugs.

This possibility is terrifying to many of us, and our terror may stand in the way of our getting help. If we are open to the possibilities, however, we find some peace. Sandra has been taking antidepressants for about eighteen months. Although she is a doctor, she resisted this treatment for years "because it meant I would have been like my sister," she now says. "I actually tolerated being very sad for years rather than treating those feelings, although I knew it was a syndrome that was treatable. I had this thought, 'Well, if I take a single pill, I'll turn into a lunatic.'"

Such treatment, like Lily's diagnosis of clinical depression, also makes us confront the last vestiges of stigma within ourselves. No matter how we feel about our obviously ill siblings—how protective of their rights or how alienated by their behavior—we are now taking the issue one step closer. We may need to reevaluate how we feel about being consumers in the mental health industry. We may need to reconsider how we define healthy.

chapter eight

LEARNING NORMAL

Sometimes, at my therapist's urging, I try to imagine what my life would be like if my family had been different, if my siblings had not developed schizophrenia. Would Daniel, the first child and only son of a doctor, have gone on to medical school? Would he now be a happily married orthopedic surgeon living in suburban Westchester with his wife and three children?

Harder still to imagine, had this happier possibility come about, is what role my brother would have played in my life. I remember Daniel taking care of me, and that might have continued. Perhaps his partially parental role would have expanded as time passed. I've tried to picture a healthy older brother in his twenties, visiting the family and grilling my teenage dates. And when our father died in the winter of 1993, I tried to conjure up a forty-something version of Daniel, standing beside me and my mother, grieving with us.

Turning the fantasy spotlight on Katherine is more difficult, even though I have more real memories of her. Given her love of drawing and of music, she might have become a textile artist, living a bohemian lifestyle in New Mexico or SoHo, or a painter, like our mother. Perhaps she would have children of her own who would have come with her to their grandfather's funeral. Maybe she would have followed her early love of pop music through a hippie stage, becoming a flower child in the late sixties, when she was in her teens. Would she, given the eight-year gap between us, have been a second mother to me?

These exercises always make me uncomfortable. In truth, almost any thoughts at all involving my siblings are just too loaded with pain and fear, and when I force myself to think back, the old queasy feeling of disorientation sets in. The few pleasant times I can remember grow confusing. These images seem so normal that either I do not believe they are my memories or I begin to think that what followed them was not real. I begin to dissociate, to talk about scenes as if they were pictures in somebody else's scrapbook. The disparity between past and present is too great, and I find it easier to not look back at all.

We have all been changed by the illness in our family. But while there may be no recovery of our earlier selves, I do try to remind myself that there is healing. For me, such a mending of old wounds has meant learning not to do things that ultimately hurt myself or set myself up for failure, and building on the strengths I do have. Healing also means that I must try to accept who I am, scar tissue and all.

In a way, my father's death brought me to this conclusion, although the nine years of therapy that preceded it certainly laid the groundwork. That December, when he went into the hospital for the final time, brought more sadness than I thought I could bear. My mother cried after every visit, and I found myself staying at the paper late into the night, working on my own projects just to avoid her phone calls. I could conjure up little comfort to give her and could barely function under the burden of my own deep and growing grief. I certainly had no time or energy for what seemed like trivial worries. My writing became more serious. And I realized, sometime in that dark month, that I had long passed my thirty-first birthday, that in between visits to my parents' house and more recently to the hospital, I had made it beyond the magical age of thirty that had been my brother's last. Although I cannot say exactly how these elements coalesced, I know that somehow, just when everything seemed so difficult, I began to truly let go of a great deal of the responsibility I had assumed since childhood. I started to realize that there was little I could do, beyond my round of visits and calls, to make anything better. There was virtually nothing I had control of, and for once even I realized clearly that none of our current family trauma was in any way my fault.

When he died that January, I was able to grieve for him. But I was also able to let much of my family burden slide off my back. With his death the last shared illusion of our family as an inviolable unit had evaporated. That winter, I realized that I would truly have to take care of myself, but also that I was capable of doing so. I initiated a more open relationship with my mother and would find over time that we could talk about our grief over the loss of my father, and then about all of our family's losses. She began finally to tell me about Katherine, how over the years they had received calls from police and other emergency workers. There were the therapists who had wanted to try to reunite my sister with my parents. She told me then also of the silent and hopeless visits they had made to Katherine's halfway house, trying to make an emotional connection with their daughter. It was a nice place, she said, like a residential hotel with a lawn and woodlands behind it. After many years and fruitless visits, they gave up. My mother had made her choices, I was learning, and I could ask her about them, but they did not have to be my choices. I began to realize finally that I was an adult.

By accepting this, I have been able to forge a happy and committed romantic relationship. But not without pitfalls, and in the stages of our acquaintance I can trace my own progress. For the first few weeks that Jon and I were dating, I lived with the fear that I could at any time make some simple slip of word or action and he would see how unworthy I was and break up with me. I worried obsessively over how I looked and what I said. In my polarizing worldview, I saw Jon as my last, best chance at happiness, the lifeguard who would keep me from drowning. By doing so, I set him up as a tyrant, modeled him on the part of my father that I feared would reject me if I was not a good girl. I didn't realize that I was not letting either of us be human, or even have much fun, until one night, about a month after we started dating, when we ran into some of my friends at a concert.

One of them suggested we meet up at a local bar, and before I could make excuses Jon agreed. We managed to leave the packed theater before they did and found ourselves standing on the sidewalk outside, looking for them as the crowd poured past. It was cold, and I felt responsible for us being stuck outside waiting for my friends. I began to talk fast, telling stories to make the time pass, when Jon turned to me and interrupted my rambling tale. "You don't have to entertain me, you know," he said. "I'm enjoying your company." I couldn't catch my breath. "You seem nervous, and you don't have to be." I gasped for air and started to see spots of light flying around. "Are you all right?" he asked. At least a minute passed before I could reply. I was so surprised and scared by this sudden intimacy that I had begun to hyperventilate. So many of my other relationships had involved my focusing on my boyfriend. I was used to drawing men out, trying to please them or somehow save them, as if they all were my beloved brother but, unlike him, still within my reach. I had forgotten that I loved my brother partly because of the early days, when he had taken care of me. And I had never before sought out a man who could give in this way, who wanted to care for me.

When we moved in together I had another shock. My way of coping with the change was to plan, much as I had throughout my childhood. I was the one who had started sorting and discarding weeks ahead. When moving day came, I was the one who had drawn up diagrams of where our furniture should be placed. And because I was the one who had already begun these plans and diagrams, I assumed them as my task. Once again, I felt responsible for making everything work, and I carried this old habit into our new home.

After the first few weeks, it became clear that we weren't dealing with money issues. I tended to do the shopping, and usually I would ask Jon to chip in half, but I felt uncomfortable asking him for the money. Instead, I wound up picking on him and sending him to do sundry little errands. Soon, he was feeling overwhelmed, attacked, and confused, and he began withdrawing from me. I saw this as him running from our problems and leaving me alone to cope, and I nearly panicked. But somehow, after one particularly bad fight, we began to talk.

At the time, I was truly surprised that he was aware of our problems. I was accustomed to being the one who did the accommodating. But the same unspoken issues that had been bothering me had been nagging at Jon, too, and as we talked, particular fears came out that startled and enlightened us both. Much to my amazement, and in direct contrast to my earlier anxiety, he was worried that I would leave him, blaming him for all the things he had not done. This anxiety was paralyzing him, he said, making it harder for him to take a more active role. Meanwhile, I was frustrated by his passivity, but as we talked I realized that I was more terrified of what it meant. My great fear was a holdover from all those other unsuccessful relationships and, originally, from Daniel. I was afraid at some level that if I did not do all the work of maintaining the relationship, that Jon, like Daniel, would break down. I worried that my newfound security would prove to be another illusion, supported only by my extreme effort. And because we now lived together I feared, more than I ever had before, that I would be stuck. Not only would another seemingly healthy relationship evaporate before my eyes, but I would be trapped into caring for someone who was not functional.

Because of this anxiety, once again, I had polarized the situation. I had focused on our problems and underestimated Jon's strengths and his love for me. Once we started talking, my panic evaporated. He was grateful to hear that my anger came out of fear and that my particular terror was one he could easily counter. He was sane and would be there for me. And I recognized, yet again, that I was still dealing with ghosts.

In that one conversation, he learned I wasn't going to leave him or constantly judge him, as long as he made an effort. I learned that he wasn't going to abandon me or collapse into someone whom I had to fear or take care of constantly, but that I had an obligation to communicate what my real fears were. I never had such a middle ground to choose from. But as I learn that we both have flaws, I am also coming to accept that this is what normal is, and that I am very happy with how we protect, support, and comfort each other.

These days, as our connection grows stronger, I am plagued by a different kind of fear. Sometimes, before sleep, usually, I start worrying about how I would cope if Jon were no longer there. It's not that I think he will leave me or that I am nervous that our relationship is in trouble. Instead, the images that invade my nights are of him dying young or being killed in an accident, and these bring me to tears, so afraid am I of losing him. In dreams, I sometimes think that I have imagined him.

In these desolate visions, I always see myself carrying on, lonely but functional. They are, in a way, the latest version of the upside-down house. I am learning to trust life, but it is difficult. Along with terror, my childhood led me to always expect loss. Happiness is scary, now that I have so much more to lose, and these dreams seem to be reassuring in a harsh way, showing me how I could manage if my world again shattered. It is hard to believe that it won't. But when I wake up, I hear Jon breathing deeply in sleep beside me, and the nightmare recedes.

Our life together isn't perfect. The dreams come back every few weeks, always startling me with their heartbreak and bleakness. When Jon and I fight, I still panic, thinking that he has ceased to love me. And then I question why I am taking this huge chance with him at all. But now I know that this middle ground is love, and that it's the best that real life has to offer. Perhaps because of my background, I have a greater appreciation of his warmth and his stability than I might otherwise. His ability to communicate whatever is going on in his head, and his interest in and validation of my thoughts and feelings, seem precious. Maybe I value these connections all the more because of the years when I felt alone, all the times I believed I had to be golden or suspected that I was cursed. And if so, that's a gift. The price was too high for me, for my parents, and especially for my brother and my sister to have paid. But maybe some of reconciling who I am now with the world around me means learning to accept the good as well as the bad, and being content.

For many of us with mentally ill siblings, the key to finding peace in our life is learning how to live with our tumultuous histories. Many of us have found ourselves in situations other than we would have planned for, had we been totally free to choose. Of course, this is true in every life: None of us has much say over our parents' choices of occupation or lifestyle, for example, or even where and how we will be reared and educated, but these factors always play into our own choices. It would be silly to suppose that any one family relationship had an overriding influence on our lifework as well as on all the choices of our heart. However, growing up with a mentally ill sibling certainly has some effect on our future and our choices. Perhaps, then, the first step to making peace with ourselves is to try to understand how these various effects have played out.

Some siblings, particularly younger ones, have seemed to gravitate toward the arts. Jane Piirto, director of gifted education at Ashland University, in Ohio, and author of *Understanding Those Who Create,* views creativity as a healthy coping mechanism. Those of us who have had to deal with more problems as children, Piirto postulates, may have learned to think more inventively. As Kyra, a pianist, explains, "Having been exposed to the dark side of life so early, I was able to play serious music and understand what was the right emotion with a degree of depth. In that way, my family troubles enriched my music."

A more well documented trend among siblings is to enter the health professions. Dr. E. Fuller Torrey has said that about half the people he knows in schizophrenia research have ill family members. For many, a sibling's illness provided the impetus toward a specialty in mental illness.

Torrey was a college student when his younger sister had her first breakdown. "I was going into medicine since about second grade," he says. "But her breakdown probably played some role in my going into psychiatry, and it played a very strong role in being involved with schizophrenia research, without any question."

His story echoes that of many siblings who have become doctors, particularly older siblings whose life courses were more or less decided before the appearance of the illness. Jeffrey was also in college, intent on medical school, when his younger sister had her first psychotic episode. Although he was not living with his family at the time and was not involved with her care, he believes the rapid onset of her schizophrenia shaped his decision to specialize in psychiatry. "I didn't know it then," Jeffrey says now, more than twenty years later. "But I became interested in families as a psychiatrist. I became interested in chronic mental illness as a psychiatrist" because of her illness, he says. A successful researcher and therapist, Jeffrey could have retreated into academia or private practice years ago. Instead, he is now involved with the self-help movement for mental health consumers; he had tried to connect his sister with such programs before her suicide five years ago.

For Jeffrey, much of his job satisfaction comes from keeping close to the people he treats. This holds true for many siblings who have become health care providers. Some talk about how taking care of our siblings, or people like them, has been a major source of motivation.

"It was a logical choice as far as what might be best for her," says Rick, who works with the chronically mentally ill on the West Coast, where he can be near his schizophrenic younger sister. "Her mental illness started a little after I started to get into psychology as course work, and I have developed that as a profession."

No other field seems such an obvious reaction to our family's crises, although many factors may play a part. For some, particularly older siblings, the choice of a career in mental health could be attributed to a caretaker trend. Many of us who wished we could do something for our siblings may have ended up devoting ourselves to their surrogates. Or perhaps while caring for our sibling, we simply uncovered natural tendencies toward healing or the sciences, or were strongly moved by the need for better treatment and facilities. Perhaps these illnesses, initially so scary, became less frightening when we viewed them through science, as problems that we had to solve. Or all of these reasons may be true, each factor playing a part in our career choice.

"For so many years I'd been trying to find ways to soothe myself," says Sandra, a medical doctor and schizophrenia researcher. Her life with her schizophrenic older sister had been traumatic, as she watched her capable sister quickly decompensate and be hospitalized. Both professionally and personally, she says, "I had done a lot of soothing myself by taking care of other disturbed people, attaching myself to other disturbed people."

These days her work, she says, gives her power over what scares her. "You have some sense that horrible things can happen," she says. "And somebody can still step back, be in control, take steps to fix things. Those kinds of life experiences were a little bit healing, and I can do that with my patients now."

"On good days, helping other people makes it feel like I've managed it," adds Maria, whose younger brother first became withdrawn and then was hospitalized with a diagnosis of either schizophrenia or schizoaffective disorder. Maria's great grief was a central motivation for her to change careers in her thirties and study social work. "Being really verbal about it is a nice defense, and being able to talk about mental illness really helps."

Many siblings, particularly those in health care, also agree that their family experiences give them an additional professional strength: a broader sense of humanity. Since we have seen our own loved ones break down under these illnesses, we are less likely to classify and dismiss those we care for in our jobs. As Jeffrey explains, his sister's schizophrenia "certainly has changed my attitude about patients and families. I'm much more empathic, I think, than I would have been."

Lincoln agrees that his experience with his brother's psychosis makes him a better counselor at the psychiatric hospital where he works. "Part of my job is to talk to families at the hospital, and I think my history has equipped me to be extraordinarily empathic with people. I truly feel like I can get behind a family member's experience and try to be helpful in a way that most people can't. The challenge for me is not to overidentify."

Sometimes our experience has given us definite dislikes, and these may have as much influence as anything on our ultimate career path. Alice, for example, thought she would study psychology after her older brother snapped suddenly in high school but found that her initial interest brought up too much old unhappiness and resentment. "I decided not to [major in psychology] because they would have made me take courses on abnormal psychology," she now recalls. "I was really angry at the fact that they were calling some people 'abnormal.' It doesn't seem logical now, but at the time it was a really compelling reason." Alice is now the overseer for her city's health insurance; she incorporated her anger into a career that helps her change and control such labels. "I still get mad at the way things are characterized," she says. This kind of dissatisfaction has prompted much advocacy work and the creation of strong antistigmatization groups, such as the National Stigma Clearinghouse, which promotes awareness and monitors media across the country.

Another woman who now works with the National Alliance for the Mentally Ill talks about channeling anger. Her fury, she says, was first directed at her brother, who often acted abusively, and later at the schizophrenia that had claimed his peace of mind. "I find it useful to apply that anger on a large scale, and for me that large scale is the National Alliance," she says. "If you feel as passionate about advocacy as you do when you feel that kind of anger, then you can communicate. And if you can communicate, then that betters everyone."

Ultimately, the same traits that influence our professional life play out in our personal life as well. For many of us, then, the challenge of discovering what healthy is for our love life and friendships involves learning how our family history has influenced our attractions and established dynamics that may be harmful.

Sandra, in addition to being a schizophrenia researcher, is now happily married, but finding the right partner took a while. Her first marriage ended amicably enough, she says. "He was never unfaithful or using drugs or anything. He was just inadequate at taking care of himself." Although Sandra was still a student when they married, she supported their family, which included their young daughter. Now she and her second husband have custody of the girl. "My relationships had been with a series of people who were needy," she says. "Until recently. Until this marriage." Her face is bright and shining. "I've grown enough that I will allow myself to be cared for by someone I can also care for."

Through her therapy Sandra has learned to recognize the patterns and weaknesses that had controlled her. Although she makes use of her ability to see beyond labels in her work, she has also learned to protect herself and strengthen her boundaries in interpersonal relationships. "Little by little over the years, I got grounded and found a way to kind of see and do things," she says. "I continue to benefit from that. Would I feel this good and be this happy otherwise? Maybe. But I have to say I have an extraordinarily happy life right now."

Debbie also found a more fulfilling personal life once she learned to let go of always feeling responsible. This involved divorcing a man who ignored her and focused instead on Debbie's sister, who has a borderline-personality disorder. "I thought at the time I was happy," she remembers. "I kept telling myself, 'Oh, your husband gets along with your family so well. He's funny. He's smart.' " Over time, Debbie saw how her husband allowed himself to be manipulated by her sister and how she had allowed herself to be shunted aside. That realization has allowed her to find a healthier relationship with a more attentive partner. "He doesn't play into my sister. He's independent. If I am missing from the room for ten minutes, he will come look for me. It's clear that he's *my* boyfriend. I feel much better at home than I ever did with my husband."

Are we ever really free from our past demons? Most of us admit to relapses, to twinges of irrational fears and angers. As I did with Jon, many siblings confess to occasional fears about their own mate's stability, expecting him or her to collapse as our once-stable brothers and sisters did. Samuel, who has two ill siblings, puts it quite clearly: "I think that perhaps when you have a sibling with a mental illness that somehow you lose your ability to trust. You've seen that anybody can break down," he says.

Alice, for example, was aware consciously that her husband was not like her older brother, who had developed schizophrenia. But when her husband lost his mother, she explains, she realized that she was monitoring his mental health. "When my mother-in-law died, we went through the grief process together," she recalls. "In the middle of the grief process, I realized he wasn't breaking down. He wasn't going nuts, and all of a sudden I started to trust him a lot more. I had, for years prior to that, always had a feeling like maybe he would not get out of bed and just become like my brother." Although she had not been aware of this fear earlier in her marriage, she now sees how her underlying anxiety had made her doubt her husband during other times of stress. Anyone she became close to, she had subconsciously worried for years, could at some point disintegrate just as her older brother had.

Carrie says she realized she had similar fears about her husband and briefly left him. While she was on her own, the connection with her older brother became clear. Her brother had had a very sudden breakdown when they were both teens, and Carrie never quite felt she could trust anyone after that, including her husband. She feared that she would end up taking care of him as well. "I told him that I didn't know if I wanted to come back because I was afraid of how much he was going to rely on me!"

Renee, too, finds that when anyone close to her becomes depressed, even within a normal range of emotions, she begins to panic. She attributes her own fear to memories of when her adored big sister developed schizophrenia. "You want them to get normal quick so there's not a chance of them kind of falling apart in front of you," she says. "Maybe because I've taken care of my sister, I have less tolerance for when other people need help."

Seemingly at odds with the great empathy that having a sibling with a mental illness has taught us, this occasional intolerance—the feeling that we "gave at the office"—may be just as common. However, many of us view it as a kind of shameful legacy that we are loath to discuss. Rikki, whose older brother killed himself after dealing with schizophrenia for nearly ten years, reluctantly describes a personal cutoff point. "When I encounter people, especially in work situations, who start displaying signs of mental illness, or get manic or have temper tantrums, I turn my back," she says. "I just will not deal with that."

With her friends, she can find more tolerance. "I'll reach out to people," says this calm young woman. "But if they do any one thing to push me away, that's it." She suddenly pushes her chair back and holds her hands up. "That's it."

Nancy, an older woman with a schizophrenic brother, reports a similar short fuse with needy friends. Although her relationships with her brother and her former husband were marked by ambivalence, she puts much clearer, and tighter, limits on her friendships. "I have a very low tolerance, and I'm out of there."

Another negative emotion that sneaks up on us is rage. Rachel still has a problem with expressing her own anger and can date this inability quite clearly to when she was a teenager and furious with her older sister, who was becoming withdrawn and psychotic. At the time, Rachel hated her sister for monopolizing their parents' attention. Then her sister was hospitalized for eighteen years, and Rachel—assuming cause and effect at some level—felt tremendously guilty. "If my anger could do that, could cause someone to be incarcerated, then that was an emotion I dare not deal with!"

For decades after her sister was hospitalized, Rachel barely allowed herself to disagree with anyone and would watch her opinions change almost without her conscious consent whenever potential arguments loomed. After many years in therapy, she can see how this guilt developed. Now a social worker herself, Rachel knows how good it can feel to assert herself and how healthy it is for her to experience a full range of emotions. But still, unless she is vigilant, she finds herself avoiding direct confrontation. When she isn't monitoring herself, she automatically apologizes whenever she disagrees with someone. "Saying I'm sorry is something that I've always done," says the fifty-two-year-old woman. "People will go, 'What are you sorry for?' I'm just sorry; I'm sorry for the world."

Many of us have had to learn that we often react inappropriately, that we sometimes respond to our ghosts and not to the present. For some this will come out as anger or guilt. For me, as for Renee, fear may provide an undercurrent of insecurity running through every new encounter or challenge. Often these traits are mingled and confused, and we will snap at our loved ones because of our fear and apologize because of our anger. These habits stay with us, and when we cannot counter them we must accept them. "It's just as much a part of you as anything," says Rikki, explaining how she feels about her brother's illness and suicide and about the reactions that have become incorporated into her own life. "It's like the color of your eyes."

Along with all these other emotions, overwhelmingly what stays with us, what we must incorporate into our lives, is grief. We may never fully finish mourning. At best, if we are lucky, as I was when my father died, each renewal of grief brings about a little more enlightenment. That's the lesson social worker Julie Tallard Johnson learned after many years of therapy, of teaching and writing, and of training group facilitators, when her cat had a sick kitten. The rest of the litter looked fine and playful, but one cried constantly and, once weaned, had trouble feeding itself. Johnson took the small creature to a veterinarian, who told her that the synapses in the kitten's brain were not connecting. "So she couldn't see what was really there," explains Johnson. "She couldn't really see where the bowl of food was. She hallucinated or had distortions." The vet advised Johnson to have the kitten put to sleep, telling her, "She'll never be able to make do on her own unless I was willing always to take care of her," says Johnson. "And so I looked at him, and I said, 'What you're telling me is this kitty is mentally ill and so we need to put her to sleep because she's mentally ill.' And he said yes and I started sobbing."

For Johnson, it recalled the pain of the condemnation doctors had made of her schizophrenic brother nearly twenty years before. This was getting the diagnosis and being informed, at the time, that there was no hope for a happy outcome. The vet had told her, she felt, "that there is no place for this kind of being," she says. And as she wept over the kitten, she realized she had not finished grieving for her brother and for all of her family's pain.

"People need to realize that once we get it, doesn't mean we're done," she says. Learning normal is a lifelong process.

chapter nine

RISKING THE FUTURE

Sometimes I think that all the madness is behind me. After all, my brother is dead, and I have been out of touch with my sister for so long that it seems like their illness belongs to my past. With their absence, much of the shame and confusion that affected all of us in the family no longer seems to be a factor in my life, particularly since I have broken many of the patterns from that time. At these times, I find myself thinking it is all over.

Most of the time, I know better.

While public awareness about mental illness has come a long way, it is difficult not to feel cursed or stigmatized by the shadows it casts on our life. A few years ago, before I met Jon, I dated a man in whom I eventually confided my family history. I told him about my brother and sister, presenting their illness in terms of how it affected me, how my early experiences had given me certain fears and strengths.

The relationship was progressing nicely, I thought, when he hit me with something I hadn't even begun to consider. "I've been thinking a lot about us," he began one evening, as we sat on my couch. "I even told my parents about you." This, I thought, was rather sweet, if a little odd. We had really only started dating and hadn't even slept together yet. Most of my friends and I wouldn't usually talk to our folks about anyone less than a potential son-in-law. "The problem is, I'm looking for someone I could get seriously involved with," he said, "and this schizophrenia thing really scares me. You see, I want to be able to have children, and you're too much of a genetic risk."

I was dumbfounded. I felt sure that I had misheard him, but I hadn't. At first, I didn't believe he was serious, but he was. He left my apartment soon after, and that's when I got angry. I realized, for one thing, that he had never asked me if I wanted to be seriously involved with him. He'd never sought to find out if I'd accept him as a lover and as a mate. He certainly hadn't asked if I wanted him for a husband or as the father of my children. The list of his sins piled up. He was a clod as well as uninformed, and worst of all he had blindsided me with his pronouncement. I told myself that when he called back, shamefaced, I would tell him that he was too much of a genetic risk. That I couldn't take the chance of my children being as stupid and insensitive as him. That I wanted to get serious about someone, but that he was too much of a jerk. He never gave me the opportunity.

That encounter was the first time I considered the possibility of my siblings' illness affecting either my genetics or potential relationships. This rejection showed me that the issues around such illness wouldn't end with my generation. My family saga would not simply wind up as I came to terms with my own wounds.

First, there was the undeniable stigma facing family members of the mentally ill, brought home all too bluntly with the words "You're too much of a risk." In some ways, when I was younger, my parents effectively shielded me from a lot of discrimination. Once my brother and sister had left home, no new acquaintances knew of their existence unless we consciously made the effort to inform them, and while my parents' code of silence isolated me in some ways, it also protected me from the curious and the cruel. But as my aborted relationship made clear, once my family history became known, no matter how Katherine's health progressed, how far I distanced myself from her and Daniel, or how well I managed my own life, there would be people who would still see me as tainted because of my family.

Second, his rejection brought home more serious concerns about the genetics of mental illness. In retrospect it seems impossibly naive that I had never realized the implications of my siblings' schizophrenia for any children of my own. But with consideration, my emotional myopia seems to fit. For so many years, I had wasted energy on pursuing dead-end relationships. I never had to face the question of whether I wanted children. Such insubstantial relationships never reached the point where I would be considered for my fitness as a mother or, more directly, as a worthwhile "genetic risk." For me, at that point, childbearing was still theoretical. The stigma could be confronted and dismissed, and the deeper issues avoided.

But were his fears legitimate? Now that I am in a stable relationship, these issues do come forward. Along with the customary concerns of any couple considering parenthood, Jon and I are also facing the very real questions that surround the genetic basis for mental illness. The conversation always, for me, comes back to one central dilemma: Is the risk greater for us than for anybody else? What I really want to know is something that no geneticist or researcher can tell me. What I am really asking is, will I have a child with schizophrenia?

Schizophrenia occurs in 1 percent of the general population, slightly higher than the incidence of bipolar disorder, most major researchers agree, says Dr. Stephen Faraone of Harvard Medical School. He, along with scientists from Yale and Columbia, have explained that first-degree relatives of people diagnosed with schizophrenia, such as children or siblings of people with the disease, may have as great as a 12 or 13 percent chance of developing schizophrenia. But for second-degree relatives—the nieces and nephews that my children would be to my sister and brother—the risk seems to drop to about 3 or 4 percent. Numbers vary, but other considerations, such as the fact that two of my siblings had diagnoses of schizophrenia, may increase my family's odds. Another factor is severity of illness; not only did two out of three children in my generation develop schizophrenia, but both became severely ill. Perhaps the gene (or gene combination) that causes the disease in my family has a higher rate of manifesting itself or is more likely to bring about a full-fledged form of the disease, as opposed to just a few symptoms. Perhaps we lack some genetic code that in other families counteracts the disease or lessens its severity. Geneticists call this factor penetrance, giving a name to whatever it is that controls how often and how strongly a particular trait comes through. As they put it, the penetrance of schizophrenia in my family may be particularly high. If we had more complete and accurate information about such things as my grandmother's delusions, perhaps we could pin down this disease a little more, but such information is unavailable. Yet because of the rate and severity of only the diagnosed schizophrenia in my generation, some researchers with whom I have discussed my family history have suggested that a child of mine could have as great as a 7 or 8 percent chance of developing schizophrenia. Of course, that still means at least a 92 percent chance of having a child with no mental illness.

That's all a genetic counselor can tell me. Unlike the case with other hereditary diseases, the genes for schizophrenia have not yet been isolated; there is no test as of yet. All we can provide are our family histories. All we can get are information and percentages. And the numbers never factor in the emotional weight of these issues. As one geneticist said to me, "Statistics are hard to read—they always look like fifty-fifty to the person they're affecting. A patient may ask his surgeon, 'What are the risks for my operation?' and the surgeon will spout out numbers and the chances of rare complications. But to the patient, there's only one question that matters. 'Am I going to live or am I going to die?' he asks. ' 'Cause that feels like fifty-fifty to me, Doc.' "

With mental illness, the questions are even more clouded. So few of these diseases are clear-cut. My brother was and my sister is exceedingly ill, resistant to treatment and so far unable to participate in society at large. But not every case of a mental illness is this severe. Many people diagnosed with schizophreniform disorders are able, with treatment, to work, raise a family, and find happiness in life. For them, these illnesses may be no more disabling than any other chronic, manageable condition, such as diabetes or hemophilia. And the same holds true for bipolar disorder, which may appear as mild cyclothymia, with its narrower mood swings, or simple depression. So many of us have coped with these conditions and still found life worth living.

The decision to have a child is made up of so many factors that it's hard to tease them apart, but this fear—of incurable illness, of a child born with such a handicap—is a big one. I am reminded of the summer I turned eleven, when I was at sleep-away camp. I had become especially close to one of my bunkmates, a girl whose limbs were malformed as a result of her mother taking the drug thalidomide during pregnancy. Partly because of her deformity, Randy was more of a reader than a jock, but so was I. We both liked to learn about what we were seeing on our nature walks, how the small tree frogs and newts we would find under leaves ate and drank. We had bonded so closely over common interests that my curiosity and awkwardness around her had faded. I had nearly forgotten her stubby arms and her awkward gait by the time my parents came up for visiting day, and it took me a little while to figure out why they looked so sad when I introduced them to her. Sometime late that day, my mother had said, almost to herself, "That poor woman." She meant Randy's mother. When I asked her what she meant, she said that she felt bad that nobody had known the side effects of the drug. That Randy was born in the early sixties and her parents did not have the choice to terminate the pregnancy once they discovered how severely deformed their child would be. Her first point made sense to me, but I got hung up on the second. I loved Randy. We shared our books. We had built a terrarium together in the nature hut. I couldn't see how the world would be a better place, how anybody would be happier, if my friend did not exist.

These days, I better understand my mother's comment, made in sorrow and empathy. Like her, I can now imagine the heartache my friend's parents must have felt when they saw their baby's foreshortened limbs, and their guilt and grief later when they learned how she had been injured by their drugs, by decisions they had made innocently, with the best medical advice then available. In their troubles, my mother must have seen a reflection of herself. No doctor had known enough to warn her of the implications of her mother's delusions. No genetic counselor existed then who could give her odds. I can also understand why my mother thought Randy's parents might have preferred to try again, to abort the injured fetus if that had been an option then, and to try for a child who would probably find this life easier and possibly happier. Perhaps if she had known how her two oldest children would end up, my mother would have decided to try again, too. The two parts of my mind don't come together neatly here. Philosophically, I don't believe in eugenics. I prefer to think, instead, that the marvel of humanity comes from its variety. But when I consider that I might have a child who has schizophrenia, I do not know what I would choose.

I can too easily anticipate that same mix of guilt and grief. I tell myself, for example, that my mothering could be polluted by anxiety. Because of what I know about schizophrenia, I say, I might always be on the lookout for early signs of illness in my child. I might think at first that such caution was sensible, that early intervention and treatment would actually render the best prognosis if a child of mine were to develop a mental illness. But what kind of effect would such surveillance have on my child, on any child? I suspect that even if I could hide the worst of my fears, the shadows hanging over me would be palpable. Perhaps my early fears and increased vigilance would re-create a different form of schizophrenogenic mother. And then I would wonder, as generations have before me, if my child's pain was my fault.

In this way, the old fears creep back in, that because of my past I am dangerous, or at least not worthy of happiness. And I begin to wonder if I have rejoined the human race after all. If I am honest with myself, I can see that these insecurities are prompted by guilt. I am the only one of us three, after all, who has such a range of options. But in that same scenario other anxieties also lurk, more pervasive and familiar than either sadness or misplaced guilt, and these make me think quite seriously that parenting is not for me. Because underneath any concern for a child, underneath any real anxiety about my fitness as a mother, is a deep dread, a selfish one that even the hint of possibility makes unbearable. What stops me cold is fear of my own child, of the possibility that I might have a child who would grow up to be like Katherine, a child who would rage and scream and threaten me.

Sometimes I imagine that I would welcome a child with any other problems than schizophrenia, and I find myself making deals with God. I play with this idea of a bargain much as I play the percentages over and over in my head. Odds are, I say to myself, my child would be fine. I tell myself that if I keep waiting, the chances are greater of having a child with Down's syndrome than a child who may have episodes of psychosis. The probability is greater that all my hours in front of a computer display terminal would damage any baby I could carry than that I would pass on an affective or thought disorder. And if I chose to adopt a baby, I would be taking other genetic risks, ones I may know nothing about beforehand. But none of this matters. When I think of having a child who might develop schizophrenia, I am eight years old again and terrified.

If only we knew more. Our basic understanding of mental illness is growing quickly but is still uneven and extremely confusing. As noted earlier, we do know mental illnesses run in families. Enough studies of twins, separated at birth, and of adopted children have been done to reveal that both schizophrenia and bipolar disorder, and possibly other mental illnesses as well, seem to be genetically based. However, genes don't seem to be the only factor.

Twin studies show the difference. Take, for example, the case of identical (monozygotic) twins, in which one twin develops schizophrenia. Since identical twins share the same genetic material, if schizophrenia were purely genetic, the other twin should have a 100 percent probability—a virtual certainty—of developing the disease. But numerous twin studies have shown that in monozygotic pairs, if one twin has schizophrenia, the other has only a 50 percent chance of developing the disease, according to Dr. Stephen Faraone. Overall, Faraone says, many studies, such as those led by Dr. E. Fuller Torrey and Irving H. Gottesman, Ph.D., have broken down the rates of inheritance to show that first-degree relatives have about a 9 to 12 percent chance of developing schizophrenia, and second-degree relatives a 2 to 3 percent chance. Studies like these conclude that schizophrenia, on the whole, seems to be about 70 percent heritable.

Bipolar disorder seems, if anything, to have a higher heritability and a stronger genetic basis. This disorder occurs less frequently in the population at large—Faraone estimates the rate at about 0.7 percent, while Torrey calls it "one-half as prevalent as schizophrenia." And yet in monozygotic twins, if one twin is bipolar, the other has a 60 to 70 percent chance of developing the disorder, noticeably higher odds than is the case with schizophrenia. The difference continues, since first-degree relatives may have as high as a 20 percent chance of developing the disease, while the rate for second-degree relatives, as with schizophrenia, drops to the single digits. In short, "if you have the gene involved in bipolar, you're more likely to express it fully at some time than is the case with schizophrenia," says Dr. L. Erlenmeyer-Kimling, professor of psychiatry and of genetics and human development at Columbia University.

However, that doesn't mean that all these relatives will be severely ill. Instead, studies seem to indicate that the greater numbers may come with lesser impact. In other words, a wider range of relatives of people with bipolar disorder will show a smattering of the disorder. Dolores Malaspina, assistant professor of clinical psychiatry at Columbia, studies the genes and vulnerabilities of mental illnesses. "Some people who carry the genes for bipolar disorder have only depression or a labile personality [with changeable moods] or depression with blips of a rather 'hyper' personality; we call that hypomania or hyperthymic," she explains. "Others may have some depressions with feelings better than good in between."

Many theories attempt to explain why bipolar disorder seems to be more heritable and yet so much more varied than schizophrenia. Some researchers suggest we may be seeing differences in the genes or gene groups that cause these diseases, others that we may be witnessing the behavioral results of these types of disorder. Faraone, who studies the genetics of both bipolar disorder and schizophrenia, points out that since bipolar disorder is likely to be less impairing and more episodic than schizophrenia is, there is a greater possibility that people with bipolar disorder are more able to lead conventional lives, to marry and have children, than people with schizophrenia. People with bipolar disorder may thus be more likely to pass on their genes, which may explain why we see these genes expressed more regularly and with greater variety in families.

Our own mental health, as parents, may also factor into all these odds. If we, in the words of Erlenmeyer-Kimling, "don't seem to have any of the personality characteristics that indicate that we're carrying a little bit more of a genetic load" of our sibling's illness, then the risk of our children developing a disease might be on the lower end of the spectrum for second-degree relatives, or around a 2 percent chance. If we have some mental health problems that may be a mild manifestation of our sibling's illness, our offspring may face a risk that is at the higher end of the spectrum, or around 5 percent. For a case like mine, especially, with high penetrance in my generation, the risks may be greater.

The little additional information we have about patterns of mental illness in families can be frightening. Bipolar disorder, for example, seems to show up earlier in successive generations, says Malaspina; the next generation tends to get it at a younger age than their older relatives did. There is also some evidence, Erlenmeyer-Kimling explains, that schizophrenia shows up earlier, and possibly more severely, in people who have a clear hereditary tendency to the disease, as opposed to the so-called sporadic cases, where the illness just appears to pop up without precedent. These shifts could signify changes in these diseases from generation to generation, like the subtle gene shifts that have been found recently in Huntington's disease. And that, in turn, would mean that if our children become ill, they stand the chance of becoming more ill, and sooner, than many of our siblings did. But, Erlenmeyer-Kimling notes, there are many other possible reasons for the second generation to be diagnosed earlier than the first. Such numbers could be due to the increased awareness of parents who have mentally ill siblings. Unlike parents from a healthy family, we may be more attuned to warning signs, less likely to deny what we see, and so we may be reporting illness more fully and seeking treatment earlier.

So little is now known that it is not unlikely that different mental illnesses may have very different modes of genetic transference. Most researchers, for example, now speculate that several genes each play a part in major illnesses like schizophrenia and bipolar disorder. And it may be that even the way these genes interact with each other varies from disease to disease. Ultimately, all we really know is that schizophrenia seems to strike more randomly. Bipolar disorder seems to be expressed more often, but with a great range of severity. We don't know why.

If only the science were further along. What we know is inconclusive and open to such a variety of interpretations as to be nearly useless, at least to those of us whose lives are so intimately involved. Every bit of knowledge heralded as a breakthrough for researchers all too often is not applicable to those who suffer. Still, even those of us who know better try desperately to read our future in the little bit of information we have.

Sometimes simply confirming that we have some knowledge can be comforting, even if it does not yet crack our genetic code. For example, one area of research being explored at several major universities is eye tracking, a visual quirk that may have a connection to schizophrenia. The theory is quite simple, born out of a correlation in families between schizophrenia and a certain jumpiness in vision. Although this trait does not seem to have any effect on thought or vision (it is, in fact, virtually undetectable without highly specialized tests), researchers have great hopes that by tracing its inheritance through families and checking this trait against schizophrenia, they will find that the two are genetically linked. Then, if the eye-tracking peculiarity can be isolated on a particular chromosome, it might provide information about the genetic basis for schizophrenia.

Right now, the research is just beginning, and there are many possible explanations. The traits may not be connected by more than a statistical fluke. Or they may both travel in the same families because of a third, as-yet-unknown genetic factor and may not be connected to each other. Or the correlation that researchers now trust may prove to be just a computer glitch and may not exist at all.

Still, one researcher could not resist using his eye-tracking tests to find out about his own genetics. This scientist has an older sister, four years his senior, who was diagnosed with schizophrenia twelve years ago. Because of her, he has concerns about having children. And although he is aware that the correlation between this vision abnormality and schizophrenia may not prove anything, he had his own vision tested recently. He found out that his eyes tracked normally. Does this mean that he, unlike his sister, does not carry the DNA for schizophrenia? He knows, as well as anybody, that it proves nothing as yet. "But despite knowing the limitations of the test," he says, "it still felt tremendously relieving."

Likewise, many of the findings of postmortem brain research cannot be directly applied to our lives yet. But for medical researchers, such as Jill Taylor, Ph.D., of McLean Hospital and the Harvard

Department of Psychiatry, the hope that it may someday provide a cure offers an emotional lift. By comparing brain tissue donated by healthy individuals with tissue donated by people who had bipolar disorder or schizophrenia, Taylor, whose older brother has been diagnosed with schizophrenia, hopes to understand the microcircuitry of the human brain, defining which cells in which areas communicate with which chemicals. Conducting this research has helped Taylor come to terms with her brother's illness. "Once I understood that my brother was the victim of a brain disease," she says, "I was able to love him again."

Using magnetic-resonance-imaging and positron-emission-tomography scans, scientists can identify specific areas of the living human brain that function differently in patients with psychiatric disorders. With these technologies, Taylor (who is also the second vice president of the National Alliance for the Mentally Ill) looks for significant scientific differences at the microscopic level, which in turn help explain the effects of chemical treatments. At this time, however, such brain mapping is still in the information-gathering stage. "Right now, it's more like how do you treat the symptom and with which drug," she says. "So many people receive so many different diagnoses for the same thing that until the psychiatric community figures out what they're talking about, nothing will happen."

While Dr. David Shore of the National Institute of Mental Health states with confidence that the genetics of these diseases will be much better understood in twenty years, even he confesses that he does not see such research having practical treatment applications within five years. And so today no researcher or genetic counselor can tell for sure whether one of our children will be healthy or ill, or even whether any illness that strikes one of our children will be mild or severe.

"People call all the time," says Malaspina, "wondering if this test or that test can be done, so they can see whether or not they carry the genes. The field is really not at that point yet. And the things we now call markers—such as abnormal eye movements—are present in at least 10 percent of the well population. They are not specific at all to the disease. They are research tools, and they are important research tools, but they really should not be guiding personal choices."

Still, researchers and scientists often recommend that siblings talk to a genetic counselor. A good counselor, one who is well informed about the genetics of psychiatric illnesses, can help a couple understand their individual family history and the complicated heredity of these and other illnesses. The counselor cannot make the difficult decisions for us but can at least help those of us concerned about our mental health legacies sort out our feelings and give us facts with which to work.

In addition to studying the genetics, researchers are seeking to understand the other factors involved in these illnesses. After all, if schizophrenia is roughly 70 percent determined by genetics, that still leaves a 30 percent variable. For all these major disorders, as Faraone puts it, "a sizable chunk is due to the environment."

The scientists who focus on these factors stress one point: Environmental causes do not mean bad parenting. As discussed earlier, there are a whole range of other influences being studied for their effect on vulnerable people, factors such as viruses, blood typing, and obstetrical complications. Perhaps some variable alters neuronal development during gestation, suggests Erlenmeyer-Kimling. That factor could be a slight variation in how much oxygen the fetus receives or some element in the prenatal nutrition. It could be, as mentioned earlier, the effect of a virus that occurred during a certain prenatal developmental period. Or it could be a trauma or delay in the delivery process that serves to trigger a genetic vulnerability. Perhaps some chain reaction of two or more factors must take place within a specific time frame to bring the disease out of genetic latency. While researchers continue to compile information, none will yet hazard a guess as to a definitive cause. Just too many factors are at work, and, as Faraone adds, "none of these findings means that everybody who has obstetric complications is going to get schizophrenia, or even that everyone vulnerable to schizophrenia is going to become schizophrenic if there are obstetrical complications. There is simply a weak association."

Ultimately, understanding environmental triggers may help our descendants, even those who inherit a genetic vulnerability. If trigger mechanisms can be understood, Faraone explains, "one could find a protective environment." Such an environment could be created by something as simple as taking a specific nutritional supplement during one period of pregnancy or perhaps by inoculating a fetus or a newborn against a common, maybe usually benign, germ. The child would still be vulnerable, but the vulnerability would not be exploited; the genetic switch would never be flipped.

For now, however, the best counsel geneticists can provide is the kind of basic health recommendations any doctor would pass on to any expectant parent. "There is no advice we would actually give that shouldn't be given to everyone," Malaspina points out. "Having adequate nutrition prenatally may be particularly important for people at risk for schizophrenia. But people always try to avoid infections like the flu and to have adequate nutrition. You can put too much of a burden on someone to think they need to do so many things magically, when we don't actually have the information to say that."

And so the dilemma remains, particularly for siblings, like myself, who feel the pressure of encroaching age. We cannot wait for research to provide answers and must make our peace with the knowledge now at hand. Our conclusions, regardless of gender, run the gamut of possible reaction.

"I cannot live through that twice," says Kyra, now in her thirties. She refers back to the years when her older sister became extremely delusional and, even when under treatment, would refuse to take her medication. "It was really a terror. Slamming doors in the middle of the night. Turning the television on at full volume at any hour, even though there was no picture on the screen. Screaming. Going outside naked in the morning, and hiding under the car with no clothes on. It was terror growing up with that.

"It's hard, because I would like children," she continues. "But I would rather not have children and be sure that I won't have to live through that again."

"I know I don't want to," agrees Rikki, whose older brother, a schizophrenic, committed suicide by shooting himself. "Who wants to deal with that? It's a total crapshoot."

"I'm totally ambivalent," says Maria, whose younger brother has been diagnosed with schizophrenia. "I really don't want to deal with a mentally unstable child. Adoption has seemed more appealing over the years, but I think it would be a shame not to have kids and maybe it's worth the chance."

"It is definitely scary," adds Debbie. "But I don't think I would let it get in the way of actually having children." Debbie has seen her younger sister become suicidal and be repeatedly hospitalized. Other of her relatives have also been diagnosed with mental illnesses, including schizophrenia. Still, she thinks she and her husband will soon try to have a child despite the genetic risk. "At least if that happens I will have an idea of what to look for and how to handle it. I feel like I would be somewhat prepared."

"I very much want to fall in love and have a family," says Samuel, who has both schizophrenia and bipolar disorder in his large family. "I do want to have children." His older brother, who had schizophrenia, committed suicide. A younger brother diagnosed with bipolar disorder and a sister with an unspecified thought disorder are both doing well with treatment. Samuel knows that he may be carrying a heavier genetic load than siblings with only one mentally ill family member. "Maybe I might end up with one child out of four, maybe three out of four that have it, but I'm willing to take that risk," he says. "For some reason, that has never been much of a consideration for me."

Gretchen and her boyfriend of three years had a number of problems, but she wonders now, a month after the breakup, how much of his retreat from their relationship was due to his fear of her family history. Gretchen's older brother had been diagnosed with paranoid schizophrenia more than ten years ago, and her cousin has the disease as well. Her boyfriend had said he wanted a large family, she recalls. "And I didn't tell him about this situation till we had been dating for more than two years. He wasn't the type who would really understand it." She has her own fears of the illness, although she maintains a warm relationship with her ill brother. "It does make you scared of having children," she admits. "And I want to have ten children. So did he. I don't know if that was a factor in us breaking up but . . ." She pauses. "He wasn't there for me in a lot of emotional ways."

Nancy, who is now a grandmother, recalls feeling "petrified" that one of her three children would show signs of the schizoaffective disorder that often made her younger brother violent. "I worried," she says, "but it never prevented me. I wanted a family." None of her children has developed schizophrenia, and she feels her fears for her grandchildren abating.

Jeffrey also remembers worrying that his two children would develop the schizophrenia that afflicted his sister. "When they were in their teens and early twenties, when they would have problems getting along with people or coping with life, I would wonder a little bit if they could become mentally ill," he admits. "But it wasn't a big worry for me."

For many of us the question remains open, and exceedingly difficult. "In recent years when dating, I've become reticent to discuss my brother because of all the issues of genetics," says Jack, whose schizophrenic older brother is resistant to treatment. "Fortunately, I can educate my friends and my girlfriends. But when it comes to my own concerns about children, about genetics, I don't know, I just don't know," he says, echoing the confusion voiced by many siblings.

The question is never simple, and even those of us who have made our choices admit to ambivalence. How could we not?

"I've decided I wouldn't have any more children, and I like children," says Clio, an older woman who grew up long before effective drug treatment became available. Three years after her daughter was born, Clio's younger brother was diagnosed with schizophrenia and hospitalized for many years. "To this day I'm very sad that I made that decision, but what could I do? What was I going to do if one of them turned out to be like my brother? I just would have felt too depressed for words."

These are the decisions we make, picking our way among scant options and information. But while discussing these choices with siblings, I sometimes sensed a dark and unacknowledged factor in our decisions, an internalized prejudice that shadows our choices. Too often, without even being aware, we have incorporated the stigma that is attached to mental illness into our own thoughts. Such thinking can permeate our entire life. For example, Clio's daughter, now in her midtwenties, is perfectly healthy. But now that her daughter is thinking of marrying and settling down, Clio cautions her not to talk about her schizophrenic uncle. "Everyone has a skeleton in the closet," Clio says. "And I think you may foreclose on your opportunities if you tell people all the bad things about yourself."

Clio has incorporated this prejudice and is passing it on to her daughter. Certainly she grew up in the era when families took the blame for mental illness. Intellectually she knows better now. Still, without realizing it, she is perpetuating the fear and the shame.

The line between stigma and healthy concern is a fine one; I, too, worry about the genes I carry. I know how horrible it can be to live with someone who is severely ill, and I can imagine how much worse it must be to become trapped inside that illness. For many siblings, especially when we talk about ourselves as possible parents, our thoughts are tangled and dragged down by guilt, fear, and judgment. Even when we deny such negative emotions, our language betrays us. Samuel, for instance, muses about the high incidence of various mental illnesses in his own family before concluding: "There's not a lot of other bad disorders in my family." He means he carries no other heritable illnesses or genetic disorders, things that would make him less attractive as a gene donor, as a father. "So I don't feel too ashamed of the genetic history I'm bringing into a relationship." Not *too* ashamed, he has said.

Even my father, toward the end, fell prey to his own sense of stigma, perhaps also to his great sense of failure as a doctor and a father. After he died, my mother and I found among his papers an obituary notice he had written for himself. In it, he listed his army service, his degrees, and the other achievements he was proudest of, his long medical practice, and me, his journalist daughter. He did not mention his other children at all.

"I mean, have you ever analyzed the kind of person who would marry a person like you if they found out ahead of time?" Clio asks me. A loving person, I answer. A secure person, one who recognizes life's unevenness and values the gifts we siblings do bring into any relationship, as lover, mate, or parent. A flawed human, like ourselves, who understands that life incorporates risk.

That's not to say that I don't have my own insecurities arguing her side of the case. But the burden we have carried has been heavy enough. We must forgive ourselves for surviving, and for being capable of joy.

Sandra, who now has a young daughter, pinpoints the problem that she wrestled with for several years after her sister became ill. "In a way," she says, "apart from whether or not the child will turn out OK, the question is, 'Who are we to be the ones to go ahead and have a happy normal family, to have children, to have a life?'

"I'm not saying that it's a necessity to have children but I think in our culture and in our lives, it's a symbol of normal life—whatever that is—that the sick ones will never have. So bigger than the question of 'Will my child be damaged?' is the hurdle for so many people of what it symbolizes to have children.

"It's like being punished for making a happy life. If you have a child it'll be damaged and it'll be your fault!" Sandra says.

Beth, whose younger brother has been diagnosed with schizophrenia, didn't even feel afraid when she was pregnant with her daughter, who is now nearly ten. "I think maybe there is an ingrained optimism in me. I look at Evie still and think, sometimes, oh, what horrible things could happen to her. What if we were in a concentration camp, would I have been able to let her be led away? But I didn't worry during my pregnancy. I was mostly in a state of constant wonderment that my body worked.

"There's so much else that can happen to a child. Maybe that's why I didn't think about it. There's still time for Evie to get sick with so many things, so many other things."

While researchers work to unravel the mysteries of DNA, we are left to tease apart our own knots of anxiety, yearning, and indecision. We need to feel secure and seek that same safety for those we love: our mates, our family members, and, if we have them, our children. We need to find that calm within ourselves, because in terms of genetics, with these illnesses, we do not know what we are working with, not yet.

chapter ten

Much of the healing process has been about finding myself, separating my own identity from that of my family, specifically my brother and my sister. Although they became ill, I grew up healthy. While I reacted first to them and then to the world with fear and confusion, I have learned to forge a life independent of their illness and my family's pathology. I have discovered that I am changed, irreparably, by the experience of my siblings' illness, but that I am not like them, nor am I merely the sum of the trauma of my early life. While my parents chose to cut me off from my brother and my sister, tried to shelter me, I have come to realize that I have, like them, many and mixed traits. And as I have taught myself to understand these internal complexities, to put all these elements in perspective I must also reach some reconciliation with my brother and sister, as they really were and are now—neither phantoms, nor ghouls, nor the fantasies of memory. In order, finally, to see who I am, I have had to look at them with honesty and compassion.

Coming to terms with Daniel has been, in some ways, easier than I imagined. He has been dead for more than ten years, and the brother I remember has much of my sympathy. With Daniel, perhaps because he was often my caretaker first and foremost, I can understand how his illness affected his behavior and separate the big brother who carried me around the house from the distracted giant who stranded me on top of the refrigerator. I can distinguish the brother who once clearly loved me, who read me bedtime stories, from the brother who also gave me nighttime terrors, coming into my room naked and aroused. Plus the story is finite: He was my big brother, he became ill, and he died. I have understood finally that I loved him no less for any of these accidents of fate.

But only in adulthood did I finally feel safe enough to ask my mother how Daniel died, to get answers to the hard questions that I knew had been kept from me ten years before. In part, I was able to ask because my father had passed on. I understood on some level that a great deal of my parents' denial had originated with his disappointment and sense of failure. My mother's great sadness had been real, but with my father gone, she seemed less intent on keeping up appearances. There was so much I didn't know about Daniel's death. Did they ever find the driver who hit him, the one who left him dying or already dead by the road? Did he say anything when the ambulance arrived? Was he delusional at the end?

Although I didn't say it then, I had also wondered over the years since his death about the nature of this "accident." All through my twenties I had told my friends that it was likely my brother had run into the road, suicidal or chased by demons nobody else could see. Perhaps he had been hiding, waiting for a speeding car to come by. Perhaps he had been in other accidents before. In the moments before my mother responded, I realized that I was anticipating some enlightenment about my brother's life, some information that might make sense of such a random end.

"You may as well know the whole truth," my mother replied. "Daniel wasn't killed in a hit-and-run accident. He killed himself by jumping off a cliff. We didn't know how to tell you then. We thought that would just make it worse."

Despite my expectations, these words left me stunned and slightly numb. At thirty-one, I had thought my family history no longer held any secrets from me. Hearing the facts of his death plainly stated was hard and disorienting. It had no romance and destroyed my final fantasy, the ideal of a poetic end. I realized, again, how little I knew.

"Anything else you want to tell me?" I snapped at her, feeling suddenly betrayed and angry. "Any other secrets?"

"No," she told me sadly. "That's it," she said, apologizing again. "We just wanted to make it easier on you." She sounded so sad that my shocked anger ebbed. I assured her that her choice had done no harm and, as proof, told her that I'd half expected some such revelation. "Even when you told me he was killed by a car," I said, "I always wondered if it was suicide, if he jumped into the road." She sounded comforted and admitted that she was glad the whole story was out. So am I. In discovering the truth I have lost my obsession with his death, and with it the hope that I will ever know what he was thinking. Perhaps my brother thought he could fly. Perhaps he simply wanted to die. Perhaps he thought that by jumping off a cliff he could escape some of his demons. Ultimately, he did. Yet none of these possibilities changes his act, and none of these mental games alters my impression of Daniel. My brother was very ill. I loved him, and he died.

With Katherine, everything is more complicated. My relationship with her was never as warm. My fear of her was greater. And she is still alive.

Sometimes the realization of this last fact amazes me. After all, I have not seen my sister for close to twenty years, more than half my life. What little contact we have had has been disjointed. A few years ago, about a month after I found out about Daniel's suicide, I called the halfway house where she then lived. I wanted, despite my fear, to know everything. In the new openness of our relationship, my mother had given me her address and, at the same time, a warning: "She hasn't wanted anything to do with us, you know. She may not speak to you at all."

This was hardly surprising. The last few years that Katherine had lived at home had been full of screams and anger directed at us all. One manifestation of her paranoia was a very direct and intense hatred of my mother. And nearly two decades later, I could still all too easily remember how terrifying Katherine's rage was, how she had killed my hamster and tortured other pets. I remember her hating us, and how my parents' decision to end their attempts at contact followed a period in which she rejected any social overtures and would refuse to see them when they attempted to visit.

I had a script mentally prepared when I called the house. Although I felt compelled by curiosity and a desire to understand, I was terrified of whom, and of what, I would find. The tension building around this call had been pressing in on me, making it difficult to breathe, much less think on my feet. I didn't want to be tongue-tied. And I knew I didn't want simply to ask to speak to Katherine. I told myself that this sudden introduction might be unsettling for her, and I admitted, too, that I was afraid of contact with her. Instead, I prepared myself to ask for the director of the residence. I thought I would explain my relationship with Katherine, although I was not sure how I would excuse what was then my more than fifteen years of silence. I would then seek the director's advice on how to make contact. Should I be put through to her directly? Would it make more sense for me to write a letter or simply a card? Perhaps, I hoped, the house director would intervene and offer to talk to Katherine about me. Perhaps she would find a way to explain to my sister that after half a lifetime of silence, Clea wanted to say hi.

When I did reach the house director, she took control of the conversation by asking me questions. When had I last seen my sister? What had her mental state been at that time? I gave her an abbreviated account of our childhood relationship. I told her, quite frankly, that I had felt threatened by my sister and spent many years afraid of her. When I then tried to explain the long silence, the lack of contact between my sister and the rest of the family, she stopped me. "We see that all the time," she said. "People burn out, and you had to get on with your life."

Those words cracked the tension that had formed around me. I had felt like such a uniquely horrible person for so long that to be told my behavior was not unusual was an enormous relief. To have my lapses understood felt like divine mercy. The phone call suddenly became much easier.

"I know that a lot of these fears are just childhood leftovers," I told the house director. "I know that as an adult, I'm much more likely to just feel bad for her, for the way her life has gone, than to be afraid. I want to make things as normal as they can be, but I don't know where to start."

"Well, here we've got a problem," the house director said, and went on to explain. Katherine was not doing well. It had been a few years since her last hospitalization, but in recent weeks her health had seemed to be deteriorating in the semistructured atmosphere of the home. Days before I called, Katherine had become extremely delusional, and the house director anticipated that she would have to be hospitalized again soon. Usually, the director told me, they would welcome reconnection with family members, because so many of the house residents were completely cut off. Usually, she said, she would suggest I send a card, just a simple greeting, and let the house resident take it from there. But not in Katherine's case. My sister was doing so poorly that they didn't want to destabilize her more. Telling her that her long-lost baby sister was trying to reach her could play into her delusions, the director explained, and said she would rather I held off making contact, promising to let me know if anything happened. I thanked her, almost as relieved by the delay as I had been by her accepting manner. I promised to call in a few weeks, just to see how things were going.

Nearly three years went by before I called again. In those years, I continued to work with my therapist, largely on isolating the childhood fears from that still seemed to cripple my life. Katherine played a major role, as I tried to visualize her in the present tense. The scary monster I saw in my dreams, I came to realize, would be a middle-aged woman by now. She would probably look small to me, at least as compared to my memories. She would probably seem older than her years, aged by the difficulties in her life. And she might be very angry at our family, both because of our long silence and because of the delusions that had led her to rage at my mother all those years before. With my therapist, I created mental images to hold up against my worst fears, but for my own peace of mind, I wanted to see my sister, to see if facing her would somehow enable me to face the pieces of myself that I had buried when my parents ended our contact. All the guilt and shame and terror no longer held as much sway as the basic need to see the truth of her. She was no longer just a nightmare figure to me. For better and for worse, Katherine was a real person. I would need to find out whether my sister would be willing to see me.

Of course, I stalled. A year went by, then another. I told myself I'd go in the spring; the travel would be easier. Still, spring came and passed, and summer did as well. My sister, I reasoned, will more likely be sad than frightening. I knew that she had never lived independently and that her stays in halfway houses had been broken by frequent hospitalizations. I knew that she was not one of the luckier ones. I continued to put off the call.

Finally November came around with the promise of Thanksgiving, family reunions, and the holiday season to follow. I could stall no longer. I realized that she might refuse to see me and would be well within her rights to reject any member of the family that had, so many years before, rejected her. But I had to try. I wanted her to know that I was willing to try.

I called the halfway house and found the same director on duty. She remembered me and never asked why I had been so long out of touch. She had a sadder story to tell.

"We couldn't handle her anymore, and we had to have her hospitalized again," she told me. "I would have called you but she specifically said she didn't want anyone notified. She said, 'No family.' So I couldn't call you. That's her right." We talked a little longer, and I asked if she could suggest any way I could locate my sister. She relented. "You didn't hear it from me," she said, and proceeded to tell me what she knew. After this latest hospitalization, she told me, Katherine had been released to a more supervised home nearby. "She didn't want anyone notified. We are not having this conversation," she repeated as she gave me the name of the other home.

I called the second home as soon as we hung up, trying to think of what excuse I would give for assuming my sister might be there. Once I got the director on the phone, the subject never came up. She was so excited to have one of Katherine's relatives contact her that she didn't question how I had found her. Katherine wasn't new to her; my sister had lived there briefly fourteen years before, and they had been happy to take her back. But she had never been willing to talk about her family. Her parents were dead, she had said then, and there was nobody else. Purely by accident, the house director had discovered that our brother had lived nearby for a short while, but Katherine had refused to acknowledge his existence as well. However, she had been a compliant resident, willing to do her few chores and obey the house rules in exchange for a modicum of independent living.

During this latest stay, the house director told me, Katherine had been different. Although the local hospital had released her, she was clearly still in a delusional state. She had refused to bathe or to wash her clothes. She had turned down flat several suggestions from her psychiatrists that she try risperidone, one of the newer medications, or even increase her dosage of Trilafon. She had refused to do anything unless God specifically told her to, and her god was growing increasingly paranoid. She had always been a fussy eater, the house director told me, but in her latest stay she had begun to accuse the house staff of poisoning her. Over the summer, which had been long and very hot, she had refused most liquids, saying that the staff had urinated in them. She had begun to hassle one of the other residents, believing him to be her husband. She decided that he was not praying enough and began lecturing him endlessly. This behavior escalated into screaming—at him, at the staff, and alone in her room. "Usually, she's so quiet. But she's got quite a pair of lungs, you know," the house director told me. Yes, I replied, I know.

The staff had tried to reason with her. The director had been in this field for more than twenty years and had gained a good amount of experience dealing with delusional residents, but Katherine was getting out of hand. The pressure she was putting on her supposed husband was affecting his fragile and hard-won emotional balance, along with his physical health. He had a lung condition, and although he had previously managed to cut down his smoking to ten daily cigarettes, the constant verbal attacks from Katherine were getting to him. His habit was back up to two packs a day.

And then Katherine had taken off. After a small breakfast she had retired to her room. She wasn't seen for hours. Nobody was worried at first; this was Katherine's usual time of day to pray. But when she didn't appear for lunch, they started piecing together a frightening tale. One of the residents had seen her get on a bus for the neighboring city. He had thought she had permission. Another had heard her say that she was moving—she and her husband were getting their own place. She had seemed so confident, the house director told me, that the other residents had assumed she was acting properly.

Nobody knew where she was for almost a week. Neither her

doctors nor any of the local hospitals heard from her. The house staff waited, fearing a call that would say she had been found dead or hurt, the victim of a crime or her own delusions. When the police finally called, just two days before I did, they said Katherine was unharmed. She had been picked up in a large city about four hundred miles away. She had been behaving irrationally in a hotel lobby, explaining to the desk clerk about how God spoke to her, and the clerk had called the cops. They took Katherine down to the department of social services, where someone had her committed to a local hospital for observation. The social workers at the hospital asked Katherine about her family. The halfway house was her family, she told them. They noted the name and state and prepared for the rounds of phone calls to get her back into a protected environment. She would be admitted to the hospital's psychiatric ward for observation; if her psychotic state continued, she would be admitted for a longer stay when that time was up. Katherine kept talking through all the paperwork and questions. The entire house staff, she told them, would be along presently. They were all moving into the hotel along with her.

The house director continued with her story, but I was lost in my own thoughts by then. How involved, I pondered, did I want to get? By the time she had finished what she knew of my sister's saga I felt overwhelmed. The enormity of my sister's tragedy and the guilt for my delayed call spurred me into a decision. When she was released by the hospital, I told the halfway-house director, I would pay for her to be transported, by ambulance if necessary, from the hospital back to the halfway house. But then the director reminded me that if Katherine was still in a psychotic state, they wouldn't be able to take her back. They shouldn't have taken her the last time, when she had been released from a hospital without being stabilized. And if she was back on her medications, responding well, the decision about what to do next would be hers. She could return if she wanted to, but only by her own choice. So much for my first instincts.

I needed more information, and so I began the first round of many calls, to local mental health facilities, to the National Alliance for the Mentally Ill, and then to the various state agencies that had custody of my sister. And I wondered what I was doing. The day before, I had wanted simply to initiate contact, and here I was getting into the loop of taking care of her. Perhaps the two had to be synonymous; I didn't know. When I called my mother to update her on Katherine's situation, she wasn't surprised, and she advised me to limit my involvement. Katherine, she reminded me, had disappeared many times before. And whenever she was picked up by the police or hospitalized, she never wanted contact with her parents, my mother said. That was why they had given up; what I wanted to do was my own decision. I was beginning to feel queasy at the expense of time and, possibly, money. Finally, an attorney at a state agency assured me that I had no legal or financial responsibility for Katherine. If I could make contact with her, I could offer my support, as much as I could afford, as much as my heart could bear, and then I could draw the line.

My sister has managed parts of her life well thus far. She has gotten her Social Security checks directly deposited into her bank account, kept her own checkbook, and made her own appointments with her caseworker and doctors. Her handling of these responsibilities made her seem, to some, quite competent. But she had never lived on her own without relapsing into a psychotic state. And this time, even in the sheltered environment of the halfway house, her condition had worsened and she had somehow managed to flee four hundred miles.

I already felt overwhelmed by what I might have brought upon myself with my phone queries and letters to state offices and hospitals. I imagined emergency calls from the police of different states. I faced the possibility that my sister might show up on my doorstep. I feared the specter of my sister herself, of who she really is and how she has lived. Against all this, I placed my best hope: that Katherine could be stabilized, that she may resume her fragile routine, living between pills and prayers. The director of the halfway house assured me that she would hold Katherine's bed as long as she could. I told myself another would open up if this one got taken. For now, Katherine would at least be safe in a hospital.

The issues surrounding my sister have become so loaded that they are difficult to pick apart. First, I have realized that just because I have tuned in during a crisis, Katherine's situation may not be as critical as it appears. She has had, I know, many other hospitalizations. She has also had other lost times, episodes of days and weeks when she has wandered off without notifying anyone or even taking any of her belongings. My parents tried to keep such disappearances from me, but I clearly recall the day when my grandmother called us panic-stricken because Katherine had used a cash gift from her to disappear. The police picked her up that time, too, and called our house, and I remember that my parents looked resigned and weary, but not surprised. Schizophrenia, I know now, often seems to be cyclical, and my recent experience may just be showing me the downside of one full turn. After past psychotic episodes, my sister has stabilized and returned to her best life. She may again. There is even some evidence that the disease abates with age, and so as my sister nears fifty her demons, and perhaps her god as well, may give her a little peace.

While I am waiting for news, I try to sort through the fears and guilt that again have come to buffet my life. This is what I find: Katherine is my sister, and I feel an obligation to renew contact with her. She scares me still, a combination of outdated childhood memories and the real horror of her current situation consuming me. All, finally, that I can figure out is that I have to start with myself. I need to feel safe. I want to redraw the borders of our relationship, but I fear that one wrong move may tear down all the shelters my parents built around me. I fear that if too many people know that I am willing to become involved in my sister's life she will be released into my care, despite the attorney's assurances and all the information to the contrary that I have uncovered. I fear that the great tidal wave of Katherine's illness may break over my life and wash away all the work I've done, destroy all the boundaries I have painstakingly built to protect myself and to guard all the love I have worked so hard to find.

I am ultimately alone with this dilemma. Jon supports me and says he understands the guilt and responsibility I am struggling with. He says he will cope alongside me with whatever I decide, with whatever we have to face, but I know he cannot begin to realize how difficult the reality can be. I put off telling my mother what I am thinking. I feel she has made her choices and should not be forced to replay that horrible triage. I also know that I want to get my own thoughts straight before I seek her input.

My therapist talks to me of how coming to terms with our humanity means accepting that at times there are no good choices. She points out how useful this dilemma is, how now, as an adult, I am getting the opportunity to make for myself some of the decisions that were made for me as a child. She also tells me that if I choose to get involved with Katherine to assuage my own guilt, I may in some ways be doing my sister a disservice. If I were to force my presence on Katherine, I might be going against her wishes and upping an emotional ante that could make her psychosis worse. If I could get her into a private hospital, Ann explains, I would be removing her from a state system to which she has become accustomed and which has the resources to take care of her—and to which she would, once all my money had run out, no doubt be consigned again. In this way I would disrupt her life and she mine, with no lasting benefit to either of us. Although I know that what she is saying is true, this doesn't matter. It may be true that I could not do much, but that is not why I am cautious about getting involved. It may be true that my intervention may make my sister's mental health worse, but that is still a rationalization for not pursuing contact. If I continue to avoid my sister, it is because I am afraid of her.

But I am beginning to realize that there truly is not much I can do to make Katherine's life better. Perhaps nothing I could do, I now think, would improve it dramatically over the long run. I am surprised that I believe this, but as the days pass, I do. My sister's life has been a series of such crises. Until she can settle into a more stable routine, until her disease frees her to accept better care (which would probably involve trying newer medications), I can do little of practical value to improve her life. I could try to have her few freedoms taken away, to have a conservator appointed to watch over her in the hope that such a move would keep her off the road and on her medications, but I do not feel confident making that choice for her, not without first talking to her and seeing for myself how she is doing. And if she wants no contact with me, I am limited further. This realization eases the guilt that has been consuming me. Yet even if there is nothing permanent I can do for her, I should do all I can, a voice deep in my belly says. *She is your sister,* the voice says. *You have everything, she has nothing.*

Several of my friends rallied when they heard of my search for my sister and the story of her disappearance. They've all warned me to protect myself, telling me that I stand to ruin my life by becoming overly involved in her care, that I have a right to my privacy and my happiness, that I should let the decades-old silence be. I feel they don't understand my dilemma. They, too, see only the rationalizations that Ann has offered. Only I can decide, for myself, how much guilt I can live with and how much responsibility, how much I will be ruled by fear of censure and by fear of my sister. Only I can unravel the knot of my own confusion and terror and find out what my sister means to me.

I concentrate on the facts: Right now, my sister doesn't want to see me. She doesn't want any family members to know where she is. She is incapable of believing anything other than her delusions. I want to move the boundaries, but I am afraid of them giving way. I want to protect my life. She won't take her meds voluntarily. She doesn't want to bathe. She's my sister. I want to become more involved, but I am afraid of her life taking over mine. I haven't seen her in twenty years. I'm her sister. Once my mother is gone, she will be my closest blood relative, and I haven't seen her for more than half my life, for nearly half her life. I may never see her again. Katherine is screaming again.

Ultimately there is probably no bigger question facing any relative of someone with mental illness than how to reconcile all the family members' lives, whether that means assuming responsibility for the ill person to some degree or cutting off contact. In some ways, we siblings have it easier. Parents, after all, usually assume responsibility for their children until they are competent. And if they are not competent, often parents become permanent caretakers, or at least the ones who forever monitor the ill child's basic care.

The sibling situation is different. We were peers to start with, not caretakers. We may have been protective of our younger sisters or championed our little brothers when we were younger, but we weren't primarily responsible for the decisions that affected their care. Now, however, and increasingly as we grow older, we feel a level of responsibility for our ill brothers' and sisters' care, but we don't have an established role.

Of course, this is not a problem that every sibling of someone with a mental illness faces. Increasingly, as drug therapies improve, some of those with mental illness who could not function are now capable of independent living. The professor who leaves his family each morning to drive to work may be reliant on his daily dose of Stelazine to control his psychotic symptoms; the health care professional who lives alone but manages his job and weekly visits to a support group may have been freed from a round of hospitals by the Trilafon that treats his schizophrenia. Such happy cases have been with us for more than three decades. And recent years have brought us wonder stories, miracle recoveries by patients who had been hospitalized long-term and who have basically come back to life after beginning a course of risperidone or clozapine. People have awakened from their delusions to find years gone, but more full and social lives beckoning.

These are the happy cases, and as treatments improve there will be more of them. But the numbers vary, and many groups manipulate the findings of studies to support their own ends. Some rights advocates stress the rate of recovery, seeing the glass as half-full, while others will exaggerate the worst statistics, definitively describing the glass as half-empty. Even apart from the political arguments about public safety and individual rights, the numbers are inconclusive.

The old clinical rule of thirds cited in numerous medical texts ran as follows: Among the most seriously ill, mostly people with schizophrenia, one third would improve and perhaps regain full health with or without treatment. One third would need treatment, probably medication, to be able to function. And one third, even with the best treatment, would never recover enough to rejoin society. That final third is probably the one that has changed the most, as the newer drugs chip away at the most stubborn diseases, and more understanding and broader-based support systems help the mentally ill manage the stresses of daily life that may trigger the onset of a psychotic state.

Some of the more optimistic, such as Dr. LeRoy Spaniol, associate executive director of the Center for Psychiatric Rehabilitation in Boston, report that up to 65 percent of people diagnosed with serious mental illnesses such as schizophrenia are capable of recovery. By recovery, Spaniol means living with various levels of support, such as assisted housing or programs such as his own at Boston University. Increasingly, other health professionals are optimistic about the recovery rate of people who have access to such support systems. These vary in type and availability. Some states, among them New York, Virginia, and Massachusetts, are developing a network of so-called clubhouses, meeting places where the mentally ill—who are referred to simply as members—can find company and social activities, as well as programs to help them with housing, vocational, and educational needs. New York also has some pioneering group homes, such as the one on Long Island that Michael Winerip documented in his book 9 *Highland Road,* and other states are beginning to follow these leads. With proper intervention, Spaniol believes, about 50 or 60 percent of people with serious mental illnesses can hold a job of some sort. Currently only about 5 percent do. Others scoff at such optimistic estimates but laud such programs for helping lower the rates of rehospitalization for many who use their services.

Whatever numbers you believe, the sad fact remains that some people with mental illness are not reachable, are resistant to treatment, or have some strain of illness that does not respond to the drugs or therapy now available. I have met with too many relatives to believe that this problem will go away soon. I have spoken with the parents of a bipolar son who fled treatment more than a year ago and has not been heard from since. He is probably homeless, if he is alive at all. I have spent hours with a friend whose brother's late-onset schizoaffective disorder has destroyed his life, and that of his wife and children, and yet who cannot see his own disorder and refuses to try medication. I have comforted a colleague whose shy, sweet father does not like to bother his children. He does not tell them when the voices have started again, even though the voices say cruel things and urge him to hurt himself. Who will care for these people?

The problem is huge, and it is as political as it is medical. While the ongoing destigmatization movement continues to push for integrating people with mental illnesses back into mainstream society, other forces are whittling away at the services that help the most seriously ill, those who may not be able to function independently at all.

Continuing cutbacks in health and social services have meant that many care providers must give priority to what will fit into their budgets rather than what is best for their patients. Because of financial restrictions, for example, many people with mental illness do not get the care that could help them function in the working world. Money for projects such as group homes and nonresidential day programs, where people with illnesses can come for support if they live independently or with families, has become harder to find, even as such programs become more accepted by the mental health care community. Even bottom-line care—the hospitalization of the most severely ill—has been trimmed to dangerous levels. Not only have the mass deinstitutionalizations of the 1970s left many people with mental illness homeless, but even those who are rehospitalized may find that they cannot always get the care they need. There are many people who with proper treatment may be able to live independently yet who cannot come out of temporary psychotic states in the amount of hospital time they are permitted, a mere ten days in some states. According to Dr. David Shore of the National Institute of Mental Health, "Unfortunately, the length of time that it takes the average person to really substantially improve on medications is longer than the length of the average hospital stay for several disorders, including schizophrenia." The result is a nearly criminal undertreatment of sometimes controllable diseases.

Budgetary cutbacks are not the only limits being placed on the care of our brothers and our sisters. These days, the trend toward less treatment for financial reasons has coincided, in an almost paradoxical way, with the patients' rights movement. Both believe that less is more, although they spring from opposing beliefs about the entitlement of people who have such illnesses. While many of the budget cuts seem prompted by a mean-spirited wish to further disenfranchise those who cannot work and are unlikely to vote, the grass-roots patients' right movement takes the stand that people with mental illnesses should have a say in their treatment. Both groups can end up advocating for less treatment against prevailing medical advice.

Practically, such groups as the National Mental Health Consumers Self-Help Clearinghouse in Philadelphia and the Massachusetts-based National Empowerment Center provide information on legal options and also push for the right of people with mental illness to refuse medication and involuntary commitment. They cite inhumane conditions in psychiatric hospitals, misdiagnosis, and overmedication with psychoactive drugs among the reasons that our brothers and sisters may refuse the care we urge on them. Despite both the advances in the efficacy of the newer antipsychotic drugs and the decrease in their side effects, these groups protest the increasingly blanket use of such drugs and point out that scientists still do not know exactly how many of these medications work. These groups also defend the right of the mentally ill to not stay in touch with family members—in short, to be as anonymous in society as any other adult.

The issues this movement raises center on the questions of competency and personal and social obligation. With a disease such as schizophrenia, which has as one of its main symptoms an inability to recognize itself, are patients the best ones to make decisions about their own care? And what about those very ill patients who may be less tormented when treated but who become paranoid and suspect the doctor (and the drug) as the latest dose wears off? In the cases of people with delusions, particularly paranoia, which may make an ill person fear an utterly uninvolved party, should an outside agent have the final say over medication? Should someone besides the ill person have such power, if the mentally ill person's health or safety is at stake, or the safety of a doctor or a family member?

Despite the heated arguments on both sides of this fight, the issues are clearly not black or white. Involuntary treatment has certainly helped many people find their center again and regain control of a life that had been spinning out of control. But undoubtedly many people have also been misdiagnosed and mistreated in the name of mental health. And even among those who have been correctly diagnosed, there may be many currently dealing with their illness who have greater self-awareness than their doctors believe. These people may be the ones most sensitive to their illness's episodic nature and may be the ones most capable of judging when psychoactive drugs are necessary and when hospitalization is called for, if at all.

Right now, there is little consensus on state-imposed care. Some states, for example, may appoint conservators or guardians to act on behalf of people with mental illness, as they have traditionally appointed conservators for the mentally retarded. Such a guardian may work with an ill person's doctors and may order a person to take medication and have the legal power to hospitalize the noncompliant. Many states are also trying or are considering outpatient commitment or "community commitment" laws, which may require a person who has been released from a psychiatric hospital to continue with some form of treatment as a requirement of continued release. Currently, although the laws differ from state to state, involuntary hospitalization (which may include forced treatment) is usually ordered by a judge when the ill person is deemed to be a danger to himself or herself or to others. That usually means the ill person has directly threatened someone or attempted suicide, although interpretations of both actions and threats can vary greatly from state to state and judge to judge.

One compromise goal forwarded by some family groups is to have power of involuntary commitment moved from the political realm into that of health care professionals. They propose to make involuntary commitment possible if a psychiatrist advises that an untreated mentally ill person is suffering severe mental, emotional, or physical distress that will cause a substantial deterioration in his or her ability to function. As another possible alternative, the National Alliance for the Mentally Ill has sponsored a national plan network to help families develop long-term care for mentally ill relatives. Called planned lifetime assistance network organizations, these groups help families set up trusts that can be used in the care of mentally ill relatives, without interfering with the relative's Social Security or disability income. Currently twelve states (California, Connecticut, Georgia, Maryland, New Jersey, New York, North Carolina, Ohio, Pennsylvania, Texas, Virginia, and Washington) have such groups, although the national organization urges interested parties to set up their own organization and offers guidelines and information. This type of planning, however, is primarily financial and serves to continue what is often a parental role in terms of paying for small comforts or luxuries and overseeing private therapies or treatment. Since all these laws differ and may be either in flux or irregularly enforced, the department of mental health in the ill sibling's home state is the best source of specific information.

Patients' groups, by and large, view these family-care-centered proposals as additional attacks on their right to choose. Handing this right from a judge to a psychiatrist or even a financial board is still improper when it belongs, they say, with the mental health care consumer. Perhaps the debate will never be resolved, and the best compromise may likely be reform of some sort that will allow for gradations of treatment and responsibility that can be customized to each individual. Despite the objections of many caregivers, from doctors to family members, the legitimate moral and ethical questions such patients' groups raise have a place in any discussion of long-term care.

For many of us, the decisions are still in the future. Gretchen, for example, sighs and shakes her head when she considers her older brother's prospects. "I hope he can go into an apartment or something," she says. Joel, her brother, was diagnosed ten years ago with schizophrenia and is now doing moderately well. Although he still lives at home, he has begun responding to newer drug therapies. Joel's counselor is trying to get him into a residential program, and he is very excited to try it. Still, the experiment may not work. Joel, now in his early thirties, has never been able to manage living on his own. And if this kind of supported-living arrangement does not work out, Gretchen does not know how the family will cope. "God forbid something should happen to my parents," she says. "I love him, and I would be there for him. I'll have him come live with me. I've already discussed that with him. The thing is, though, it's a lot of work."

Gretchen is still single, but she hopes to marry and have a large family of her own. Right now, she lives in a different city from the rest of her family and has not been around to help with Joel's care as much as she would like. "It's so hard," she says, "but I have to do things for my own life now." She does not know how the future will allow her to manage both the full personal life she dreams of and the caretaking role she has assumed, but she hopes that somehow she will balance it all.

Kyra, whose older sister is much less responsive to treatment, cannot see herself in a caretaker role. "I will not," she says, and then repeats, "I will not. I think there is enough money in the family that I actually won't have to think about that. I can't live through that."

What will happen if her family's money will not support an independent life for her sister? "I don't care," she replies, with a deep sigh of resignation. "I wish she were dead. She will end up in an institution, I think." She pauses and remembers how vivacious and healthy her sister was when they were both younger. "It's too bad. It's a waste of life. She was very creative and very talented in some areas. As a seamstress and a tailor, she was among the best. Now she has got so much pain and no one can seem to deal with her, and I see no signs of change."

"In my family and in myself there are two really opposite kinds of pulls," says Jack. His older brother lives on his own, despite frequent psychotic episodes. "One is to completely disengage, like my other brother. The other is to become overly involved and burn out, which I think my sister has done. I struggle with both of these. My compromise is to be physically far away. I mean, when I was still living near them in Atlanta, my mother used to call me at two in the morning, saying, 'He's doing this.' And I'd say, 'Call the police.' And she'd say, 'I can't do that.' And my thought was, 'Well, shit! You can call *me* at two in the morning!' So I'd hang up and call the police, and they'd bring him to the hospital because my mother was afraid. I don't have to do that kind of stuff anymore because I don't live a mile from her anymore. My sister does now and she deals with this kind of thing regularly. I think the whole issue of burden doesn't get talked about enough. I'm just struck by how overwhelming it all feels."

Since most of us will outlive our parents, this is a problem we will have to face. As I found out after my father's passing, the death of a parent rearranges the family constellation. We tend to feel more responsible, more aware of the consequence of our actions, once we are truly on our own. Many of us will actually be left with the care of our siblings, will inherit our parents' burden of responsibility for them. That is not an easy role to take on, but it is fairly common.

"I started to realize in the last few years that my dad is getting older. He retired at sixty-five, had a heart attack at sixty-six. My brother lives with him now, but of all the children in the family, the burden will fall on me," says Maria, discussing the long-term care of her schizophrenic younger brother. "My youngest sister feels like since she's younger, it's not her responsibility. My older sister has a borderline-personality disorder. So I will have the financial and legal say over my brother's life. I've already made a big push to get more active about my brother's treatment and housing, and tried to make some changes. He's very clean. He's been doing his own checkbook, and he's been living the winters by himself while my dad goes to Florida. He's able to do that. I picture that he'll live by himself and that I'll check in on him."

Sandy has already assumed most of the care for her younger brother. He has schizophrenia and lives in a halfway house, but she has taken on her late parents' role of visiting him and taking him out for a Sunday dinner. "It's hard," she admits. "Even if we're just going out to McDonald's, I get embarrassed. I just have to at some level accept the fact that unless I'm going to scrub him down, wash his clothes for him, tell him what to wear, and generally not treat him like an adult, that he is going to embarrass me. I can't push him on everything, so I just kind of give up."

Although Sal works in a psychiatric hospital, often with patients who are more ill than her schizophrenic sister, she finds that the burden of dealing with illness in a family member is heavier. "It's difficult. And it's almost doubly difficult knowing that you've been to all these support groups and that you're supposed to be a professional now and know how to handle this."

The key, for those of us who choose to have some kind of interaction with our mentally ill siblings, may be to know our own abilities and our own limits, what we can give and what we must keep for ourselves for our own comfort and safety. We cannot ask ourselves to bear more of the burden than we are able to. And we must learn, somehow, to forgive ourselves for what we cannot take on.

Julie Tallard Johnson uses an example from her own life to illustrate the value of drawing clear lines. Her brother, who has schizophrenia, was beginning to decompensate one winter several years back when he showed up at her door. "He had walked fifteen miles to my house in forty-below windchill," she recalls. Although he was in a residential treatment program, he wanted to stay with her, in her apartment. "He was pre-psychotic and I thought, 'Oh, God. If I say no, he'll freeze.' But I said no. I didn't let him in. I thought if he could make it out there he could get back. Then I sat and wept for the rest of the night. But he didn't die, and I set my boundaries for the rest of my life."

Her story underlines a basic truth for families with mental illness: There are no right answers. We are all burdened, even those of us who have changed and adapted and made our peace. "For many years," says Rachel, "I would see my sister twice a year, on her birthday and at Chanukah." This distanced relationship changed when Rachel began studying social work and met a colleague who worked with her sister. "He went on and on, raving about my sister, saying, 'She's so funny.' He couldn't stop talking about her in this positive way, and it was very genuine. And I began to see my sister in a positive way."

Rachel made plans for a special visit to her sister but admits, "The stress of that was a lot for her. By the time I arrived she was beginning to lose it. She was laughing in her hysterical way, overloud. The person at the table with us said, 'Callie is a little bit upset today. It's OK, we all get like that sometimes.' For the first time I saw her in an environment with her peers. It was the beginning of my being able to accept her as she was. Since then, I'm in contact with her. I see her. I speak with her every day. She's been very interested in the work that I do. When she's in a good state, she's been very helpful to me. She loves being in that role. At other times she gets very angry. We have a relationship."

Rachel and her family have, in some ways, an ideal situation. Rachel's sister is aware of her limitations and accepts the facts that she must take medication and stay in a supportive environment. She has a good living situation, a model residential facility that allows her as much independence as she can handle, along with excellent psychiatric care. And Rachel has found a role that works for her as well. She is very involved in her sister's life and believes that when her parents pass away she will assume the position of primary caretaker for her sister. That thought does not make her life easier.

"I dread my parents' dying 'cause I'll be the caretaker," says Rachel, echoing the sentiments of many brothers and sisters. "I often wish that she will predecease them."

For many of us, the premature death of our siblings may offer the opportunity for resolution. But admitting that we would prefer such a simple out can be very difficult, even in the most extreme cases, in which mental illness has engendered fear and abuse.

"My brother is very sick now; he's dying of AIDS," says Lincoln. His older brother Charles has never been diagnosed or treated, although he has been imprisoned several times for irrational and threatening behavior and sexually abused Lincoln when they were both younger. Neither Charles nor his and Lincoln's mother ever admitted that Charles was ill. Lincoln, now a mental health professional, suspects that schizoaffective disorder has been the source of Charles's wild mood swings and paranoid delusions. "Charles has lived in the streets. He's shot heroin and he's shared needles with people. Now he's slowly dying and he lives at home with my mother. Periodically, he still has psychotic episodes, and he threatens her. At one point last year, he almost set the house on fire. My mother allows this to happen. And now he's dying.

"I don't really feel sad about it," admits Lincoln, who at fortyfour has undergone more than a decade of therapy to understand his family's dynamics. "Maybe someday I will. Instead, I find myself hoping that he does die soon so my mother has some hope of resolving something for herself. I'll be very relieved to find out he has died."

There is little good to be salvaged from such pain, and this may be our final lesson. Resolution, I now think, can come only when we face what has happened to ourselves and to our family members. We must be honest about who we are and who our siblings are. We have to look beyond society's horror-movie projections and beyond our own unrealistic hopes and childish fears. Only then can we accurately assess our wounds and our blessings. Only then can we draw boundaries that make sense for ourselves and our families. Only then can we finally mourn and move on.

I do not know yet when my resolution will come. My sister is still in a hospital as I write this, or so I believe after many phone calls and conversations with hospital administrators, advocates, and the legal representatives of three states. Patient confidentiality and her wish not to be contacted prevent me from knowing for sure exactly where she is being treated. Still, I have let the staff of the hospital where I believe she is know that I am interested in opening communication. I have informed several relevant state agencies of our relationship and of my desire. If my sister wants to be in touch, someone will let me know.

In the meantime, there is the chance that some caretaker will reach her, or that some inner voice will cease to cavil, and Katherine will consider trying different drugs. In that scenario, the world opens up. Perhaps no drug will help her, not yet. But perhaps one will, and then maybe my sister will be able to leave the hospital for good. With some help, perhaps she could even experience the kind of independent life she has never really had. She could get her own place, perhaps find a job and begin to interact with people who would never have any reason to know about the lost decades, unless she chose to tell them.

I realize that this is a long shot, that paradoxically until Katherine is healthier she will probably reject many things that could make her healthier still. And that leaves darker options. There is the chance that my sister will be released from the hospital and disappear again. In this way, she could vanish from my life permanently, although not in a way that I would ever wish. She could end up like so many other people with mental health problems: on the street, abused, the victim of crime. In this wealthy nation, it is possible that my sister could die of exposure or starvation. It is also possible that I would never know.

The middle ground that I hope for is good care and release into another halfway house. Ideally, the one she had grown accustomed to will find a room for her, make another space if her bed has already been filled. Ideally, Katherine will find some peace in the structured daily routine there and within the limited range that her illness allows, and in which she was content for many years. If this comes about, and if Katherine is willing to let me be informed of her whereabouts, then I will probably begin to write her occasional cards. Nothing personal, just greetings from Hallmark, perhaps with the religious motifs that she finds comforting. And I would not expect any letter back. In some ways, I would be happier not to hear any reply. After all, she scares me. And part of coming to terms with my own life has been learning that I can neither judge nor ignore my emotions. I loved my brother, despite his illness. I am afraid of my sister, but she is the only sibling I have left. I would like to know something of her. I cannot care more, but I cannot care less either.

As much as I may wish it, I may never be totally free of my fear of my sister. At least I am learning not to be ruled by a habit of panic. If I never tried to contact my sister, I would feel guilty. I would wonder what could have changed, what could have been said, and that silence is too loud for me to bear. I do not want to be her caretaker, nor, if she regains her equilibrium and can enter a halfway house again, do I want to upset her balance by a sudden rush into her life. I do not want to raise expectations that I cannot fulfill. But I feel I want to give Katherine what I have sought in my own life: acknowledgment. That is the best I can hope for, the most I can offer. That would mean peace to me, a kind of truce, perhaps even bring some moments of comfort to her in her illness as well as provide a respite from some of my own conflicts. I would settle for that; I could learn to be happy with that in the future.

Now is what's difficult. Because Katherine is screaming again. In my imagination, I hear her. But this time I am not in the same room or even down the hall. This time, I am in my own house. I am getting on with my life.

recommended reading

Bank, Stephen P., and Michael D. Kahn. *The Sibling Bond.* New York: Basic Books, 1972. The landmark book of studies of these relationships.

Goodwin, Frederick K., and Kay Redfield Jamison. *Manic-Depressive Illness.* New York: Oxford University Press, 1990. The authoritative medical text compiles exhaustive studies as well as practical information.

Herman, Judith Lewis. *Trauma and Recovery: The Aftermath of Violence—from Domestic Abuse to Political Terror.* New York: Basic Books, 1992. A thoughtful and readable book that may be applicable to family members.

Jamison, Kay Redfield. *An Unquiet Mind: A Memoir of Moods and Madness.* New York: Alfred A. Knopf, 1995. A professor of psychiatry talks about her own bipolar disorder.

Johnson, Julie Tallard. *Hidden Victims, Hidden Healers: An Eight-Stage Healing Process for Families and Friends of the Mentally Ill.* Edina, Minn.: Pema, 1994. A psychotherapist's approach to overcoming trauma.

Kaysen, Susanna. *Girl, Interrupted.* New York: Turtle Bay Books, 1993. The novelist's first-person account of a hospitalization.

Keefe, Richard S. E., and Philip D. Harvey. *Understanding Schizophrenia: A Guide to the New Research on Causes and Treatment.* New York: Free Press, 1994. A readable and concise book.

Lamb, Michael E., and Brian Sutton-Smith, eds. *Sibling Relationships: Their Nature and Significance Across the Lifespan.* Hillsdale, N.J.: Lawrence Erlbaum Associates, 1982. A collection of essays by psychological theorists explores many aspects of these relationships.

Marsh, Diane T. *Families and Mental Illness: New Directions in Professional Practice.* New York: Praeger, 1992. A very readable study of the interaction between such illnesses and family dynamics.

Merrell, Susan Scarf. *The Accidental Bond: The Power of Sibling Relationships.* New York: Times Books, 1995. A study of ten sibling groups shows how the relationships influence other areas of our lives.

Swados, Elizabeth. *The Four of Us: A Family Memoir.* New York: Plume, 1993. The playwright's autobiographical account of growing up in a family that included a brother with schizophrenia.

Torrey, E. Fuller. *Surviving Schizophrenia: A Manual for Families, Consumers, and Providers.* 3d ed. New York: HarperPerennial, 1983. A comprehensive guidebook to the disease, complete with many contacts for further information.

Winerip, Michael. *9 Highland Road: Sane Living for the Mentally Ill.* New York: Vintage, 1994. A journalist's account of the establishment and the day-to-day activities of a group home.

acknowledgments

This book has depended on the support and cooperation of many people on many levels, so many, in fact, that I'm sure I will be leaving some out. If I have, please forgive me and believe that I am grateful. Of all those I have presence of mind to thank, allow me to name:

The many experts at hospitals and universities across the country who shared their time and resources, sending me articles and recommending books. Julie Tallard Johnson, Dolores Malaspina, Jill Bolte Taylor, E. Fuller Torrey, and David Shore in particular went out of their way to answer my questions and shared their knowledge in comprehensible, human-scale terms.

On less scientific matters: Rosalie and her crew at A.D.S. and Simson L. Garfinkle provided technical and moral support. Various *Boston Globe* colleagues gave me encouragement and guidance, most notably Peter Canellos, Vicki Croke, and the Living/Arts copy folk, and of course Ande Zellman, Julie Michaels, and Vicki Hengen at the Sunday magazine.

And most of all: my agent Jonathan Matson, for remaining upbeat and returning my phone calls, and Betsy Lerner, my editor, for keeping her perspective and my focus throughout this project. My mother, for her bravery in the face of painful memories, and my father, who always believed in me. Ann Porter, who accompanied me on this journey, particularly for her confidence that I would emerge safe at the end. My friends and readers, particularly Louise Kennedy, who lent me her sharp editor's eye and constant support, and Brett Milano, writer, wit, constant friend, and catcher of the unintentionally ridiculous phrase. And, of course, Jon S. Garelick, for his warmth, confidence, and love. Without you guys this would have been a very lonely year. Finally, let me use this space to thank all those with mentally ill family members who opened their lives and hearts to me. So many of you gave me your time and your trust that I am overwhelmed by your generosity. This book could not exist without you.